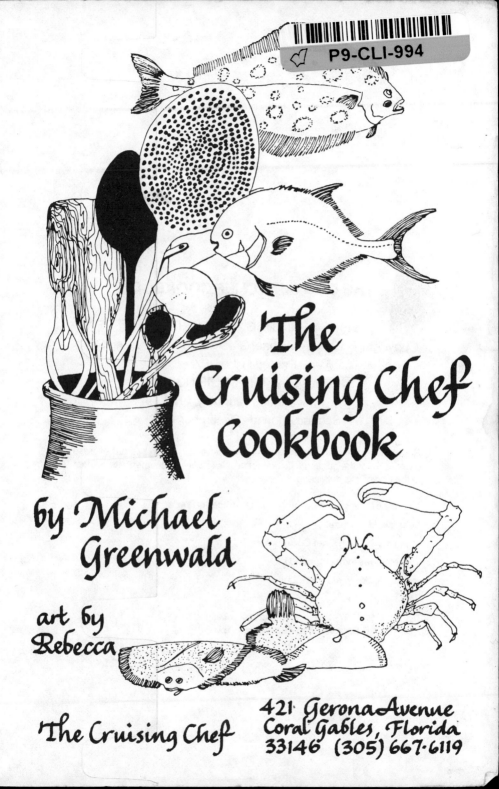

The Cruising Chef Cookbook

by Michael Greenwald

art by
Rebecca

The Cruising Chef

421 Gerona Avenue
Coral Gables, Florida
33146 (305) 667·6119

THE CRUISING CHEF COOKBOOK

FIRST PRINTING - OCTOBER 1984
Copyright © 1984 by Michael Greenwald (The Cruising Chef)
Printed in the USA
Previous title - THE CRUISING CHEF
First printing - January 1977
Second printing - December 1978

Library of Congress Cataloging in Publication Data:

Greenwald, Michael

The Cruising Chef Cookbook

Includes index, appendix.

1. Cookery, marine. 1. Title.

TX   84-072396

ISBN   0-931297-00-1 pbk (previously published by
TAB Books, ISBN 0-8306-6864-0 pbk)

preface

This book has been written for lovers of fine food who must work in a small galley under adverse conditions with limited facilities. The great majority of recipes call for common, easily found ingredients that store well and last a long time. They are our living experience in a belief that the sailor should dine sumptuously on tasty nourishing meals that satisfy the appetite and delight the soul.

The majority of recipes in this book are simple, one-pot affairs that can easily be made underway. They have been tested repeatedly on seven ocean crossings and 34,000 miles of cruising.

Pressure cooking is recommended wherever possible because of the speed, fuel economy and superior flavor which results. We feel that the pressure cooker is the finest tool a cruising chef can have and its mastery well worth the effort.

The joy of having sailed far and eaten well linger in the mind long after the bitter, hard times have been reduced to laughter. Only the essence of the moment, the lust for life, and the joy of it all remain islands in the mind's eye more green and scented than anything dreams can bring.

Michael Greenwald

contents

1 the galley

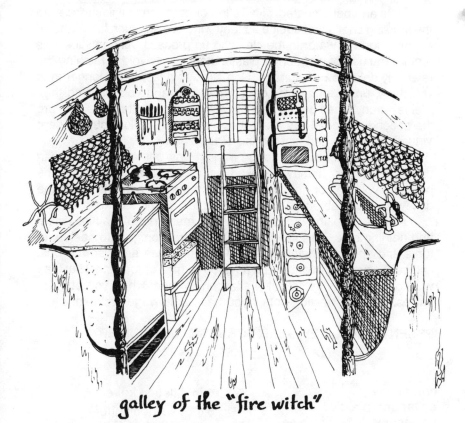

galley of the "fire witch"

There's no use denying it, being a cruising chef is a demanding job. The galley is much smaller than your home kitchen and all storage space is at a premium. The sink is much smaller than you are used to and usually lacks hot water. Counter space is also at a premium. This means that you will have to develop the habit of washing and stowing galley gear as it is used, not just at the end of the meal. Work flow planning is much more important than at home, where you have enough space to spread out and set half completed items aside. Your visits to the fridge or ice box must be carefully planned to avoid losing its precious cool. Make a list of what needs to come out of the box for the whole meal, then remove it all at once. Find a few spots where you can wedge things such as bowls of chopped food or batter. Buy a few high sided plastic trays into which you can set food which is apt to slide. Most of all, have patience. You just can't expect to make culinary accomplishments as easily as on shore. Don't be discouraged if you feel all thumbs in the beginning, with a few miles under your keel they will call you Master Chef.

Pots and pans coated with Teflon or other non stick surface are the cruising chef's first choice as they will save so much labor and so many gallons of water in the cleaning up process. All non stick pots require the use of wooden or plastic utensils to avoid scratching the relatively delicate pan surface. Non stick pots last much longer than you think, up to four years of constant use and you will sing their praises many times before new ones are needed. Stainless pots are the second choice. They are not non stick like Teflon, but they are virtually immortal and last the life of the ship.

If your vessel is big enough for just one pot, make it a 4 quart pressure cooker. It may be used as a pressure cooker with the pressure valve on or an ordinary pot with the valve off. Its use in the galley is so valuable that we have devoted a whole chapter on it.

All other cooking utensils should be made out of stainless steel and nothing else. This includes all hardware from potato peelers to forks and spoons. Stainless steel kitchen knives are also the best choice. Their edge might not be as good as high carbon steel but they will not rust. Be sure to get a sharpening steel when you buy the knives. Look for nesting pots if you have a stowage problem.

ESSENTIAL GALLEY GEAR FOR A SMALL CRUISER

corkscrew
collander, plastic
fish scaler
bottle stoppers, 6-8
shakers, salt, flip top
pressure cooker, 6 quart
10 in. omelette pan (pg 115)
10 in. heavy pot with lid
7 in. pot (2) with lid
5 in. pot with lid
2½ in. paring knife
5½ in. chopping knife

6 in. filleting knife
8 in. serrated knife
cleaver or hatchet
mixing bowls (3)
12 in. spatula/scraper, wood
large wooden spoon
egg spatula, stainless
grater, flat
ice pick
potato peeler
can opener, heavy duty
measuring spoons

ABOUT STOVES

When selecting a marine stove, first consider what type of fuel best suits your needs.

ALCOHOL is the safest, cleanest and most odorless of the liquid fuels. It is ideal for the weekend cruiser whose family may be sensitive to the smell of burning kerosene. Alcohol is safe because it evaporates if spills or leaks occur. In addition, liquid alcohol burns at a low tempertaure, reducing the chance of injury from an accidental fire and the fire is extinguishable with water.

Alcohol and kerosene stoves burn vapor, not liquid. The liquid fuel is converted into vapor when it passes through a preheated tube in the burner head. Liquid fuel stoves are preheated by igniting alcohol in a little pan beneath the burner head. This can be an aggravating and occasionally exciting procedure. The pan must be filled, not half-filled or overfilled. If the pan is half-filled, the burner will not get hot enough. When the stove is lit, burning fuel will run in all directions. It will then be necessary to turn the burner off, let it cool, then start over again or use a torch to reheat the head. NEVER TRY TO REPRIME A HOT BURNER. The alcohol will vaporize and possibly explode. Many an eyebrow has been lost this way. If a priming pan is overfilled, burning alcohol will run everywhere. Nothing enlivens that morning cup of coffee like shaky, hung-over hands. Burning alcohol runs merrily across the counter tops, onto the floor, over bare feet, adding to the alcohol damage begun the night before.

KEROSENE vapor is intensely hot and produces the most heat per ounce. Alcohol is the coolest and least efficient. Add 10-15% to your cooking time if you use alcohol and skip recipes that call for high heat. Alcohol burns cleanly, as does kerosene, unless the burner head becomes clogged. The blue flame then turns yellow, producing soot. The best way to prevent clogged burner heads is to filter the fuel when filling the tank. Mineral spirits produce a cleaner, hotter flame than kerosene. Use it when possible.

PROPANE is hot, odorless, easy to use and highly explosive. It is best tamed by the development of good habits, especially turning the propane off AT THE TANK after use. An electrically operated solonoid should be mounted in the line at the tank. The solonoid is activated by a switch near the stove. it is fail-safe, so it must be removable in the event of power failure.

Aluminum tanks are much more expensive than steel but are worth the price as they are lighter and do not rust. Store the tanks OUTSIDE, not in a locker or down below. Leaking propane runs like water, especially on a cool day. It seeps through flooring and seeks the lowest spot in the boat – the sump under the engine. What a glorious bang it can make when the engine is started! Small tanks are easier to handle than large ones. Propane is available almost everywhere in the world, but tank fittings vary from country to country. If you cruise, it is best to carry a spare fitting, a few pieces of copper tubing and a flare tool. A local fitting can be used to make an adaptor.

In isolated places, propane is often available only in tanks. A tank-to-tank adaptor can be made and the full tank inverted over the empty one, partially filling it.

The tube from the tank to the stove should be made of copper, as short as possible, easily inspected and protected against chafe. A short neoprene tube connects the stove to the copper line. Propane lines should be inspected frequently for leaks with a brush and soapy water, not a match. Propane is an excellent fuel if used properly.

STOVES should be inspected carefully before purchase. The oven should be well insulated and should have an automatic cutoff if it uses propane. The burners should produce a large, hot flame. Stainless steel stoves look great but they are expensive. The most commonly sold American stove is in our opinion the worst unit ever made, uninsulated, poorly built, hard to repair, incredibly expensive but beautiful. Ah, well. The Italians say "sometimes one must suffer for beauty." Perhaps a camper stove would be a better choice.

A microwave oven is a true joy on a boat, odorless, cool, quick and easy to use, but requires considerable A/C power. When driven by a generator or dockside power it is a true delight.

No boat is complete without a small back-up burner with its own fuel supply, such as a gas camping stove with spare cartridges.

THE FOOD GRINDER

A small food grinder is nearly indispensable as a timesaver and opens up many culinary vistas which are otherwise closed. There is nothing like a handy food grinder when the chicken, that you proudly bought for a pittance from the local natives, turns out to be made of old tires and golf balls. There is no way to salvage the dinner that night, but the chicken salad the next day will certainly mitigate the disaster! A food grinder is also indispensable for grinding tough mollusks such as surf clams, welks, conch (for fritters) and big quahogs. In fact, a grinder will take the spine out of all tough meat, fish or fowl, allowing you to enjoy the flavor. In addition, it is ideal for reducing vegatables such as garlic and carrots to a consistency which recipes call "finely chopped" or "minced."

THE COFFEE POT

Look for a squat pot which will not easily tip. Stainless steel pots look better and last longer than aluminum. A good way to make filter coffee is with a funnel and thermos. Place the filter in the funnel and the funnel in the thermos bottle. Wedge the thermos bottle in the sink to avoid tipping. Use a large funnel to avoid spills in rough seas.

POTATO BAKER OR STOVE TOP OVEN

A potato baker can be used as a small oven to make casseroles. The type with a thermometer in the top is best. A "medium" kerosene flame produces approximately a 325° oven. A good addition to your galley if space permits.

HERBS, SALTS, AND SPICES

The following list contains 17 frequently used herbs, salts, and spices. The five with double asterisks are essential. Those with single asterisks are most useful, and the rest round out the complete galley gourmet rack. Seasonings are the basic ammunition of the galley gourmet—they are relatively cheap, last a long time, and many times make dull food distinguished. So take along as many of the following as you can store.

** Basil leaf, crushed   ** Thyme
** Celery seed   * Bay leaf
** Garlic salt   * Curry powder
** Marjoram, crushed   * Pepper corns

* Cloves, whole
* Sage

* Tarragon

Dill Weed
Fennel
Nutmeg, powdered

Bouquet Garni
Ginger powder
Oregano

And, of course, plenty of salt and pepper. Salt that doesn't come in a plastic bottle is just about useless on a boat. So are salt shakers made of aluminum or open-topped table shakers. They all permit the salt to become damp and unusable. Salt shakers with self-closing caps are good for long cruises, but small disposable units work better for weekends.

Fresh herbs are really the best for cooking, as their flavor is not marred by drying. When using fresh herbs, do not forget that their rich, robust flavor is more powerful then when dried. Never use more than ½ of what the recipe requires. Fresh herbs can sometimes be purchased in native fruit markets around the world. There is just no substitute for their delightful fresh flavor. In addition, they can be dried for future use. The best way to dry fresh herbs is to hang them in a bunch, upside down, in a cool, airy place. Direct sunshine isn't good for drying, as it weakens the flavor of the herb. Oven drying is permissible as a second choice over the air-dried method. Preheat the oven to 200°. Place a thin layer of the herb over the bottom of a pan and place in the oven. Turn the oven off at once and dry for 6 hours. The herb must be crackly and dry to the touch or it will mildew in the jar. If you are using the oven-drying method, be sure to test for dryness and repeat the heat treatment as often as necessary. Oh, yes, and don't get greedy like we did and buy a ton of it in the market. The natives will love you, but even dried herbs lose their potency after six months.

salon of "barcarolle"

MONOSODIUM GLUTAMATE

Monosodium glutamate (MSG), a form of sodium usually extracted from wheat protein, is not a spice. It was developed by D.Y. Chow, of the National Dyes Company in Hong Kong, to enhance the flavor of food. The Chinese and Cantonese use it frequently. MSG used to excess, like most things, is not good for you, and that is a fact. Fresh foods, properly cooked should not need it, for the natural flavor of well cooked food is sufficient. Canned meats, vegatables, soups and stews can probably use a bit but check the contents of the can, it may have MSG in it already. A bit more will do absolutely no good. Should the canned or frozen food not contain MSG, a pinch or, more precisely, about 5 per cent of the quantity of salt used is enough.

On a recent cruise, we tied up at Ostia Antica, the old seaport of Rome on the Tiber River. A group of scientists from the University of Rome were there accumulating data to support the theory that Rome fell not only because of Barbarians from the North but because the Romans used lead tartrate to preserve their wines. Lead, as everyone knows today, is a deadly poison causing lapses into insanity, sterility, and incipient tuberculosis. The wealthy Romans drank more wine and therefore ingested more lead. Perhaps the fits of Nero and his friends were the result of this subtle poison. This is not to say that MSG is so dangerous. It is merely a reminder for you to observe your diet intake and avoid excesses of preservatives and artificial junk.

DOING THE DISHES

A gallon of water is sufficient to wash the dishes of a meal for four people, particularly if you have easy to clean Teflon pots. Yes, it can be done! If you don't have sufficient water, wash with hot salt water and rinse in fresh. This reduces salt stains and corrosion. If you are able to wash with fresh water, put the entire ration in a kettle and heat it. Pour the hot water on the sponge or rag, not on the plate. If all this sounds like too much trouble, why not try this easy man's way. We have a friend who has a hole in every plate and utensil. He simply runs a line through the hole and throws the whole mess, pots, plates, etc., over the side. Underway, the motion of the water takes off all the excess debris, leaving only a fine oil. In port, the crabs do the work. It sure makes cleaning up easier!

PLATES

Most yachtsmen use plastic plates because they are unbreakable. Plastic plates, however, scratch and become dull quite easily. Plastic glasses look beautiful in the shop, but quickly craze from warm or cold drinks. They have the additional negative feature of retaining the smell of many drinks. Enamelware has all of the advantages of plastic, and none of the disadvantages. Its big drawback is heat retention. Being handed an enamel mug of soup is like getting a burning coal dropped on your palm! Heavy china plates have none of the disadvantages of either plastic or enamel. But, they do break. Long distance cruising chefs often prefer them, and basic white plates are cheap and always in stock.

If you have the space and don't mind paper plates and cups, we heartily recommend their use. With such a variety of sizes and shapes now available in super-strong materials why not go this easy route. Saves plenty of water, too. Remember, however there will be plenty of trash! See page 36 for hints on how to solve trash problems.

2
food stowage and storage

The best tasting food comes from the freshest materials, not from cans. If you plan to sail for a long period, say weeks or even months, careful preparation of your fresh foods will double or triple their useful life. Needless to say, refrigeration will greatly extend the life of all fresh foods. But if the space in the refrigerator is limited (isn't it always), or if you have none, do not despair. There are many ways of having real, fresh food for the duration of the cruise without refrigeration. A number of the most useful methods of food preservation are included in the following list. You can consult the indicated page for additional information.

The fruit and vegetable dip, page **28**, extends the life of unrefrigerated food by killing surface bacteria and mold.

Searing and salting meat, page **249**, preserves it for several weeks without refrigeration.

Eggs, if properly treated, last for months without refrigeration.

Hard brick cheese with pepper forced into its surface and packed in vegetable oil will last many months.

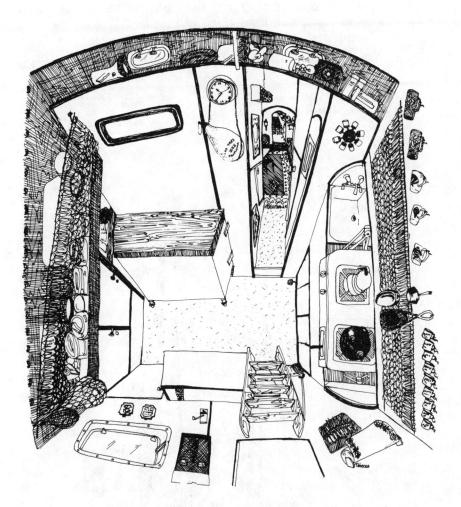

galley of "barcarolle"

Butter will last a year without refrigeration if melted and clarified (skimmed off) then poured while hot into a freshly scalded small jar and capped. (Try to keep in a cool place).

In many countries outside the USA you may purchase sterilized whole milk that needs no refrigeration. Condensed or powdered milk can be watered to taste almost like fresh.

barcarolle

Canning your own meats and vegetables is easier than you think; the results are invariably far superior to commerically tinned goods.

Generally, food normally refrigerated, such as mayonnaise and ketchup, will last several days without refrigeration. Purchase small units to permit consumption before spoilage.

Unrefrigerated food usually spoils more rapidly if exposed to air. Wrap food in plastic, or even better, coat it with vegetable oil. Cooked meat or raw fish, for example, if brushed with oil, will last much longer; the oil will not affect the taste of the meat.

PREPARATION OF TINS FOR EXTENDED SHELF LIFE

For cruises of normal length it is usually necessary to write only the contents of the can on the lid and varnish over it. This can be done with great speed and the varnish keeps the lid shiny and legible for years. So, if the label mildews or falls off, you won't have to play "can roulette." But cans do rust, even if they are not actually wet. If you plan to stock for several years, or leave supplies on the boat for an indefinite period, it is probably better to protect the entire can.

Melt one pound of paraffin wax in a bucket. Take it outside and mix in one gallon of gasoline. Dip the can, label and all, into this mixture and allow it to stand outside for at least a day to eliminate the smell of the gasoline which completely evaporates. Cans will stay bright for years and resist occasional contact with salt water. The paraffin/gasoline mixture was not originally developed for use with tins; windjammer sailors used to dip cotton coats in such a solution to make them waterproof. The coats worked well but had a bit of a greasy feeling to them, hence the name "slicker" or "oil skin."

We have used this paraffin/gasoline solution to waterproof sunawnings. Ordinary canvas painted with this mixture becomes quite waterproof and resistant to mildew.

STORAGE OF DANISH TYPE SALAMI AND DRY SAUSAGE

Both of these meats are expensive but will last up to a year without any refrigeration. The best way to store these items is to hang them, but having a dozen salamis and a few hams bashing about in a seaway can be a nuisance. Try wiping them with a cloth saturated with three parts water and one part bleach. Then put them in an unused double thickness grocery sack. New sacks are cleaner than used ones and this decreases the chance of spoilage. Check the sack periodically to be sure oil has not seeped through it.

STORAGE OF AGED HAM

Country cured ham, Spanish ham, and Italian prosciutto have been cave-aged three to five years; they are eaten without cooking. This is one of the rare exceptions to the "cook until white rule." Trichinae do not survive in cyst form for more than two years. These hams are expensive but extremely delicious. Because they often drip fatty oil, they are usually sold with a little drip pot attached. These hams will last years without refrigeration if handled properly. They must be purchased on the bone and not sliced. The best storage technique is to hang them inside a paper bag allowing essential air to circulate. To use, cut off enough from the bottom for a week's supply and generously salt the exposed bottom of the remaining ham.

WINE

How often we have met Americans sailing along the coast of Spain, Italy, or France who, while in port, take their plastic jerry cans to a bodaga and buy the cheapest wine possible. It always staggers us to see them proudly carrying their prize costing just 30 or 40 cents a liter when a dollar could buy some of the best bottled wine of the region. Not only do they have an inferior product, but also a wine that is "fresh" and does not travel well. Nothing really dramatic happens; the wine just gets a little more astringent while sloshing around mile after mile until it is only good for salads, if that. Buy the best wine you can afford. The memory of the fine taste will linger long after the pain of spending the money is forgotten.

Wine ages more rapidly on a boat because of the motion. This is an advantage, because you can purchase inexpensive new wine that would not be really good on shore for a year or two. On board it will be ready after a few months of "lee rail aging." Wine labels should be varnished to prevent their loss by moisture. They may be stored upright in the bilge. When handling a great quantity, bundle the bottles into fours to prevent their falling over and being contaminated by sea water in the bilge. The motion of the boat will keep the corks moist.

Robust reds usually last longer than whites. In addition, reds require no refrigeration to serve. Whites should be purchased fresh. White wine more than three years old becomes thin after an ocean crossing. Champagne is an exception. It travels well and, indeed, may be improved by the motion. Don't be snooty and think good wine comes only from France. Some of our favorite wines came from Morocco, Algeria, South Africa, and the United States.

Never, ever, buy a case of wine without opening a bottle and sampling it. If it is palatable in the shop, it will be even better after it has had a chance to breathe. Foolish indeed is he who trusts the recommendation of the wine merchant, for no two tongues are alike.

Wine contaminates easily; it's better to buy a fifth and finish it in a day or two than pour a bargain half gallon over the side. Besides, wine in large jugs does not travel well.

A bottle of wine weighs about 2½ pounds and makes much better trim ballast than lead, even if it's not as compact. After you drink the contents, just fill the bottle up with chlorinated water and replace the cork. You now have a fine drinking water reserve.

PURCHASING LARGE QUANTITIES OF BEER

Being beer lovers we must admit to the satisfaction of having a lazarette bulging with a supply of beer that will last for months. But beer in metal cans, especially aluminum, does not hold up well. The metal is thin and tends to develop corrosion holes which spoil the beer. These holes are not only caused by salt moisture but, in some cases, by the motion of the boat and the vibration of the engine. Varnishing the cans helps greatly to protect against corrosion.

We use a pint of varnish in 3 pints of mineral spirits. Wearing rubber gloves, dip the whole six pack in the solution and hang it from a bent wire to dry in the sun. When the cans are dry, slip a single piece of cardboard up the middle of the pack between the cans to reduce vibration damage.

A better idea for long life storage of beer is to buy it in glass bottles. The caps may be daubed with paraffin or varnish if the beer will be stored for more than six months. The disadvantage of glass is its weight. If weight is a great consideration, perhaps it is best if you purchase half cans and half bottles, using the cans first.

Beer in many foreign countries is often both good and cheap. Spain, for example, has several excellent beers that are far less expensive than U.S. brands purchased in America. Since quality and price vary so much from one country to another, it is a good idea to ask other sailors about beverages in the lands you plan to visit. Why bring coal to Newcastle?

CREATING A COOL

Citrus fruits last months, particularly if washed in the fruit and vegetable dip. Citrus drinks, lemon favored tea, even soda pop with citrus always have a cool taste even if not chilled. The temperature of bottled drinks usually can be lowered 10-20 degrees by wrapping a wet dish towel around the bottle and standing it in a bowl of water in the shade. This same procedure using alcohol instead of water is even more effective, but expensive. Perhaps having a small bottle of alcohol to chill the wine for special occasions would not be extravagant.

The sea is always cooler near the bottom, so try tying the items to be chilled to a long line and dropping them over the side.

If the area where you are sailing has cool nights, consider taking along a bucket of sawdust. Items chilled at night are then plunged into the sawdust keeping them cool all day. Be sure that the sawdust is kept dry.

Most camping stores sell canvas water bags. The canvas becomes saturated with water and provides a cool drink if hung in a shaded, breezy spot. Cloth or blanket-covered canteens accomplish the same purpose as canvas water bags but don't drip. They must be dipped in the sea periodically to resaturate.

VEGETABLES

All fresh vegetables should be removed from their containers which should be thrown away immediately and not brought aboard, if possible. The vegetables should then be soaked for a half hour in water containing a tablespoon of Clorox bleach per 2 gallons of water. After soaking, pat dry with a freshly laundered towel. The Clorox forms clorine gas that kills the mold and bacteria which normally cause spoilage. You are, in effect, sterilizing the skin and, thus, extending its life. Allow the vegetables to stand for an hour in the sun. While thoroughly drying them, the sunlight also aids sterilization. The poisons in the bleach are completely destroyed by the air and sunlight. Most vegetables should be stored in shallow fruit boxes or dish drainer trays capable of holding only one layer. The boxes should be scrubbed first with a strong bleach solution and allowed to dry thorougly. Storage in such containers reduces bruising and allows easy inspection. Inspect your fresh stores frequently and eat the vegetables with bruises first.

The life of many vegetables can be extended by keeping them covered with a cloth dampened in chlorinated water (1 tablespoon per 5 gallons). However, they cannot be covered and forgotten or mold will develop. The produce should be wiped every few days and a fresh cloth substituted. Vegetables having stems, such as artichokes and asparagus, can be kept alive and reasonably fresh by removing the dead bottom of the stem and placing the rest of the plant on a damp towel.

FRUIT

Fruit should be dipped, dried and stored in exactly the same manner as vegetables; however, do not store the two together.

Easily damaged fruit such as pears and peaches should be lightly stocked. Favor tough varieties such as oranges and apples. All citrus fruit will last for a month or more if first dipped, then dried and hung in a mesh sack. Be sure to hang the sack where it can swing unobstructed with the rolling of the boat. The citrus fruit should be inspected a few times a week. Should mold appear, dip each piece in a double strength solution of the fruit and vegetable dip. Citrus fruit plays a particularly important role in the galley of the blue water cruiser. It can be eaten whole or used to make juice for a thirsty crew. Thirst invariably turns out to be a bigger problem than anticipated.

Many fruits can be purchased green. This is excellent for an extended cruise because green fruit usually takes 5 to 9 days to begin ripening. Always carefully examine green fruit for bruises or mold since such imperfections usually destroy the fruit before it ripens. The ripening of fruit, particularly bananas, may be accelerated by dipping in the sea and placing in a sunny, breezy spot.

GRAPES

Grapes should be washed thoroughly in the fruit and vegetable dip. They are then cut into fist-sized, or smaller bunches. Jam a single grape onto the freshly cut stem of each bunch. This sacrificed grape furnishes moisture to the rest of the bunch. Keep the bunches in a towel dampened with chlorinated water. Treated grapes will last up to two weeks without refrigeration.

BANANAS

Bananas purchased in the United States are just a few days away from ripening. Finding rock hard green bananas is a futile task. But it is possible to find them in this desirable condition in the Caribbean, the Canary Islands, South America, and many areas of the Pacific. In these places bananas are incredibly cheap and make a joyous sight hanging from the backstay. We heartily recommend that you submerge your bananas in fresh water (not salt water) before bringing them aboard; banana bunches are a favorite hiding place for spiders, especially tarantulas, and for small snakes, especially boas. Even if you are certain there are no tarantulas in your bananas, wash them. A tarantula's body hair is extremely irritating and can produce an allergic reaction.

COCONUTS

Coconuts are found throughout the world in tropical and semi-tropical climates. A cruising chef should become familiar with the many virtues of this excellent food. In addition to being tasty and thirst quenching, coconuts travel extremely well and may be stored in the bilge if it is not oily. If possible, coconuts should be obtained green. They may be consumed this way or allowed to turn a mottled yellow which is a sign of maturity. Coconuts with brown husks are quite mature and somewhat past their prime. The meat has become hard and the juice is reduced but strongly flavored, delicious and good for cooking. Green coconuts are full of a tart, flavorful, slightly effervescent water which always seems to be cool. It is extremely thirst quenching but has a laxative effect when drunk to excess. Three or four nuts per day per person is approximately the maximum. Green coconut meat is gelatinous, mildly flavored, extremely delicious and just begging to be cooked into something. Mixed with chopped fruit, honey, lemon, cinnamon with a touch or rum, it is a fine dessert. Added to cooked rice, it imparts its own subtle flavor. Stirred into sauces such as hollandaise or sour cream, it makes a new creation. Green coconuts are also traditionally eaten "on the half shell." The top is whacked off with a machete, a small spoon-like edge of husk is removed to help eat the delicious jelly. The water is first drunk, then the nut is cut in half to finish the snack.

Mature nuts are hard to open and no truely effortless method to accomplish this has been discovered. The Caribbean natives drive a stake about 4 feet long into the ground at a 45 degree angle with the projecting end burned to a hard point. The stake is straddled; the nut is raised high above the head using both hands. With a hard swing, the nut is brought down onto the point of the stake. I have seen a coconut husked in about three seconds this way but always thought I might need my fingers for typing, so I never tried it myself. A safer method is to bounce the nut repeatedly off a pointed rock. Unfortunately, the nut often cracks and the "milk" is lost.

Extremely mature, dried out nuts are opened for the meat which is called copra. It is used to make coconut oil which is delicious for frying fish and chicken and imparts a bit of its own flavor to the food. Copra is also good shredded and used for dessert toppings because it is strong-flavored and sweet.

VEGETABLE SHELF LIFE

This list summarizes the shelf life of non-refrigerated, supermarket vegetables. If vegetables are refrigerated, their shelf life approximately doubles. If vegetables are personally picked, add a week to their listed shelf life. The assumption is that the cruise is in a temperate climate.

NAME	SHELF LIFE	STOWAGE	COMMENTS
Celery	3-4 days	Store upright in bucket of lightly chlorinated water	Goes limp quickly
Corn	7-10 days	Cool	Cover with a damp cloth
Cucumbers	9-14 days	Cool	
Eggplant	2-3 weeks	Cool	Buy large size pare away spongy dead outer layer
Onions, Bermuda or Spanish	2 weeks	Warm & dry	Tasteless & mushy after 2 weeks
Onions, Cepa or cooking	6-8 weeks	Hang in mesh sack	Remove shoots as they appear
Artichokes	3 weeks	Upright	Cut bottoms. Wrap in damp towel
Asparagus	7-10 days	Cool	Cut off bottoms. Place in can with damp towel in bottom
Green beans	1 week	Cool	Get very tough after a week
Peas	1 week	Cool	Cook with ½ tsp of bak-ing soda to restore color
Beets	3-4 weeks	Dry	Do not remove roots and entire stem
Broccoli	1 week	Hang	Soak bottoms in lightly chlorinated water

NAME	SHELF LIFE	STOWAGE	COMMENTS
Brussels Sprouts	3-4 days	Cool, dry	Do not cover. Remove outer leaves before cooking
Cabbage	4 weeks	Wrap in damp towel	Soak for 2-3 hours in veg. dip, shaking occasionally to assist penetration
Yams	4-6 weeks	Dry	Remove any roots or eyes before stowing
Cauliflower	7 days	Wrap in cooking oil impregnated rag	Remove leaves
Green Peppers	7-10 days	Cool	Turn red & yellow as they ripen. All colors edible
Radishes	1-2 weeks	In jar of fresh, chlorinated water	Wash in veg. dip before storing
Squash, Summer	7-10 days	Oil well	Wipe often with Cooking oil
Squash, Winter	4-6 weeks	Dry	
Zucchini See Summer Squash			
Garlic	2 months	Hang braided or in mesh sack Dry	
Carrots	3-4 weeks	Cool	Leave roots on. Cover with damp cloth. Change daily.
Potatoes	5-6 weeks	Dry	Remove eyes as they appear
Turnips	3 weeks	Dry	Leave roots on.

NAME	SHELF LIFE	STOWAGE	COMMENTS
Apples	3-4 weeks	Cool Dark	Do not bruise.
Apricots	7 days		
Avocados	2-3 weeks		Purchase rock hard and check carefully for bruises.
Bananas	3 weeks	Dark	Buy on stalk, all should be completely green, rock hard. See page 30.
Berries	5 days		Not good cruising fruit. Easily bruised. Wash in chlorinated water.
Citrus	3-5 weeks		Keep relatively cool. Wipe with fruit-vegetable dip weekly.
Grapes	2 weeks		Washed in fruit dip, cut into bunches, page 30. Wrap in towel dampened with chlorinated water.
Mangoes	14-20 days		Buy rock hard, green; check for bruises, store in a bowl as mangoes emit resin as they ripen.
Melon	7 days		
Peaches	4-7 days		Purchase rock hard. Wrap in fresh tissue paper
Pears	10-14 days		Purchase rock hard and green
Pineapples	2-3 weeks	Upright	Purchase green
Pomegranates	2 weeks	Cool	

MEAT

The only area where the lack of refrigeration hurts is in the fresh meat department. You will notice, however, from the meal plans in the next chapter that man can live without fresh meat. However, meat can be kept for approximately two weeks in a simple homemade freezer. The best container is an old packing crate. Two inches of sawdust or polyurethane granules (they don't absorb water as sawdust does) go in the bottom. Next comes at least 1½ inches of dry ice. Next the meat, foil wrapped, frozen rock hard, and clearly marked. Then another inch of insulation on the sides and on top. The secret of success is to layer the meat in the order of consumption insuring that the box is open to the air as little as possible. Do not be alarmed by the gas escaping from this container; is only the dry ice evaporating. A good idea is to place the crate in a big sack, or sheet, because the loose packing material can make a mess.

REFRIGERATION

Refrigeration doubles the life of most fruits and vegetables. If you have a large refrigerator, you can have fresh food on the menu every day of your voyage. Our only suggestions for chefs in this enviable position are to keep away from delicate stores like peaches and to wash everything in the fruit and vegetable dip to retard mold.

KEEPING FOOD ON ICE

Many yachts have ice chests, which can be a godsend on a short cruise. There are several facts about using ice chests that are important to know. We have all heard that ice is only as good as the water used to make it. In most areas ice is made from the drinking water supply. However, some ice is made for commercial purposes such as chilling trawler fish. It is not intended for human consumption. The best guarantee is to find another yachtsman who bought some ice the day before. If he is still functioning normally, the ice is most likely just fine.

When using an ice chest it is extremely important that fruit and vegetables are not lying directly on the ice. Temperatures below 34° damage produce. Meat should be securely wrapped or it will impart its flavor to the ice and everything else it touches. Algae and some molds are hearty growths that can thrive in an ice chest. It is always a good idea to wipe the inside of the box with a strong bleach solution both when changing ice and at the beginning and end of a cruise. Never let ice water stand in the bilge, even in a fiberglass boat. It is almost invariably contaminated with bacteria which will multiply and foul whatever they touch.

Dry ice is really excellent for a cruise, especially if it is used a little at a time and kept well insulated. If well wrapped, big blocks of dry ice should keep for two or more weeks. When it evaporates there is very little water residue. Dry ice is, of course, much colder than regular ice and fresh stores must be kept off it. The blocks in the bottom of the ice chest should be wrapped first in aluminum foil, then newspaper, and finally slipped into a plastic bag to prevent the newspaper from fouling the ice chest. As the ice on top is used, the blocks on the bottom are unwrapped and utilized.

MAKING A STOWAGE PLAN

Sketch a plan of the stowage spaces in the boat and assign each a letter. The large, dry spaces are for items such as packaged pasta, wet places for prepared tins, dark, cool spots for fruit and vegetables, hot areas for grains and cereals, and the bilge for glass and plastic bottles. Keep a space near the galley for a miscellaneous handy reserve. Try to keep like items together and in the same location. With a little organization, you will have everything at your fingertips. Fresh stores should be kept in an easily cleaned and highly accessible location.

Eggs are best stored in plastic travel packs available at camping supply stores. These packs will store anywhere but first sterilize them with bleach. Cereals must be inspected for and protected against weevils, see page 296. Hygroscopic (water absorbing) items, such as salt and bouillon cubes, must be stored with grains of rice in a tight plastic containers.

THE TRASH PROBLEM

The word "trash" and the word "problem" seem to be used together both on land and at sea. But on land the problem is usually someone else's, at least after the odoriferous bundle hits the bottom of the trash can. At sea the problem is yours alone. How you handle it is a matter of conscience and necessity.

There is nothing more ghastly than sailing into some isolated place only to find the litter of some thoughtless person fouling the beach. If you are near land go ashore with a few pints of mineral spirits and thoroughly burn your trash, or, better, bury it.

No matter how ecology-minded you are, there comes a moment on extended sea voyages when the only sensible place for that pungent bundle is in the sea. It is not as bad as it sounds. Organic garbage is quickly eaten by sea creatures. Glass bottles and jars are inert and will eventually be reduced to sand. Cans rust away. Beer cans should have holes punched in them so they sink. The only hazard is plastic products, especially foam such as styrene and urethane. Sheet plastic, used for garbage bags, settles to the bottom forming an impermeable membrane. No one knows if it ever breaks down in those sunless depths. Styrene and urethane are eventually reduced to individual plastic bubbles which seem to have the lifespan of a grain of sand. Some believe these bubbles are affecting fish reproduction. Their effect is cumulative since they do not dissolve in body tissue. The next time you walk along a tide line, look carefully; you may be amazed at how many tiny plastic bubbles you may see. The great ocean currents usually carry these products out of sight. But in the Mediterranean you cannot sail half an hour without seeing plastic trash. Reduce your contribution of plastic trash by not using it. Buy paper cups and plates, or use china ware. When plastic products are used, wash and store them for disposal ashore. They can be burned when you make a landfall.

The sea, once believed capable of absorbing unlimited pollution, is a delicate, organic solution that can be rendered incapable of supporting life. It doesn't matter who the villain is, does it?

SHIPBOARD PESTS

You must be certain that there are no live pests aboard at the beginning of a cruise. Roaches are the worst problem. In comparison to a house, the problem of ridding a boat of roaches is tremendous. They hide in air pockets and are, therefore, resistant to non-professional fumigation. Sprays, baits, and residuals are merely methods of containing the problem. Once infested, it is questionable that any of these techniques will remedy the situation. Large boats (above 43 feet) present greater problems because of space between double walls, panels, ceiling and air conduits. How many roaches constitute infestation? If you come aboard at night and see three roaches, you have a real problem.

The first assault must be massive, for roaches are an adversary not to be underestimated. Buy one of every pesticide available. Use them all at once (except the fogger). Baits, usually tablets or meal, and residual liquids contain boric acid. The liquids are painted along corners and over surfaces. If you can't find them at the store, make you own as follows. In a paint can marked "POISON" combine:

½ pint water
2 tablespoons honey
2 teaspoons boric acid powder (available at drugstores.)

A safe insecticide like our water, honey, boric acid solution will not cause you grief—unless you drink it at tea time!

Roach-resistant shelf paper is also good for your first assault, but it loses its potency in a few weeks and the surviving roaches become resistant to it.

Three days after your first efforts, fog the whole boat. Lift floor boards, access plates, cabinets, and lockers. Remove drawers, shake out sails, and destroy cardboard cartons. Put all paper trash bags in a neat pile and stomp all over them. This is a favorite home of roaches. Seal air vents, tape refrigerator, and store exposed food on deck. Then, you're ready to use foggers; some in the bilge, one under the galley sink, in the galley, the head(s), the salon, quarters...everywhere. If possible, sleep on deck that night. The longer the boat remains sealed, the better. Refog in 10 days to kill just-hatched roaches. If you see a roach within three days after fogging, you have lost the battle. Call an exterminator and have him gas the boat.

Roaches are miserable but not deadly. You can live with them, and aside from a feeling of disgust and the several gnawed cartons, they will casue you no harm.

MICE

These little animals can cause much damage to your vessel but, fortunately, are easily dealt with. Use traps and bait, but keep your toes out of the traps! All capitannerie du porte, or pest control officers, in every port are charged by international law with the responsibility of rendering assistance in the destruction of ship board pests. They almost invariably give willing assistance in the form of fresh bait and traps which are supplied free or at nominal cost.

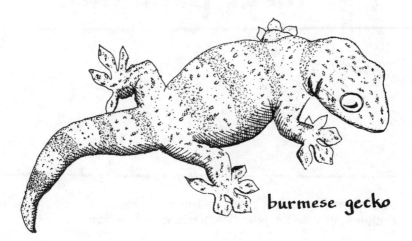

burmese gecko

NATURAL PREDATORS

Cats usually eat insect pests and some may be willing to kill mice. In addition, it is quite unusual for a mouse to come on a boat that smells of a cat.

We had a friend who became infested with large roaches while sailing through Burma. He bought an 8-inch lizard called a gecko in a market place. Its name was Alfred. Alfred slept in a shoe box during the day; at night he quietly ate roaches. Sometimes he hung from the ceiling. Our friend claimed Alfred was quite friendly, made great efforts to avoid being stepped on, and never kept union hours. When it ate itself out of business, our grateful friend fed it hamburger.

3
meal planning

Meal planning is an asset in the most modern, well-stocked kitchens; in a ship's galley it is a matter of survival.

MEAL PLANNING FOR A SEA VOYAGE

Everyone realizes that meal planning for ocean voyage is different from planning for a coast cruise. The stores for an ocean passage must be balanced and complete, while a coast cruise allows more freedom. You can take advantage of bargains, stocking heavily in some areas and not at all in others.

Many people planning a long cruise seem to envision themselves as sons of the Flying Dutchman, touching shore but once a year to take on stores. Even the slowest boat will cross the Atlantic Ocean in 45 days and the Pacific in even less. So taking on balanced stores for six or more months is unnecessary. The essence of good planning is to provision for the ocean passage, generously allowing 15-20 percent excess for delays, then filling any remaining storage space with local bargains.

The definite bargains in the USA are whisky, clothing, fruit juices (an excellent buy), bottom paint, line, yacht gear, and oil (which costs $2.30/pt. in some places). Some of the cruising areas of the world have such a high cost of living that nearly everything is more than in the USA. Take Bermuda, for example. In 1970 we paid $2.00 for a head of cauliflower. In the Bahamas nearly everything is 40 percent more expensive than in the USA.

"barcarolle"

In the Marquesas, imported goods cost nearly double. Japan, Australia and New Zealand, to name a few, have similar high tariffs on imports. It is almost always a safe bet to stock items not produced in your expected cruising area; it will probably cost much more as an import. We love American artichokes packed in oil, but these are difficult to find and very expensive outside the USA. Such expensive gourmet items, if locally produced, are usually a good bet. But think of how silly it would be to stock cheap, heavy items like tinned soup, vegetable oil, or flour which are inexpensive everywhere.

A frequent error which many long distance cruisers make is to purchase large quantities of food in commercial supply houses. This is a mistake for several reasons. First, the actual savings over regular supermarket prices is usually less than ten percent. Often this amount can be saved if you ask the supermarket manager for a discount. Second, commerical supply houses often do not carry the exact brand you desire. You may end up with several cases of something you really don't like. Third, it is far better to have a wide variety of goods rather than a huge quantity of one or two things. After all, variety is the spice of life.

Fourth, and our final reason why commercial supply houses are not recommended, is they usually do not stock the smallest sizes of some tinned goods. Purchasing cans that are too much for one meal invites trouble. Unrefrigerated open cans are the first step to a good case of food poisoning.

If you purchase case lots in their original crates, be sure to open them on the dock and not on the boat. Cardboard cartons often contain roaches, silverfish, or their eggs. If a few of these pests get loose at the beginning of a long cruise, your life may be miserable, indeed.

Having made a number of ocean crossings, often with guests and crew, we have learned the best way to prepare for a cruise is to make a week's menu. We include everything, right down to the midnight snacks. Show this menu to everyone in the ship's company to make sure there are no strong objections. Then make a list of ingredients for each recipe and multiply by the number of weeks in the voyage. If the voyage is an ocean crossing, make two meal plans, one for the first two weeks and the other for the rest of the voyage when the delicate, fresh stores, like lettuce, are gone. This approach works very well for meal plans, but snacks and beverages often end in short supply.

puerta josé banus

If the weather is hot and the crew are not seasoned, the beverage consumption can be fantastic. Allow at least four big glasses of ready-mixed beverages, such as beer, wine, and juice, per man, and a potential five glasses of mix with water drinks such as quick lemonade, ice tea, mint tea, and powdered juice. This approach will not only provide beverage diversity, but also provides a hedge against water tank contamination.

Once we lost our entire fresh water supply four days out of the Canary Islands on a transatlantic delivery. A cover plate cracked, allowing diesel fuel to contaminate the fresh water. We faced a 4,000 mile crossing to Miami with 5 gallons of emergency water and 2 gallons of battery water. Fortunately, we had a large reserve of bottled juice and wine. Between the bottled liquids and a small amount of collected rain water, we honestly can say that we did not suffer for a moment. How different the picture would have been without bottled stores!

Try to keep away from nutritionally limited snacks, such as candy and potato chips. Nuts are a great snack. Although they are expensive in the USA, prices are higher nearly everywhere else. Salami, cheese, and dried fruit also make fine snacks. Oatmeal cookies are particularly good because they do not become stale quickly and are easily revived by heating. Hot chocolate and an oatmeal cookie make a great dogwatch snack. Prepared snacks, such as hard boiled eggs, deviled eggs, stuffed celery, hot soup (kept in a thermos), or even more hefty snacks, such as ready-to-eat chili, beef stew, or chowder, are recommended.

TESTED TRANSATLANTIC MEAL PLANS

These menus and the accompanying ingredients were tested on a four week transatlantic crossing from the Canary Islands in 1972. Galley facilities consisted of a two-burner kerosene stove and a work top area of about 3 square feet. There was no oven, no refrigeration, and a very small sink. As we discovered, elaborate facilities were unnecessary to produce pleasant, acceptable meals.

We did not stick to all of these menus. All food entries are completely interchangeable to suit your needs. Make new dishes from leftovers, change lunch for dinner, and skip breakfast, if you wish. The menu and the stores list assure that needed ingredients are aboard. Dave, the owner of the boat, was a fussy eater who didn't like anything highly seasoned. Mayonnaise was even too much for him. Bacon and eggs were his favoriate meal.

the mate

the foredeck

So this meal plan should be particularly acceptable, especially for those "morning after sailors," as well as those trying to get their sea legs.

The second meal plan from yacht BARCAROLLE is for more sophisticated palates. The usual approach is to buy the final fresh stores at the last jumping off place for the voyage. Buy the full projected list of stores for the length of the voyage, then purchase an additional load of fresh perishables for immediate use. This gives the necessary hedge against a slow passage and eliminates the hassle of guessing how long the fresh stores will last.

We have included the following two meal plans not as suggested menus for your cruise, but to show how well one can eat at sea and how easy stores projection really is. It is far better that you include your own favorite recipes and take into consideration the tastes of your crew.

YACHT CORRINA MEAL PLAN
(Without Refrigeration)

	BREAKFAST	LUNCH	DINNER
MONDAY	Oranges Fried eggs Bacon Toast, jam Coffee	Tomato soup Ham sandwiches Baked beans Pudding	Beef stew casserole with peas, carrots, potatoes. Tinned pineapple. Tinned cake.
TUESDAY	Hot applesauce Soft-boiled eggs Tinned ham, fried Toast Coffee	Hot dogs Fried onion rings Deviled eggs Tinned apricots	Hot tuna casserole Buttered noodles Carrots Loganberries with cream
WEDNESDAY	Hot cereal with raisins Tinned sausage Toast Coffee	Applesauce Macaroni Buttered peas Cookies	Spaghetti with tomato and cheese sauce. Green beans with bacon. Fried garlic bread
THURSDAY	Mushroom omelet Sausage Toast Coffee Grape juice	Lentil soup Sardine pate on crackers Salami and cheese Rice pudding	Potato pancakes Applesauce Sliced cold ham Chocolate pudding
FRIDAY	Pineapple juice Soft-boiled eggs Tinned pastry Bacon Coffee	Tinned roast beef French fried potatoes Pineapple rings Cookies	Curried chicken Rice pilaf Turnips Butterscotch pudding
SATURDAY	Oranges Cold cereal Cheese omelet Bacon Coffee	Tuna fish salad Cold noodles Buttered peas Tinned cake	Cornbeef hash with potatoes and onions Buttered peas Apricots
SUNDAY	Grapefruit French toast Bacon Coffee	Chiliburgers French fries Tinned peaches Chocolate	Candied ham Mashed potatoes Buttered green beans Chocolate

*SNACKS: Cheese slices   Oatmeal cookies
             Chocolate   Oranges, Grapefruit
             Mixed nuts   Hard-boiled eggs

YACHT BARCAROLLE MEAL PLAN
(Non-refrigerated Menu from Long-Lasting Stores)

	BREAKFAST	LUNCH	DINNER
MONDAY	Fried eggs Bacon Toast Oranges Coffee	Lentil soup with bacon, sliced onions. Carrot & raisin salad Fruit Beer	Glazed ham. Green peas. French fried potatoes. Zabaglione with Gran Marnier. Red wine. Expresso
TUESDAY	Mushroom & onion omelet. Crackers with cheese Sliced apples Hot tea	Spaghetti Carbonara. Olives. Artichoke-pickled beet platter. Red wine	Atria beef. Steamed carrots, olives & onions. Beer Chocolate pudding Coffee
WEDNESDAY	Scotch eggs Tinned ham, fried Toast with soy Butter Coffee	Split pea soup with leftover ham chunks, croutons & onion slices. Fish pate on crackers. White wine	Tuna casserole French fried onion rings. Steamed carrots and turnips Dessert fruit omelet White wine. Tea
THURSDAY	Buckwheat pancakes with maple syrup. Tinned sausage Oranges Hot chocolate	Melted cheese sandwiches. Bean sprout salad with boiled eggs. Pineapple juice	Bean 'n bacon dinner. Chinese fried carrots with soy sauce. Tapioca pudding. Nuts. Provolone and port red wine. Expresso
FRIDAY	Hot cereal with dried fruit Bacon. Coffee Cinnamon toast	Kippers on toast. Potato salad with garlic mayonnaise. Crackers, apples, cheese. Ice tea	Salmon croquettes Artichokes with Hollandaise. Carrot & raisin salad. Sliced fruit Beer. Coffee
SATURDAY	Cheese omelet Hash brown potatoes Toast. Coffee	Ham sandwiches with onions, mayonnaise, mustard, garlic. Cole slaw. Beer	Lentil burgers Steamed cabbage or sauerkraut. Pan cake, w. whipped cream. Beer or red wine
SUNDAY	Fresh corn bread with syrup Tinned sausage Orange & apple slices. Coffee	Boston soy bean soup w. bacon & onion. Cruising Salad Nicoise fruit salad. V-8 Juice w. lemon	Spanish fritatta omelet. Melted cheese on crackers. Applesauce. White wine

BARCAROLLE MEAL PLAN (con't)

SNACKS:

Mixed nuts

Coconut chocolate
  chip cookies

Walnuts, Parmesan
  chunks & port

Fruit cake slices

Apples

Tinned cheese

Oatmeal cookies

Dried apricots

Sunflower seeds

Oranges

Artichokes on crackers

BEVERAGES:

Beer (2 per man per day)

Red wine

White wine

Port

Sherry

V-8 juice

Pineapple juice

Grape juice

Tea

Coffee

Grand Marnier

FOUL WEATHER RESERVE FOOD: Beef stew in individual tins

SAMPLE FOOD TALLY SHEET

Each meal is broken down into its component ingredients and tallied on a sheet. We submit here two lunches from the Barcarolle menu as examples. Each meal serves four. When tallying ingredients, be sure to include everything you need to complete a week's menu. Multiply the ingredients by the number of weeks at sea. If you have an alternate week's menu, tally these ingredients also.

I. Curried lentil soup with bacon, page 107
    Sliced onions,
    Carrot and raisin salad, page 315
    Fruit
    Beer

II. Spaghetti carbonara, page 290
    Olives
    Artichoke, pickled beets
    Red wine

MEAT

Bacon, lbs./

CARBOHYDRATES

Lentils, cups ////

Spaghetti, lbs. /

BEVERAGES

Red wine, bottles /

White wine/

Beer, tins ////

49

VEGETABLES, TINNED
Olives, black, tins /
Artichokes, jars /
Pickled beets, tins /

MISCELLANEOUS
Bouillon cubes, chicken //
Olive oil, cups ¼
Eggs, dozens ¼
Parmesan, grated, cups /
Honey, cups ¼
Mayonnaise, cups ¼

SPICES
Bay leaf /
Curry powder, tablespoons /
Ginger, tablespoons /
(salt & pepper)

FRUIT
Raisins, cups /
Apples //
Oranges ////

DRINKS (not included above)
V-8 juice ////
Grape juice, qts. /
Tea bags ////

VEGETABLES, FRESH
Onions //
Garlic, halves /
Carrots, dozens ½

SNACKS (not included above)
Cookies, bags ½
Cheese wedges ////
Nuts, tins ½

MEAL PLANNING FOR COAST CRUISES

On coast cruises fresh stores are accessible. The essence of good planning is to load the heavy and bulky items, such as beverages, canned goods, sugar, etc., at the beginning of the cruise when transportation is reliable. In addition, it is always a good idea to have the ingredients on hand for at least a week's meals in case the vessel is becalmed or caught in bad weather. Remember, most food except meat and a few delicate vegetables will keep without refrigeration for more than two weeks. It never hurts to have a supply of apples or oranges, green tomatoes, and potatoes on the shelf. Remember, however, stores will be accessible. Why not enjoy fresh eggs and produce while they are available.

On the other hand, if you know very little about the area you will cruise, stock for a longer period of time. Frequently, we have dropped the hook in a place when the chart shows a nearby town, only to find that the nearest grocery was four miles away. How glad we were to have the ingredients for a fine meal on board.

4
pressure cooking

As was said in Chapter One, if your ship is big enough for just one pot, make it a pressure cooker! This wonderful tool, used only occasionally in the home, becomes the unvarying pot of choice in the galley. It may be used as an ordinary pot. But if the sea becomes rough, the lid may be clamped on, effectively preventing spills no matter how rough the weather. With the lid clamped on and the pressure valve in place the pressure cooker reduces cooking time by 65 to 90 per cent. Contrary to popular belief, the pressure cooking of recommended foods does not impair their flavor or texture. We believe that statements to the contrary invariably come from those who have not fully mastered the use of this incredible tool. Some foods unquestionably taste better and are more nutritious when pressure cooked. Vegetables stay crisp when pressure steamed, tough meats become tender, and infuriatingly long cooking items like brown rice are finished in less than half the time. Fuel savings with a pressure cooker are even greater than time savings. The tiny flame needed to keep the pressure regulator jiggling uses a pittance of fuel. If you have made a great cauldron of something delicious and have no place to store it, the pressure cooker becomes a fine refrigeration-free hermetic container.

The pressure cooker reduces cooking time by increasing the boiling temperature of the cooking liquid. Normally, it is impossible to make water boil above 212° F. If you increase the flame, the water boils faster, but the temperature remains the same. There is, however, a direct relationship between pressure and temperature. This is the reason why water boils below 212° F at high elevations where atmospheric pressure is less. The opposite is also true. If the pressure inside a pot is increased, the boiling temperature of water is also increased. At 5 pounds additional pressure, water will boil at 227° F. At 10 pounds, the temperature is 240° F, and at 15 pounds additional pressure, water will boil at 250° F. This last temperature decreases the cooking time of food from the first jiggle of the pressure regulator by 75 to 90 percent. Boiled new potatoes, for example, normally take 25 minutes to cook. But in the pressure cooker they take just 2½ minutes—a time saving of 90 percent!

It is commonly believed that pressure cooking impairs the flavor of some foods. This is not true. Because pressure cooking is rapid, it is easy to overcook food; overcooked food, of course, never tastes right. We have attempted in this book to give minimum cooking times. In many cases it will be necessary to simmer the dish for an additional 5 to 10 minutes to correct the seasoning, consistency, and cooking time. A common cause of overcooking is failure to realize that pressure cooked food will continue to cook, because of internal heat, long after the flame has been turned off. If the food is delicate, it is essential to stop this cooking immediately. The best method is to pour lots of cold water over the pot. Sea water works fine, but it does mar the pot's finish. An ugly pot cooks just as well, however, so don't worry.

The pressure cooker not only decreases cooking time, it also decreases the necessary amount of cooking liquid. Vegetables, for example, can be steamed in a scant cup of water. Baked beans normally take up to 5 hours of regular oven cooking, and 5 to 7 cups of water for each cup of beans. But in a pressure cooker, 30 minutes at 15 pounds is sufficient and 2½ to 3 cups of water per cup of beans is plenty. But too little water can be disasterous. The pot cannot be "watched" like a standard one, so additional water cannot be added at just the right moment.

There is no culinary disaster like burning a pot of pressure cooked food. The ghastly awful smell is usually the first warning, but by that time it's far too late to save the meal. Just a few minutes after the horrible smell, the safety plug in the pressure lid melts. At this point you have not only ruined the meal, but caused the pressure cooker to become so badly encrusted with charred food that drastic measures are necessary to save it. Be sure to follow the recommended liquid requirements most carefully and do keep an eye on the pot while it is in action.

USING THE PRESSURE COOKER

A pressure cooked meal is always simmered for some few minutes before putting the lid on. Meats and chicken are thoroughly browned in oil or butter. This sears the flesh, seals in juices, gives better color and helps equalize the cooking time with the vegetables. When the added liquid is rapidly simmering, the pressure lid is clamped in place and a half minute later the pressure regulator is added. The flame is reduced to medium. When the pressure regulator gives a loud, definite snort or jiggle, the timing of the meal begins. The flame is reduced to low, or just enough heat to allow a jiggle every half minute. Tuning an ear to the "rhythm of the pot" is extremely important. Should the jiggling action suddenly cease, it is possible the pot has run out of water or the pressure vent is blocked. In this case the flame should be turned off and the pot immediately cooled with water. While cooling the pot, keep your face away from the safety plug. Should the plug blow out (an extremely rare occurence), you woundn't want your chin to be the backstop! If the pressure vent is blocked, clean it with a pin or toothpick and be sure that the pot is not too full—never more than ¾ full of solid meat or chicken and not more than half full of heavy soup or boiling potatoes.

When the cooking time is reached, turn off the flame and cool the pot. The lid will open easily when the pressure inside the pot is reduced. Never try to force the lid open; pressure inside the pot locks the lid on. There is a pot full of super-heated steam under that lid, and you will get it in the face if you try to force it open!

IMPORTANT RULES FOR PRESSURE COOKING

Never fill the pressure cooker more than ¾ full, and never more than ½ full when making thick soups or heavy sauces— these sputter and may block the pressure vent.

Season pot contents lightly; correct the seasoning in the final, lid-off moments of cooking. There is less liquid to carry the seasoning and added flavors are intensified under pressure. Try to use the cooking liquid as a sauce, since it contains many nutrients.

Bring the pressure pot up to the first jiggle over medium heat, then reduce the flame to the minimum necessary to produce 2-3 jiggles per minute. **Never** use high heat.

Timing a pressure cooked meal begins with the jiggle of heavy snort of steam—not with the steady hiss which begins much sooner.

When cooking delicate items, such as vegetables, stop cooking by internal heat immediately—pour cold water over the pot. Less sensitive soups and stews may be allowed to cool gradually.

Never force a pressure lid open. The lid is locked by steam pressure you will be badly burned should you force it.

Equalize the cooling time of ingredients by cutting the less delicate items into smaller pieces.

USING THE PRESSURE COOKER IN BAD WEATHER

The hardest job we know is to make food in bad weather. Most galley chefs instinctively turn to tinned food; no one can really blame them. It is only the veteran blue water chef who can patiently combine basic ingredients in a galley which is wildly gyrating through an arc of 50° while simultaneously dropping off the crest of a twenty foot high wave. The most that can be expected from the galley in really mean weather is something hot, nourishing, and edible. Perhaps, the easiest is an individual tin of stew that has been heated in the pressure cooker and poured into a mug, followed by a bracing mug of buttered rum. Forget about the hour, it's always rum time when the sea is sweeping through the cockpit!

When heating the tins, open and nestle them in the pressure cooker using a bed of aluminum foil to prevent tipping. Add 3 cups of water and pressure cook, with the lid on, pressure regulator off, for 6 minutes after steam starts coming from the hole. The contents of the can will then be piping hot.

Hard-boiled eggs can be made in a pressure cooker, lid on, pressure regulator off. Use two cups of cold water and not more eggs than will cover the bottom of the pot. Cook 5 minutes after steam comes from the pressure vent. Soft-boiled eggs take 3½ minutes.

For other recipes, reduce cooking time 25 percent for lid on, pressure regulator off cooking. If the pressure cooker is used with the pressure regulator on during bad weather, never fill the cooker more than one-half full; one-quarter full, preferably. This reduces the possibility of vent blockage due to the motion of the boat.

PRESSURE COOKING MEAT

Meat should be browned before pressure cooking to seal in flavor. The cooking times listed in the following table do not include the browning time. Remember, all pressure cooking times begin with the first jiggle of the pressure regulator.

MEAT (serves 4)	COOKING TIME IN MINUTES AT 15 LBS.	REQUIRED AMOUNT OF WATER FOR COOKING
Pot roast of beef, 3-in. thick, approx. 1½ lbs.	20	1¼ cups
Short ribs of beef, stacked loosely, parboiled 5 min.	20	1¼ cups
Hamburger stew, 1 to 1½ lbs. mixed with vegetables	10	¾ cup
Beef stew, bite-sized chunks with mixed vegetables	12	1½ cups
Beef or veal shanks	20	¾ cup
Swiss or flank steak	15	1 cup
Rump, camel, young, 2½-in. slice	20	1 cup
Chicken, cut up Add 10 min. for old bird	10	1½
Lamb shoulder approx. 2½ to 3 lbs.	25	1½ cups
Lamb stew	15	2 cups
Mutton, trim excess fat approx. 2½ lbs.	25	1½ cups

MEAT (serves 4)	COOKING TIME IN MINUTES AT 15 LBS.	REQUIRED AMOUNT OF WATER FOR COOKING
Ham shank or shoulder approx. 2½ to 3 lbs.	25	1 cup
Ham, 2-in. slice, uncooked approx. 2 lbs.	15	¾ cup
Oxtails in a stew, trim excess fat	20	2 cups
Pork shanks	22	2 cups
Pork shoulder 2 to 3-in. cut, well browned	15	1½ cups
Pork chops, in a stew	20	2 cups
Pork ribs, parboiled, first, to remove excess fat	8	to cover
Rabbit stew, add 4 minutes for hares	12	2 cups

PRESSURE COOKING VEGETABLES

Vegetables are most nutritious and flavorful when steamed in a pressure cooker. Place a rack, trivet, or makeshift unit* in the bottom of the cooker to keep the vegetables off the water. One and one-half cups of liquid is used when cooking requires more than 10 minutes. Use one cup of water when vegetables require 10 minutes or less cooking time. The water on the vegetables may be seasoned with aromatic spices, such as lemon peel, thyme, or rosemary. Season lightly; vegetables are

*A handy makeshift trivet can be made from aluminum foil placed on aluminum foil balls or long bolts—even wadded chicken wire.

easily dominated by seasonings. Just a pinch of the desired herb is enough to season pressure steamed vegetables for four. When the cooking time has elapsed, the pot should be instantly cooled with salt water. Additional cooking time can make mush out of vegetables.

Vegetables with similar cooking times may be mixed with no intermingling of flavors. This technique is particularly nice when used with vegetables of different colors, such as green beans and yellow summer squash. After becoming familiar with this technique, try mixing vegetables with different cooking times. Simply slice the slower cooking vegetables into smaller pieces than the faster cooking vegetables.

FRESH VEGETABLES

VEGETABLE	COOKING TIME IN MINUTES AT 15 LBS.
Artichokes	10
Asparagus	2
Beans, fresh green or wax	3 to 4
Beans, lima or fresh soy	3
Beets, large, quartered	5
Beets, small, whole	10
Broccoli, flowers	2
Brussels sprouts	4
Cabbage, shredded (white)	3
Cabbage, shredded (red)	4
Cabbage, wedges	4 to 5
Carrots, sliced thinly	2
Carrots, small or cut up	4
Cauliflower in flowers	3
Celery, stalks	4
Corn on the cob	3 to 5
Eggplant, in ½—¾" rounds	3
Kale (collard greens)	4
Okra	3
Onions, sliced or chopped	2½
Onions, small whole	5 to 7
Parsnips in ½—¾" slices	2
Peas, green, shelled	2
Potatoes, sliced or diced	3 to 5
Potatoes, small whole	8 to 10

VEGETABLE	COOKING TIME IN MINUTES AT 15 LBS.
Potatoes, yams or sweet, quarters	6
Pumpkin wedges	9 to 12
Turnips, cut up	3 to 5
Spinach	1 to 2
Squash, soft summer	3
Squash, hard winter	10 to 12
Tomatoes, peeled	2
Zucchini	2½

DRIED VEGETABLES

Some recipes for cooking dried vegetables specify soaking overnight in water. We usually never do this on board; if pressure cooked, the beans listed below turn out just fine. Never add less water than is specified. These beans absorb water while cooking and burn easily.

VEGETABLE (1 CUP DRY)	COOKING TIME IN MINUTES AT 15 LBS.	REQUIRED AMOUNT OF WATER FOR COOKING (4 QT COOKER)
Black eyed peas	10	2 cups
Northern beans	22	3 cups
Kidney beans	30	3 cups
Lentils	25	3 cups
Lima beans	25	3 cups
Navy beans	30	3 cups
Pinto beans	12	3 cups
Soy beans	30	3 cups

Fifty percent of the watery additives, such as tomatoes, tomato paste, may be counted toward the water requirements of these beans. Old beans occasionally take much, much longer to cook, page 104; don't be surprised if the cooking time is insufficient.

green heron hunting

PRESSURE COOKING SOUPS AND CHOWDERS

Pressure cooking drastically reduces the cooking time of soups and chowders with absolutely no loss of nutrients. A pressure cooker seems just made for soup cooking; it works so efficiently. But some important DON'Ts must be considered.

1. Never fill the pot more than ½ full, because the contents can bubble up and block the pressure vent.
2. Never add less water then the recipe specifies; some dried ingredients readily absorb water and the food may burn. It is better to add a bit more water than necessary, pressure cook less time than specified, and simmer to the right thickness later, with the lid off.
3. Do not combine delicate vegetables with long cooking meat, unless, of course, you don't mind mush. It is best to pressure cook the meat first, then add the vegetables and simmer until done, lid loose.
4. Most pressure cooker manuals do not recommend making split pea soup or cooking barley. They claim these items tend to jam the pressure vent. We have made both soups many, many times without difficulty. Just be sure to fill the pot not more than half full and do not use high heat to produce the first jiggle.

Soup can be "home canned" right on board. Cook it 10-15 minutes in a regular pot, then pour the soup into glass jars and cook for the required time in the pressure cooker.

We have specified pressure cooking for soup in most of the recipes included in this book. As a rule-of-thumb the times in the chart below may be useful.

SOUP	COOKING TIME IN MINUTES AT 15 LBS
Meat soup (on bone)	35
Legume soup (dried bean)	30
Chicken soup	30
Beef dices (soup)	30
Ham dices and bean	35
Vegetables in broth	8
Fish chowder	6

A reminder: If there is a great difference between the cooking time of several ingredients, it is better to add the more delicate ones just before the soup is cooked. This results in crisp, delicious vegetables that have not lost their flavor to the broth.

A favorite trick of ours is to add a small handful of delicate fresh vegetables such as peas, tender beans, carrot shavings, or grated cabbage to the soup as soon as it is completely cooked. The internal heat of the soup cooks the added vegetables just crisp and the fine flash of color spices the meal.

PRESSURE COOKING DRIED FRUIT

Dried fruit makes a fine dessert and cooks beautifully in a pressure cooker. Fresh fruit may be added, but after the pressure cooking is completed. Put the fresh fruit in the pressure cooker with the flame off, the internal heat of the pot will cook it sufficiently.

Dried fruit should be soaked in enough water to cover for an hour prior to cooking. All other ingredients, except fresh fruit, should be added at this time.

The recipe below, made with any type of fried fruit, is a favorite "end of the passage" treat.

2   cups dried fruit
4   cup raisins
2   tablespoons lemon juice
3   tablespoons brown sugar or honey
1   tablespoon rum
1   teaspoon cinnamon
4   cups water

Pressure cook for 2 minutes. (If using figs or prunes, cook for 6 minutes.) Cool slowly.

PRESSURE COOKING CEREALS

When pressure cooking cereals, follow the liquid recommendations carefully. Cereals absorb a lot of water while cooking and, therefore burn easily. Add a tablespoon of light oil or butter to the pot to prevent frothing and clumping. Bring the water to a boil, then add the cereal, a little at a time, making sure the water does not stop boiling. Then close pot and time the cooking from the first jiggle of the pressure regulator.

CEREAL (1 CUP DRY)	COOKING TIME IN MINUTES AT 15 LBS	REQUIRED AMOUNT OF WATER FOR COOKING
Corn meal	10	3½ cups
Cracked wheat	15	3½ cups
Grits (not precooked)	14	3 cups
Oats (not precooked)	5	2½ cups
Rice, page 295		

IT IS BEST NOT TO PRESSURE COOK...

FISH, which is delicate and easily overcooked (except in chowders).

PASTA, which froths and foams while cooking, easily blocking the vent pipe.

MILK PRODUCTS, which tend to scorch. This includes cheese.

FRESH FRUIT, which cooks so quickly that it is impossible to control cooking time (this does not apply to preserves).

EGG PRODUCTS, which become insufferably tough when pressure cooked.

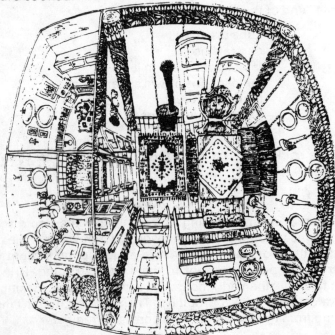

5
soup, my love?

The morning, swinging at anchor on a tranquil bay, is always the best time. The sun is always shining then, a high fire in the sky and noon seems always just around the corner. There is a sort of languorous fatigue left over from the night before or the day before; a fatigue that makes us move slowly and awkwardly like slow motion dancers in the sunlight. We see the world with eyes grown young in the night. Colors seem purer then. Fresh coffee is fragrant and overwhelming; the taste of an orange is a new experience. We are mostly silent together and look at each other like strangers, as though there were some question to be answered, but we cannot find the words to ask. The sun always seems to be shining the next morning but even if it were to rain, the rain would be a friendly rain, warm and gentle and full of spice smells of damp earth, the browns and greens of life casting their fragrance like confetti to the wind.

The night before may be just as good, those first few minutes of safety and shelter when the anchors are down and the running lights put out. Then there are only the gentlest sounds—the muted creak of a block, water slapping lightly against the hull, and the occasional whisper of the wind. Exhaustion hangs heavily about us, but for a few minutes we are beyond sleep and there is time for a glass of cognac and a last look at the stars. The cockpit is quiet then, in the darkness, almost a temple with the big oak tiller pointing silently at the stars, the compass a glowing pool of red and the cockpit seats like pews, deserted in the moonlight. Those few minutes, the first minutes of rest and safety, with the sails furled and the anchors down, are as strong and mellow in their intensity as the

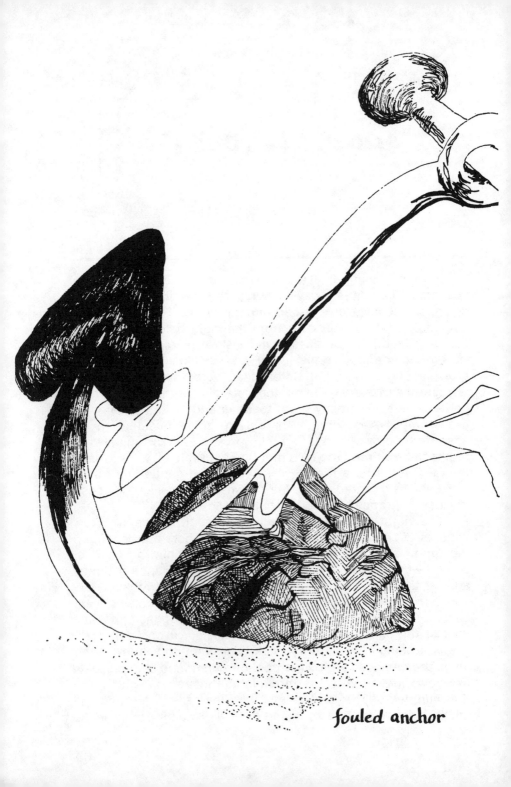

fouled anchor

taste of liquor. The anchor light shines far above us from the masthead. It sways gently in the darkness when all other lights are out. Even then, in the darkness, behind closed eyes, there is the sound of the waves. Perhaps it is only in the mind. That sound is always with us when we are at sea and the night is rough. The whitecaps cast themselves upon us, muttering as they pass in a welter of foam. They seem almost to stalk us like wild beasts. We left them this time at the mouth of the bay, and as we sailed away into tranquil water we heard them yammering behind us like voices calling from far away. We heard that sound afterwards, in the darkness, when the anchors were down and the lights out, behind closed eyes when sleep first comes. But perhaps it was only the blood against our eardrums like the sound of the sea in a shell.

We never leave port in bad weather, preferring to sit at one of the many little bistros by the quay, watching the sea gulls patrol the shore, drinking coffee, listening to the waves, far away, thinking of how mussels in wine would taste for lunch. We sat thus once in Port Sollar (Majorca) watching the wind move the almond trees high up on the hill. The hills are very sparse. Only a few goats can live there. And the almond trees. They seem to be cast from the same gnarled rock from which they grow—heavy, twisted, black trunks in fields of stone. We watched the wind move the almond trees and sat drinking coffee, talking intensely with a stranger about God, paradise, pollution, the Fiji Islands where he had lived, and the quality of young breasts in Ibiza. We left when the storm blew itself out and sailed off in the sunrise.

But I sometimes think of the Mediterranean as the girl with green eyes. There is often a surprise behind her smile. A day of sunshine, a night of stars: but by first light the wind was blowing hard from the North and it was time to shorten sail. That is a job of which we are never fond. We always wait too long, hoping that it is merely a vagrant breeze and soon will pass. Sometimes it does. We talked about that, too, with the stranger in the cafe and asked him if he were ever afraid at sea, knowing the answer in advance but wanting to see how he would phrase it. "Well," he said, "sometimes all that I want to do is get into some port and give peace a chance." Then he laughed and we all had another round of cognac. The sunlight was so good then and the almond trees swayed in the wind. Setting the heavy weather jib is the worst part of the job. It is absolutely necessary to work in the bow, on the very front part of the bow, the part that rises majestically up into the air on the crest of the waves; then comes majestically down, burying itself heavily beneath the sea. It is like cresting the hill in a roller coaster about every thirty seconds, feeling that funny feeling in the pit of your stomach as the seat drops away and the rush of the wind, then the leaden weight of arms and legs as you, coming down, meet the bow, going up. The only difference between the bow and the roller coaster, aside from the water and the bashing that you are taking from the rigging and lifelines is the fact that when the bow goes up on the crest of a wave flinging you into the air, it also moves sideways, so that unless you are somewhat careful you will find upon descending that there is only green water waiting to break your fall. As a consequence, your arms and legs find it very busy work looking for a place to attach themselves. This makes the job of snapping the 15 or 20 piston hanks of the jib to the stay a trying experience. We set the jib, then double reefed the mainsail, water running like sweat from our red foul-weather suits.

The stranger in the cafe, whose name was Fred, has lived for 3 years on one of the small Melanesian Islands in the Fiji group south of Suva. Rebecca, John, Fred, and I sat around one of those little cafe tables hardly bigger than a dinner plate, littered with empty cups and glasses. Sunlight danced upon us through the tree leaves and the air was warm and filled with the smells of summer. We talked of the people who lived in the Fijis, about attempts to civilize them—give them television sets and jobs—and how that had failed so miserably and how they seemed to find everything humorous that Fred thought was serious and relevant. Then we talked about Gauguin—the kind of life that his paintings portrayed and whether some remnant of that society existed. Then we swam in the sea.

Nightfall in rough weather, when land is somewhere just over the horizon, a time for decisions. The sea sinks fewer boats than the land, for the land is silent and unforgiving. A Polaris shot at dusk tells us that we are 18 miles north of our projected landfall in a comfortable upwind position. The seas have gotten very steep and are now breaking regularly. The chart shows that we will have to pass between several small, unlighted rocks of undetermined height, with positions that seem to wander from one chart to another and which, in fact, have the PA (position approximate) symbol next to them. One of them is decorated with a wreck which is supposed to be awash. We have already hit a wreck several years back and are not particularly interested in trying the trick again. So, we are looking very hard at the Gulf of Oristano ten miles to the north, which also has several unlighted rocks and a wreck. Apparently, they do not lie directly in our path and should not cause us grief—if we are where we think we are. The Gulf is to windward of our present estimated position which means that we will have to pay for our change in plans by pounding to windward for the next three or four hours, taking waves regularly onto the boat, being generally uncomfortable indeed. Wind, wind, you lousy North wind, there are but cold stars in a black sky and uncertainties from you. I see none of these in the swaying of the almond trees on a sunny day. Why do I love you when your hate is so cheap? On that sunny, windy day in Mallorca we watched goats lying beneath the almond trees shaded from the hot afternoon sun, then went down and swam in cold water, diving from high rocks. We drank white wine chilled in the sea and warmed ourselves on huge boulders as separate in their roundness as islands beneath the sun. The almond trees grew on the hills high above us and were mostly black and silent in the sunlight. The goats were there too. When the sun was low we climbed the hill and walked through the trees. We stopped to rest when we reached the top and turned for the last time to look at the sea, far below. It seemed different then than the way it looked when we were lying among the rocks with the sea around our ankles and the sun touching our flesh. That is always the case then you are close to the sea; it is always different then. On that sunny day the goats were lying among the almond trees, the sea sparkled for joy and was as green and filled with promise as the cold wine in our mouths. We were drunk from the sea as we were drunk from the wine and the sunlight. But high up on the hill, among the almond trees with the sun going down the sea looked blue and silent and we felt that there were things that we would never know about. And on the night off Cardinia when we searched the horizon hungrily for land, the sea was as black as the sky and it was difficult to tell where the sea left off and the sky began or whether there was, in fact, any difference between them, and it was all just dream. We saw only the whiteness of the breakers as they came to us, muttering to themselves. And we felt them as they tumbled beneath us with a phosphorescent glow. But we never actually saw the sea, though we were closer to it then than when we stood among the trees, listening to goat bells and watching the sunset.

We could have reached from the deck and touched the sea but we did not. It was not a friend that night and though we knew it was there and could have touched it, we did not, but looked instead into the night toward the land, trying to touch it with our minds.

At last there was a light. We thought at first that it was a star on the horizon. Then, as it grew brighter we thought that it might be a ship on the rim of the sea which would come toward us, unfolding itself from a point of light and go rushing past, leaving us a little sad as though at the parting of a friend. But the light did not move and we finally knew that it was not a ship. We thought then that perhaps it might be a fishing boat working with lights, rolling in the heavy seas. But finally we knew that it was a beacon, though far away, and we counted the flashes and the seconds of darkness before the light. We watched the beacon for a long time as though to be really sure that it was the particular beacon that we wanted. But we continued to look hungrily at the light after we knew what it was, as though we could taste it and it somehow satisfied a craving. We watched the light with the darkness all around us and it seemed that we were stationary on a carousel with the boat going up and down and it was really the light that was moving toward us. And we watched for the rocks and the submerged wreck that would kill us in the darkness. We stared ahead into the night but it was hard and cold like a stone and we did not know how to touch it, so we looked at the beacon which bloomed like a flower far away, and we watched it through the binoculars, hoping somehow to bring it nearer.

And then through the glasses we could see a glimmer of foam at the tower's base, the sea lacing its fingers through the fingers of the shore and we could hear the dull boom of breakers, not from the shore but from abeam of us. We knew then the location of the wreck and that we had passed it. Something was gone from our minds, a weight which we had not known was there. But it was gone and we knew then that it was fear.

Then we passed the light and in our human way cared no more about it but looked instead ahead, into the night, searching for some deep pool of silence in which to drop the hook. As we passed into calm water, the hatch was thrown back and Rebecca popped her head out. "Care for a cup of soup, my love?"

6
soup

Sometimes when it is late at night and I am off watch, I awaken to the feel of a lumpy sea and the sounds of Rebecca making soup in the galley. This is invariably a first warning that she has spotted a falling barometer and suspects that a blow is in the wind. Rebecca knows well the value of a hearty, nourishing soup that will last for days. A big mug of it, handed up to the man at the helm, seems, at times, like an offering from the gods. What better food is there for the beleaguered sailor who must have one hand for his boat and is left with only one to feed himself? Soup seems to nourish the very soul.

We care nothing for the stocks and bouillons, the consommes variously garnished, which shapren the appetite, but do not stick to the ribs. Any of the lovely chilled madrilenes have no place on a cruising boat at all. All of these potages have their place in the world and we love them, but not on a boat. Every recipe in this section has been included with the idea of providing a hearty meal-in-a-bowl that is both satisfying and relatively easy on the chef. You will find many shortcuts which would undoubtedly outrage the sensibilities of a Cordon Bleu chef, such as the liberal use of tinned consomme or bouillon cubes as a soup stock, or the flagrant use of a pressure cooker to reduce cooking time. In most instances where a tinned sauce is suggested, provision has been made to partially replace some of the flavor which is thereby lost.

caldron

Particular emphasis has been placed in the following recipes on utilizing the meats and vegetables at hand. After all, many of the places where you will shop will be poorly stocked compared to your local supermarket. Consider carefully when replacing vegetables: Is the missing legume crisp or soft, rich or subtle flavored, sweet or tart? By categorizing component parts of a taste, you may well be able to approach the desired flavor.

There is absolutely no substitute for fresh food—soup is no exception. But many frozen and some tinned soups are really quite tasty; a good supply of both, or either, is a godsend to the cruising chef. Know the comfort of a well stocked food locker filled with hearty, easy to fix soups that can be made as a hot snack or as the basis of a square meal. But when you choose prepared soups, keep the following simple facts in mind.

FROZEN SOUPS

There is no sense in buying a frozen soup that is only as good as canned. The canned variety will last longer, especially if the refrigerator fails. Lean toward frozen creamed seafood soups, bisques, chowders, Vichyssoise and rich, fresh vegetable soups, such as fresh pea and minestrone. These frozen soups are far superior to the canned variety because they more nearly preserve the delicate flavor and texture of the fresh soup.

CANNED SOUPS

The best canned, or tinned, soups are those that, when made fresh, require considerable boiling and contain ingredients that do not readily break down when cooked. The best among these are the legume soups, split pea, black bean, and lentil soup. Also quite good are some of the tougher vegetable soups, such as corn and tomato, and chicken or beef consomme. But, in our opinion, there is nothing as useless as delicate tinned vegetables, such as carrots, peas, green beans, or okra. They are invariably soggy, tasteless, and lacking in food value. It is best to avoid any tinned soups containing them. Soups containing pasta, such as chicken noodle or chicken rice, are quite popular with most crews, but it is undeniable that the pasta is soggy and the chicken scarce. With a little more effort, fresh pasta could be made and either leftover or tinned chicken added to tinned consomme.

Tinned soups may be considerably improved by adding one or more of the fresh ingredients from which the soup was originally made. In addition, diluting condensed soups with either milk, stock, or wine is better than using water. A number of more specific suggestions are found later in this chapter. Generally, we have discovered that most tinned, condensed soups call for more diluting than is desirable. Therefore, dilute slowly, adding half of the liquid first, and the rest after checking the consistency and taste of the soup.

A considerable amount of the flavor lost in canning soup is caused by the breakdown of important fruit and vegetable acids that are sensitive to heat. Some of these can be replaced partially by the use of lemon juice, a little minced onion, or even vinegar. If a soup tastes a little bland, draw a half-ladle from the pot and try experimenting with it. If the result is a failure, the whole pot will not be a loss.

FREEZE-DRIED SOUPS

For some reason unknown by us, freeze dried soups range in quality from poor to absolutely awful. Regardless of the type, they all emit a similar, unpleasant odor, and have a somewhat gluey consistency, giving one the vague feeling that corn starch or whey has been liberally used to replace missing body. The clear soups, such as minestrone, vegetable, chicken and noodle, are the worst offenders, but the thicker ones, such as split pea, seafood bisques, and creamed soups, aren't much better.

Our personal choice is to have them aboard only for emergencies. For this they are very good, because we are assured no one will touch them until everything else is gone!

THICKENERS

There are two ways to make a soup more substantial: by adding starch to the liquid, thereby thickening it, or by adding other foods such as grated hard-boiled egg white, pasta, chopped or minced vegetables or rice to the pot.

Starch Thickeners

Some chefs disdain the use of starch thickeners but they will not damage the taste of food if used in moderation. ARROWROOT has the lightest taste, works the fastest and is the most effective per spoonful. Unfortunately, it is sensitive to heat and becomes gummy if boiled or overcooked. Arrowroot is added as a thickener when the food is completely cooked. This is perfect for the first sitting but care must be exercised when reheating.

Corn starch is the second choice and does not overcook. Flour's main virtue is its availability but its taste is the most noticeable of the three. When using starchy thickeners, an excessive amount should be mixed in cold water, stock or wine. All the lumps should be worked out. The mixture should be added slowly to the simmering (not boiling) pot.

Allow a few minutes for the starch to thicken and add more as necessary. Don't guess and dump it in; you know what will happen!

Vegetable Thickeners

Vegetables such as carrots, squash, potatoes can be overcooked into a mush and added as thickeners. Fresh vegetables should be used as old ones impart a bitter flavor to the soup.

Rice and Pasta Thickeners

Quick-cooking rice or pasta can be added to a soup or sauce to absorb water and add body. But these thickeners add a starchy taste to soup. They are better parboiled and washed before use.

DEGREASING SOUP

The best way to degrease soup is to let it cool, then ladle soup off the surface into a narrow jar. The fat floats to the top and is more easily removed than from the pot.

HEAVY WEATHER SOUPS

People who don't get seasick like hearty soups in bad weather. They should be made in the pressure cooker with the lid locked on to prevent spills. It is especially important to get some liquid into a seasick crewman, even if he doesn't want it. As we all know, seasickness is caused by an inner ear disturbance, not an upset stomach. Each time the person is sick he loses body fluids and soluble ions. He gets weaker and weaker without soup. Even death can occur. Chicken broth is best, just like your mother told you. It should be served warm immediately after a bout of seasickness. The ill one will thank you, usually later. An additional virtue of chicken soup is that it may be served at either end of the sufferer, but if served unconventionally, it should not be heated. A crewman near death from seasickness will make an astonishing recovery if stern fed chicken soup with an enema bag. Remember, you read it here first.

A WORD ABOUT SOUP MEAT

The flavor of most soups and chowders is enhanced if appropriate pieces of meat, fish, or fowl are added to the pot. Remember, however, the flavor of the meat is largely contributed to the soup. If the meat is to be eaten, it is usually best to separate it from the soup. Serve it on the side with a rich sauce that will complement the somewhat depleted flavor. Listed below are some good sauces for soup fish, meat, or fowl.

Horseradish sauce for boiled or corned beef
Mustard sauce for meat and fish
Garlic sauce for beef
Hollandaise for fish
White wine sauce for fish
Curry sauce for chicken

CURRY GREEN BANANAS AND CHICKEN IN THE BUCKET

A soup from the Blue Mountains of Jamaica! One fine morning we were swinging on the hook just outside the yacht club in Montego Bay, Jamaica, when we saw a small ketch working its way into the anchorage. She was a lovely sight from a distance, with everything hung out to catch the last gusts of the dying morning breeze. But as she approached, we could see that she was a case of butterflies at sea, of God protecting fools and drunks. Her sails were made mostly from old bed sheets held together with grommets, assorted pieces of blue jeans, and flour sacks. The largest and, undoubtedly, strongest pieces were the flour sacks, but she did have a fine looking main halyard that might once have anchored the Leonardo. She has been many colors in her life; they all showed somewhere or other. Her predominant colors were red and white, and she flew an absolutely huge American flag that the crew used as a sun awning. Her name was Felicidad and she had a sunburst covering her stern. The wind died before she approached the dock. The motor was apparently inoperative, so the crew broke out oars and bits of wood to row, looking for all the world like a bunch of ants towing a crumb of bread. The Dockmaster was very British—all crisp Bermuda shorts and knee socks. He was in no way interested in the current addition to his yacht club and plainly told them so, but agreed to let them take on water if they would leave thereafter. The crew was a jolly lot of American hippies with a huge black Jamaican cook named Jesus. We agreed to tow them across the bay with our dinghy, and Jesus invited us to lunch aboard the Felicidad. Things were a bit chaotic below; the color scheme was approximately the same as the exterior. The "galley" was the inevitable single burner primus with a bucket that doubled as a pot. Since there was no head room, Jesus has to cook with his top half sticking out of the midships hatch. In the bucket that day was chicken curry with green bananas and pieces of coconut in a soup, which just covered the other ingredients. The green bananas were quite starchy, similar in flavor to potatoes and surprisingly filling. It was a really fine, completely satisfying meal, which, to that stoned crew, and with a cook named Jesus, must have seemed like a gift from God.

CURRY GREEN BANANAS AND CHICKEN IN A BUCKET

Serves Six

1 chicken, skinned and cut into twice as many pieces as usual: legs in two pieces, breasts in fours.
4 tablespoons curry paste, page 277
4 slices bacon
1 cup green pepper, chopped
5 carrots, sliced
1 apple, sliced
  coconut chunks to taste (optional)
3 cups chicken stock
3 cups water
½ cup rice (15-20 minute variety)
2 teaspoons parsley, chopped
4 cloves
1 tablespoon each salt and pepper
4 green bananas, quartered both ways
½ cup each almonds and raisins

1. In a large pot or bucket, fry bacon; remove bacon.
2. Fry the curry and the chicken in bacon grease for about 15 minutes.
3. Add remaining ingredients except apple and green pepper; continue to cook until bananas are tender like boiled potato.
4. Add apples and green peppers; simmer until peppers are tender. If soup appears a bit thin, add 1 teaspoon corn flour to ½ cup cool chicken stock; stir into the pot. The soup should have the consistency of cream. Serve with sliced fruit, such as peaches and apples sprinkled with lemon juice.

GAZPACHO

Gazpacho is the wonderful cold vegetable soup of Spain. It is a hot weather delight with its tangy taste, and is a lot of fun to eat. There are actually more than 30 different varieties of Gazpacho, each a regional specialty. Gazpacho Malagueno, for example, is made with grapes and sliced almonds, while Gazpacho Andalusia has more to do with onions, tomatoes, and green peppers—not a grape in sight. Our Gazpacho recipe does not come from Spain at all, but from the Spanish island of Mallorca.

One sunny day, we sailed into the snug little harbor of Port Sollar on the north side of Majorica. The harbor is entered through a narrow break in the cliffs, the sheer, rock face opening grudgingly gives access to the bay. We approached this formidable channel in the early hours of morning, with sea mist swirling around us, wetting our foul weather gear, and increasing the silent brooding of the high, dark cliffs.

puerta banus tower

We had no motor and reached the mouth of the cut on the last vagrant morning breeze. We drifted in utter silence on the dark water—the black rock sheer and shining in the early light. The lighthouse, far above us, was staring blindly with its extinguished eye. Finally, rowing in the dinghy and towing our yacht Fire Witch, we passed between high rock into the lovely bay. Completely surrounded by soft, green mountains the bay was just a basin, like the hollow of a hand—full of sunlight, light breezes and clear water. Protected by the mountains and the narrow entrance, Port Sollar is one of the loveliest harbors in the Mediterranean. A wide, tree-lined promenade, dotted with little shops and restaurants, runs completely around the bay

By the time we had worked the Fire Witch to her berth by the key, it was time for lunch. We had this wonderful Gazpacho Andaluz—just right on a hot summer day—followed by caricolles con salsa, which turned out to be tree snails in a fresh garlic mayonnaise. It was the perfect tribute to a perfect day.

This recipe for Gazpacho Andaluz has been slightly modified to suit the convenience of the cruising chef, and to satisfy the stomachs of the crew. As described it is a two-pot meal that serves six. Gazpacho Andaluz is invariably served cold, or at least cool.

GAZPACHO ANDALUZ   Serves Six

- 3   large, fresh tomatoes, peeled, seeded, and chopped
- 1   can tomato soup (condensed) and
- 2   cans water
- 2   green peppers, seeded and chopped
- ⅓   cup olive oil
- 5   cloves garlic, minced
- 3   tablespoons lemon juice
- 1   teaspoons sugar
- 1   cucumber, chopped and seeded
-     Salt and pepper to taste

1. Add all the above ingredients, to a stainless pot and let stand in a cool place overnight.
2. Add enough of any or all of the following vegetables to make 2 cups:
   - **cauliflower**, chopped
   - **radishes**, sliced
   - **celery hearts and leaves**, finely chopped

turnips, finely chopped
palm heart, chopped

3. Season with heaping teaspoon of one or more of the following herbs. Use fresh herbs, or soaked dried herbs for an hour in water.
   chives
   tarragon
   basil
   dill
   celery seed, well crushed

4. Chill in refrigerator, or cool place for 3-4 hours minimum; overnight is better.
5. Add, just before serving, 2 large potatoes, diced and boiled. (This is definitely not part of the typical Andalusian recipe but it seems to sit well. It adds a lot of body to the soup, and makes it a hearty, robust meal. The Spaniards omit the potato, adding, instead, a generous handful of croutons. Take your choice.)

CHICKEN IN THE POT   Serves Six

Use fresh or canned chicken for this one pot, one burner recipe. When whole chickens are canned, they are sterilized by boiling them to bits. These canned birds are not too palatable, but they do well enough in this recipe, if added last—about 2 minutes before removing from the heat. If the can is stored in a cool place and the fat is congealed and is readily removable, the broth that surrounds the chicken may be used. If not, this broth will make a greasy soup, so stick to stock.

1   **chicken, cut into small pieces, skinned**
3   **tablespoons butter**
    Pinch of salt and pepper

1. Fry chicken in large pot over medium heat for about 30 minutes, or until the meat is just cooked through. Stir occasionally to avoid burning the meat.
2. Add:
   4   **cups chicken stock, or the equivalent bouillon and water**
   1   **bay leaf**
   5   **whole pepper corns**
   1   **teaspoon parsley**

1½ cups macaroni added slowly to avoid cooling
the liquid
3 medium carrots, chopped
1 large leek, chopped (if available)

Simmer for 5 minutes, watching time carefully.
3. Add one or more of following vegetables, enough for
two cups:
1 onion, quartered
Celery, finely diced
Green beans, chopped
Peas

Simmer and cook until the vegetables are almost
cooked, about 4 minutes.
4. Remove from heat and allow to stand for 5 minutes.
Serve in soup bowls. (Removing the vegetables from the
heat a little early prevents them from being over done for
the second helping, or the next day.)

CHICKEN SCRAP SOUP
1. Pressure cook 20 minutes:
**All available chicken scraps including skin, feet,
gizzard, heart but excluding the liver
2 cups chicken consomme**
2. Remove the scraps and add:
**1 cup diced, parboiled potatoes or pasta
2-3 cups cut up vegetables
½ teaspoon celery seed
2 onions, quartered**
3. Pick the meat off the bones and add it to the soup. Salt and
pepper to taste. Degrease the soup (pg 72) if necessary.

MINESTRONE   Serves Six
1 cup garbanzos pressure cooked 30 minutes
1 teaspoon each thyme, oregano, marjorum,
sage
3 cloves garlic, coarsely chopped
1 teaspoon parsley
1 cup tomatoes, chopped and drained

3 stalks celery, chopped
2 large carrots, sliced approximately ¼ inch
thick

1½ cups macaroni
3 quarts salted water
1 teaspoon olive oil
4 oz. salt pork or bacon, diced small
1 teaspoon sweet basil
1 tablespoon tomato paste
1 cup fresh peas or green beans
½ small cabbage, shredded
2 quarts water
½ cup plus 2 tablespoons, grated Parmesan cheese

1. Pressure cook garbanzo beans in salted water for 30 minutes.
2. Add all ingredients except cheese; simmer for 20 to 30 minutes. Vegetables should be almost cooked; **not** soggy!
3. Correct seasoning. Mix in Parmesan cheese and serve.

MINESTRONE—THE EASY WAY   Serves Four
1. Add to **1 can minestrone soup:**
   Onion, fried and chopped
   Carrots, sliced and boiled
   Cabbage, lightly boiled
   Any available fresh vegetables
2. Add:
   ¼ **cup red wine**
   1 **teaspoon wine vinegar**
   ½ **cup grated Parmesan cheese**
3. Add:
   finely diced, well cooked bacon or salt pork;
   ½ pound
   ½ **lb bacon or salt pork, finely diced, well cooked**

SOUP FROM THE ANGELS
Certainly the most aristocratic fish stews and chowders come from humble origins. Bouillabaise, rumored in legend to have been brought directly from heaven by angels, merely tastes heavenly. It was certainly the creation of some rough French fisherman, as a method of using unsalable, ghastly looking fish, such as rascasse or sea ravens. It is sold today in some very fancy places at some very fancy prices, but bouillabaise never forgot old friends. It is just as likely to find it knocking around on

castle on the strait of gibraltar

some very smelly fish boats in some very isolated ports—such democracy is hard to find!

The French are very fond of saying that the real bouillabaisse is made only in southern France. It is true that the ancient, classic ingredients come from the Gulf de Lion and can only be approximated in other parts of the world. But the main ingredients of a great bouillabaise are a mixture of fresh fish and the skill of a fine chef. It is the wonderful taste that counts, not the fanatical adherence to a list of ingredients. So if you have invited some culinary impresario to taste your fine fish stew and he pokes around suspiciously with his spoon, hunting for the rascasse that is not there, we suggest you tell him the story of our friend Sam.

Sam was a shrewd Nassau fisherman who single-handed a 34-foot livewell smack to the vast stretch of reefs and shoals called the Yellow Banks. Sam was a well-equipped sailin' businessman. The fish were trapped in straw cages, then transferred to a huge bait well that took up the entire midship section. When Sam couldn't sell his entire catch (which was rare), he smoked what was left in his on-board smoke house, and sold the smoked fish at a higher price the next day.

Like most fishermen who service Nassau, Sam tied his smack, the Miss Jane, 'longshore near the Paradise Island Bridge, and sold his wares directly from the bait well to the shoppers passing by. What a delightful way to buy fish! The small conch boats, loaded high with hundreds of brightly colored shells, were tied by the quay. The tap, tap, tap of the conchmen's hammers punctuated the air. The huge mollusks were slipped from their shells and eaten on the spot with a dash of lime. A big wire basket full of scuttling, rustling crabs stood near the curb, and a huge sea turtle, flipped on its back, glared balefully from the sidewalk. Little boys were selling turban shells, piled high like walnuts in the shadow of the bridge. Near them a fat lady in a big straw hat has hung five huge green moray eels by their heads and was preparing to skin them. She sharpened her knife on the cobble stones.

Sam stood with his long knife, knee deep in the cockpit of Miss Jane. The sail, a coat of many colors, hung loosely in lazy jacks and afforded some protection from the sun. The livewell was a living reef with sunlight brightly dancing. There was a school of blue angels, a school of jacks, a big grouper motionless on the bottom of the tank, and a bright snapper dashing

nassau fisherman

about nervously. We picked a fat grouper; after a short discussion, a bargain was struck. Sam went after the fish with a net, following a brief chase around the tank, much splashing and an occasional oath, the big grouper was gleaming and flopping on the carving block. Ah, what joy! Fresher fish could not be found.

When a tourist or obviously green hand came to make a purchase, Sam generously offered to fillet the fish free of charge. He had a quick tongue and ready smile; his customers seldom noticed fine pieces of meat accidentlly left on the head, tail, fins, and backbone that were flung in a garbage can. The greenhorn paid for the fish by the pound, but got only the fillets laced on a palm frond. Sam was a master at the game and was seldom caught. But when he was caught a look of astonished disdain clearly said, "Who would want this trash?" That night the garbage can miraculously became the ingredients for some of the finest soups and chowders we have ever tasted.

When the market closed at sundown, all the other fishermen would "come along" the Miss Jane with a cup or bowl, smoke their pipes, and wait for His Majesty Sam to "finish the pot." About eight o'clock, when the dishes were washed and the pipes smoked out, Sam would go home a mighty contented man.

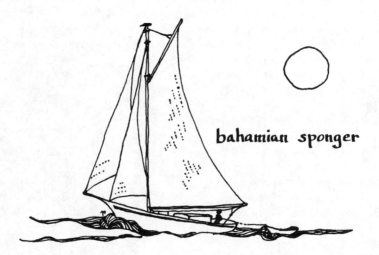

bahamian sponger

spear-fishing in jamaica

Since most of the following recipes were created "on the hook" over some nameless reef, they are particularly useful to the cruising chef. Sam's galley had only a two-gallon bucket, which doubled as a bailer; you may be assured that these are all one-pot meals. The secret of success for all fish stews, chowders, and soups is to add the edible fish pieces last, cooking them just long enough to be tender. If the fish is overcooked, it loses all of its flavor to the soup and becomes mushy and tasteless.

Fish bones, tails, fins, and heads, crab shells, lobster bodies and shells, shrimp shells and tails, even conch scraps are used, but in a different way. They are first simmered or boiled for 15 to 20 minutes in liquid to extract all of the flavor and thickening agents found in fish backbones. After discarding the scraps, the stock is ready to use in Sam's Sunday special bouillabaisse.

We would venture to say that there is no trace of French in Sam's ancestry. He would not tell us where he got the recipe for this lovely dish, and we can verify that he did not find it in the Sunday Times, because Sam can't read. His name for it was merely "Sam's Fish Stew." Call it what you like, this dish is a fair approximation of the fine Mediterranean bouillabaisse, but using tropic zone fish.

Bouillabaisse has many ingredients and is not generally associated with sailing food. But the secret of fine bouillabaisse is lots of fresh fish, the kind that a bunch of hungry divers might take from a reef on a windless Sunday afternoon. And since those divers can't always spear exactly what they want, the hodgepodge of mixed ingredients is just what the galley needs for a fine bouillabaisse. This recipe overfeeds six. Don't worry, bouillabaisse tastes even better the next day.

SAM'S SUNDAY SPECIAL BOUILLABAISSE   Serves Six

1. Begin with fish stock described on previous pages.
2. Remove bones. Add and simmer 15 minutes:

  1 lb. canned Italian tomatoes, coarsely chopped
  3 large onions, coarsely chopped and sauteed
  ½ cup celery leaves, chopped
  ½ cup celery, diced
  1 teaspoon saffron
  4 garlic cloves, roughly crushed
  2 tablespoons fennel
  2 tablespoons salt and pepper

¾ cup olive or vegetable oil (olive oil preferred)
1 teaspoon thyme
3 bay leaves, broken up
3. The quantity and variety of fish depends, of course, on what you have caught. The list below is merely a suggestion. Add to the pot:
   3 to 4 **Florida Lobster, sliced into about 5 sections**
   2 **lbs. grouper, cut into 1½-inch squares**
   1 **lb. snapper, cut into 1½-inch squares**
   1 **small moray eel, skinned and sliced into ½-inch pieces**
   2 **lbs. grunt, cut into 1½-inch squares**
   ½ **lb. shrimp, shelled and deveined**
   18 **small clams, mussels, or cockles**
4. Cover ingredients with:
   2 **cups white wine**
5. Boil over high heat for 8 minutes. Serve as a stew with chunks of toasted garlic bread. Your crew will sign for another voyage.

SAM'S ONE POT FISH STEW

This recipe uses fish fillets. Any delicately flavored fish may be used—the more varied the fish, the better tasting the dish.

SAM'S ONE POT FISH STEW

1. Fry together in pot:
   3 **medium potatoes, diced**
   2 **onions, diced**
   ½ **cup celery with leaves, chopped**
   8 **slices bacon, chopped and cooked with the onion**
2. When onions are golden, add:
   2 **cups half and half**
   6 **peppercorns**
   A generous mesh sack with fish bones, heads, tails and fins
3. Simmer for 10 minutes, then discard contents of mesh bag. Do not let the mixture boil as this will curdle the milk.
4. Turn off flame; skim surface to remove any floating debris.

5. Add:
   1½ to 2 lbs. fish fillets, cut to bite size
6. Simmer for 7 minutes or until fish is just done. Serve at once. Add:
   Dash of dry sherry
   1   teaspoon paprika
   Salt to taste

"village belle"
bahamian
sailing dinghy

YELLOW BANK CHOWDER   Serves Six
1. Boil at high heat for 15 minutes in enough water to cover:
> **1 to 2   lbs. fish bones, heads, tails, fins, shrimp, crab or lobster shells—any or all**
> **½   cup celery with leaves**
> **1   carrot, sliced**
> **1   teaspoon salt**
> **½   teaspoon pepper**
> **1   teaspoon thyme**
> **1   teaspoon marjoram**
2. Strain; use this stock as chowder base.
3. Saute until golden:
> **6   slices bacon**
> **2   onions, diced**
> **3   medium potatoes, diced and parboiled 10 minutes**
4. When onions are golden, add:
> **1   16 oz. can Italian tomatoes, drained and chopped**
> **2   bay leaves**
> **6   peppercorns**
> **2   chicken bouillon cubes**
> **1   teaspoon thyme**
> **1   teaspoon marjoram**
> **Fish stock, enough to cover, plus one inch**
5. Simmer 15 minutes. Serve with cheese and crackers.

NORTH ATLANTIC BOUILLABAISSE   Serves Six

We created this cold water version of bouillabaise at the little island of Flores in the Azores. We had lots of help finding the ingredients; the little children of the island, fishermen before they could walk, were glad to supply all of the rascasse, rouget, and eels needed in exchange for chocolate chip cookies. Such fine barter is getting scarce, even in the Azores.

1. Make a fish stock, see recipe above.
2. Cook over medium-high heat until onion is transparent:
> **½   cup olive oil**
> **1   medium onion, chopped**
> **6   cloves garlic**
> **1   teaspoon orange rind**

1 teaspoon fennel
1 teaspoon saffron
1 bay leaf
½ teaspoon celery seed, or 1 teaspoon celery salt
1 teaspoon pepper
3. Add:
    1   16 oz. can Italian tomatoes, drained and diced
        Fish stock
    2   cups white wine
4. Add fish, enough to make 4 pounds; any or all of the following:

    2   lobster tails, cut into 4 pieces
    24 mussels
    4 to 5   small squid, sliced
    2 lbs. fillets of any or all: pompano, snapper, halibut, perch, or bass
    6 to 12   shrimp
    1   small moray eel
    2 to 3   small rock fish, if you can find them

5. Simmer 5 minutes over medium heat; avoid overcooking the fish. Serve with crusty French garlic bread and a tossed salad.

ZUPPA DI VONGOLE WITH FRESH OR TINNED CLAMS

Serves Six

The Italians are inordinately fond of little clams. They call them all vongole, though a number of different species are sold under this name. Perhaps for culinary purposes the Italians have the right idea; any little clam will taste quite similar when cooked into a rich tomato recipe. But occasionally, in other parts of the world, delicious little clams are judged to be too much trouble to be worth bothering about. This is truly a regrettable attitude; after all, we think nothing of expending the energy and time to get a walnut out of its shell, while the steamed clam is just begging to be eaten. Nevertheless, should the cruising chef find himself with a dirth of small clams and plenty of medium ones, the same recipe can be followed by adding chopped clams and their juice.

1. Saute in large pot until onion is golden:
   1 medium onion, diced
   2 tablespoons parsley (add after frying if chopped)
   1 whole bay leaf
   3 large garlic cloves, finely chopped
   ½ cup olive oil
   ½ teaspoon salt
   ½ teaspoon pepper

2. Add and simmer for 10 minutes:
   1 cup tomato sauce
   1 cup tomatoes, chopped and drained
   Salt and pepper to taste
   1 tablespoon wine vinegar
   1 teaspoon sugar

3. Add:
   2 quarts of vongole, or
   1 pint of chopped clams and their juice.
   Simmer 10 minutes, stirring occasionally.

Tinned clams are also acceptable, though, of course, their flavor is not as good. Add them and an additional ½ pint of clam juice. Simmer just 2 minutes. In either case, serve individual portions in bowls or heavy weather plates and sprinkle with fresh parsley. Buon Appetito!

living room of the haj

MUSHROOM BARLEY SOUP

Mushroom barley soup is another of those wonderful, hearty meals-in-a-bowl that is just as good at the dock as under way. It can be made with those beautiful black Chinese mushrooms, sauteed for a few minutes in a little oil, or with tinned mushrooms or sliced, dried mushrooms—any sort of mushroom you can find. I first came to know this fine dish when I was working as a laborer in Les Halles, the Paris fruit and vegetable market of days gone by. What a marvelous place! During the day the district was virtually deserted; but very late at night, or in the early hours of the morning, trucks would begin arriving from all over France with fantastic things to eat. There were no stalls; the trucks would park by the curb and sell direct, stacking the farmers' wares in the street.

When the first rose petals of dawn touched the roof tops, the farmers began to fill their vans with the empty boxes that had held their fruit. When the first commuters rushed along these streets a few hours later, they found them silent and deserted. All that remained were a few pigeons patrolling the curb, the scattered ashes from the chestnut vendors' fires, and an occasional fractured box. The fairy world of night was gone.

Mushroom and barley soup was a favorite of the French farmers and laborers who worked in Les Halles. Considering how thoroughly they were surrounded by fine food, mushroom and barley soup had some tough competition! This is another one of those hearty meals that keep well for days as a **pot au feu**; pork scraps and carrot ends, mutton bones and par boiled barley can always be added—a virtually immortal, endless pit of fine flavors.

MUSHROOM AND BARLEY SOUP   Serves Six

1. Fry in large pot:

    ½ **lb. salt pork, bacon or, best of all, ham hock**
    1 **large onion, diced**
    Any available ham or mutton bones, especially knuckles.
    Saute until the onions are golden.

2. Add:

    1 **lb. quick-cooking barley**
    2 **chicken bouillon cubes**
    4 **cups water**

>   2   teaspoons caraway seed
>   2   teaspoons salt
>   1   cup dried mushrooms.

3. Bring to boil and simmer until barley is tender, about 30 mintues. Keep adding a little water to prevent barley from burning.
4. While barley is boiling, saute in pan:

>   3   teaspoons butter
>   1½ cups fresh mushrooms or tinned mushrooms, drained.
>   4   garlic cloves, coarsely chopped
>   1   teaspoon parsley
>   1   teaspoon salt
>   1   teaspoon pepper
>   1   teaspoon marjoram
>   2   big carrots, sliced lengthwise in quarters

5. Keep adding butter as mushrooms absorb it, but do not let pan become saturated.
6. Add contents of pan to pot. Simmer another 10 minutes.
7. Soup should be thick, more like porridge. Salt and pepper to taste. Serve with a cold, white wine.

MUSSEL BROTH SOUP   Serves Two

>   2   lbs. mussels, debearded and well scrubbed
>   2   teaspoons parsley, chopped
>   1½ cups dry white wine
>   2   shallots, coarsely chopped (optional)
>   2   small onions, diced large
>   2   tablespoons butter
>   ½   bay leaf
>   1   teaspoon thyme
>   2   egg yolks, well beaten into cream
>   2   cups heavy cream or unsweetened, evaporated milk
>   ½   teaspoon salt
>   Pepper

1. Put all ingredients, except cream and egg yolks, into pot; simmer 15 minutes.
2. Pour soup through sieve.

3. Return liquid to pot; add cream and eggs. **Do not boil.** Simmer over very low heat, stirring contantly until soup just begins to thicken. Remove from heat and serve
4. Serve mussels hot, without shells, on buttered toast, garnished with finely chopped celery. Or serve floating in the soup.

QUICK FRENCH ONION SOUP

Hearty onion soup, the way the French make it, is a serious affair. Long afternoons, sometimes even days are spent simmering a small mountain of beef bones and scraps, carrot ends, celery leaves and fine herbs into a rich stock—the heart of the soup. The second stage of straining, chilling, skimming, and restraining the bone-laden pot is equally time consuming; but that rich, sparkling stock gives real French onion soup its unbeatable flavor.

This approach is, of course, quite impossible on a boat; unfortunately, canned beef consomme (not bouillon) must be used. By adding a few little extra touches, some wine, a bit of brandy, you can some very close to the wonderful taste of from scratch French onion soup.

QUICK FRENCH ONION SOUP   Serves Six

> 2   10½ oz. beef consomme cans
> 4   cup dry red wine
> 2   tablespoons brandy
> ½   carrot, well chopped
> 3   tablespoons butter
> 4   tablespoons olive oil
> 2   tablespoons flour
> 4   large onions, sliced
> ½   teaspoon garlic powder
> 6   slices French bread
> ½   teaspoon marjoram
>   Celery leaves, if available

1. Peel and slice onions; separate the rings.
2. Saute onions and butter in large pot over high heat, stirring frequently until onions are soft.
3. Add flour, a little at a time; continue stirring until onions begin to turn golden brown. Remove onions; set onions aside.

4. Add to pot:
   - **2 cans consomme**
   - **4 cup red wine**

   - **½ carrot, well chopped**
   - **½ teaspoon marjoram**
   - **A few celery leaves, if available**
5. Stir, making sure flour is not stuck to bottom of pot.
6. When soup simmers, reduce heat and simmer 5 minutes. **Do not boil.**
7. Add onions, brandy, salt and pepper to taste; simmer 5 minutes.
8. While soup is simmering, make soup toast in a fry pan. Add to fry pan:
   - **Enough oil to grease the pan**
   - **4 teaspoon garlic powder**
   - **6 bread slices without crusts**
   Fry bread over medium heat, adding oil as necessary to prevent burning; brown on both sides.
9. To serve: Put a slice of the toast in a bowl; pour a generous ladle of the completed soup over it. **Bon Appetite!**

FRENCH ONION SOUP GRATINEE

Gratinee means with cheese; if you have some Gruyere cheese, a casserole dish, and an oven, your quick onion soup becomes a grand main course.

1. Put the soup in casserole dish; cover surface of the soup with soup toast; sprinkle generously with grated cheese.
2. Melt cheese at 400°, then brown it quickly with broiler.

CORN SOUP   Serves Four

This recipe is hearty and easy to make; don't let its length intimidate you. As is true of everything in the world of food, fresh ingredients will invariably make better tasting, more nourishing meals. If fresh corn is available, by all means use it; but canned corn, as every corn freak knows, is fairly tasty.

1. Fry in pot until onions are golden
   5   slices bacon, chopped
   1   small onion, diced
2. Add:
   2   cups water
   1   medium potato, diced
   1   bay leaf
   1   teaspoon parsley
   1   teaspoon salt
   1   teaspoon pepper
3. Bring to boil; simmer until potatoes are just soft, about 20 minutes.
4. Add, stirring occasionally:
   3   cups corn kernels
   2   cups milk, previously mixed with
   2   teaspoons corn flour
   If the corn is fresh, steam it before removing from the cob. Day old, leftover cooked corn-on-the cob is just fine. Use a sharp knife, and don't cut too deeply. If using tinned corn, choose the whole kernel variety. We prefer whole kernel white corn because of its fine flavor and tenderness.
5 Bring to a boil; turn off heat. If a thicker consistency is desired, remove one cup of chowder liquid; cool for a few minutes. Add to the cup:
   2   egg yolks
   Mix thoroughly; add to soup. **Do not boil** after eggs are added.
6. Just before serving add:
   3   tablespoons butter
   Generous dash of paprika

POTATO SOUP AND VICHYSSOISE

Potato soup sounds less fancy or complicated than vichyssoise, but the latter is actually nothing more than cold, creamed potato soup. These two recipes are easy to prepare. The secret for potato soup is lots of fresh leeks, while for vichyssoise, it's the liberal use of sweet cream. Restaurants often cheat outrageously on the cream, substituting milk and corn starch or arrowroot to obtain the right consistency.

POTATO SOUP   Serves Four to Six

A one pot recipe that feeds four to six

1. Saute in pressure cooker for 5 minutes until onions are
   golden:
   - **4   leeks, whites only, well chopped**
   - **2   onions, well sliced**
   - **3   tablespoons butter**
   - **4   medium potatoes, peeled and sliced very thin**
2. Add:
   - **4   stalks celery**
   - **4   cups chicken stock**
   - **½   teaspoon salt**
   - **½   teaspoon pepper**
   - **½   bay leaf**

3. Pressure cook for 3 minutes after first jiggle, or until
   potatoes are quite soft. Remove bay leaf and serve.

VICHYSSOISE   Serves Four to Six

1. Puree, liquify or force strain potato soup.
2. Add **2 to 3 cups heavy cream;** chill.
3. Serve garnished with **chopped chives, green onion
   ends** finely chopped, or **one teaspoon of seeded, finely
   chopped cucumber,** for each cup of soup.

man-o-war cay fishboat

DEEP SEA SPLIT PEA SOUP   Serves Six

1   lb. dried split peas
2   qts. water
½   lb. of salt pork, bacon, ham, or salami; but best of all, ham hocks
2   chicken bouillon cubes, crumbled
1   cup onion, chopped
½   cup celery with leaves or (1 teaspoon celery seed, crushed)
1   bay leaf
1   teaspoon thyme
1   teaspoon fennel
2   cups milk
5   pepper corns
2   tablespoons sherry (optional)
2   carrots, chopped

(**Note:** Most pressure cooker manufactures advise against cooking split peas in cooker because it sputters, easily clogging the steam vent.)

1. In pressure cooker fry meat and onion until onion is golden.
2. Add water, peas, celery, bay leaf, fennel and bouillon; pressure cook for 20 minutes over low heat.
3. Add remaining ingredients except the milk and wine; simmer uncovered until the carrots are soft. The soup should be about the consistency of porridge at this point. If soup is too lumpy for your taste, pick out the meat and force soup through a sieve; add meat.
4. Add milk, wine, salt and pepper to taste; reheat and serve with croutons or grilled cheese sandwiches.

Split pea soup is just as good the next day, perhaps better. Since the split peas will absorb more water, it may be necessary to add water as you reheat. Add it slowly and avoid over-watering the soup; split pea soup is traditionally served thick and hearty.

IMPROVED CANNED SPLIT PEA SOUP   Six Servings

1. Thin with **milk** instead of water.
2. Add **pork meat** and **onion;** follow step number one above.

3. Add **2 carrots,** well chopped, **½ teaspoon celery salt;** simmer until carrots are soft.
4. Add **2 teaspoons sherry.**

CRUISING CREAMED SCALLOP SOUP ST. JAQUES

Serves Two

- **2   cups water**
- **½   lb. potatoes (2 medium), chopped**
- **1   egg yolk**
- **¾   cup scallops, pen shells, surf clam muscles, or ray wings**
- **¼   cup heavy cream or evaporated milk**
- **½   cup dry white wine**
- **½   bay leaf**
- **¼   teaspoon thyme**
- **1   clove garlic, minced**

1. Pressure cook potatoes, onions, bay leaf, thyme, water, salt and pepper for 5 minutes, or simmer in pot 1 hour.
2. Add scallops and garlic; simmer gently for 5 minutes.
3. Remove bay leaf; pour soup through a sieve; finely grind solids and recombine.
5. Bring to boil and turn off.
6. Add beaten egg yolks and cream. Stir constantly until soup thickens, returning briefly to flame if it does not. **Do not let soup boil.**

SHRIMP BISQUE OR SOUP   Serves Two to Three

This bisque can also be made from, or in combination with, lobster or oysters, fresh or tinned.
1. Combine in double boiler or over very low heat:
   - **4   tablespoons butter**
   - **1   teaspoon grated onion**
   - **½   teaspoon celery salt**

   Saute lightly, stirring constantly for 5 minutes.
2. Add:
   - **1½   pints seafood, shelled, deveined and coarsely chopped**
   - **2   cups milk**
   - **½   cup cream or 2 cups condensed milk with ½ cup water**

Pinch of salt and pepper
Pinch of paprika
Saute and stir until milk steams.

3. Add:

2   teaspoons parsley, finely chopped
½   cup dry white wine
Saute another 2 to 3 minutes. Serve over fried, buttered toast.

MANHATTAN CLAM CHOWDER   Serves Four

Small, tender clams of any sort may be used; but if these are unavailable, larger clams, beaten, then ground, will do.

Bahama conch chowder may be made using the same recipe by substituting thoroughly beaten and ground conch or welk for clams, page 149. Limpits may also be used. They should be removed from their shells, eviscerated and beaten, then chopped or ground.

If live clams are used, they should be degritted overnight in sea water and corn meal, page 144, then steamed open and the liquid used in the chowder. If it is not possible to soak them overnight, the clams should be eviscerated and washed to remove intestinal grit.

Steaming is done in a pan with a lid. Add the clams and half cup of water. Steam, lid on, for 5 to 10 minutes until all clams are open. Pour the juice into a tall glass and allow the sediment to settle.

1 **pint deshelled mollusks**
4 **slices bacon**
1 **medium onion, chopped**
1 **cup clam juice**
2 **cups potatoes, diced**
2 **cups Italian tomatoes, drained and chopped**
1 **cup carrots, sliced**
1 **bay leaf**
   Salt and pepper

1. Cook bacon; remove from pan.
2. Add   the   onion to bacon grease; cook over low heat until onions are transparent, about 5 minutes. Stir occasionally.
3. Add potatoes, carrots, water, clam juice, and bay leaf; simmer until the carrots are just soft.
4. Add tomatoes, green pepper, well crumbled bacon, clams, butter. Continue to simmer for 10 minutes, or until the potatoes are just done.
5. Salt and pepper to taste; serve with fried toast or crackers.

IMPROVED CANNED MANHATTAN CLAM CHOWDER
                                              Serves Two

1. Use **clam juice** instead of water to dilute; add a few drops of **lemon**.

2. Add more **clams, conch, limpits** prepared as for previous recipe.
3. Saute ½ **carrot**, diced and parboiled, with ½ **onion** in a little **butter**. Cook until the onion is golden. Add to soup.

PORTUGUESE COCKLE SOUP   Serves Four
1. Prepare as for Manhattan clam chowder; but leave bivalves, always small and tender, in their shells and add to pot.
2. Add, during step number four of Manhattan clam chowder recipe:
   - 1 **cup tomato sauce**
   - 2 **tablespoons port or sweet sherry**
   - 1 **teaspoon marjoram**

NEW ENGLAND CLAM CHOWDER   Serves Six
New Englanders have as definite an opinion about the best version of clam chowder as they do about which is the best anchor. They consider Manhattan chowder an "infernal invention," a bastard child, and other things not fit to print. So, if you have a few good old boys from New England in your crew, think twice about making Manhattan chowder.

- 1 to 2 **pints mollusk meat, chopped, or small clams**
- 4 **slices bacon, chopped**
- 1 **large onion, chopped**
- 3 **tablespoons flour**
- 2 **cups water including the steaming liquid from mollusks**
- ½ **bay leaf**
- 3 **cups milk or half and half**
- **Salt and pepper**
- 2 **potatoes, cubed**

1. Steam open and treat mollusks as in Manhatten Chowder.
2. Fry bacon in large pot; remove it and reserve.
3. In bacon drippings, add onion; saute until transparent.
4. Add all other ingredients except milk and flour; simmer 10 minutes.
5. Add milk and flour, pre-mixed to avoid lumps.
6. Simmer until soup thickens but **do not boil.**

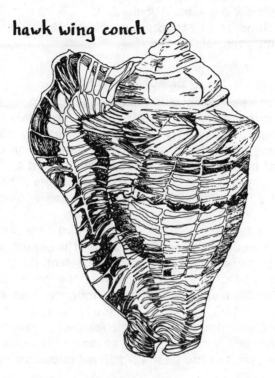

hawk wing conch

CONCH INN CONCH CHOWDER Serves Four

This is such an outstanding recipe for conch chowder; you must try it if you have a few conch about.

2 stalks celery, finely chopped
2 medium onions, finely chopped
4 tablespoons olive oil

1 16 oz. can Italian tomatoes, drained
5 fresh okra, if available
2 bay leaves
3 conch, finely chopped
1 carrot, sliced
2 potatoes, cubed (pressure cooked for 1 minute) Water to cover

1. Saute celery and onions in oil until tender.
2. Add tomatoes and tomato paste; stir.

3. Add remaining ingredients; just cover with water and a little white wine, if desired.
4. Simmer until potatoes are tender, about 15 to 20 minutes.

BLACK BEAN SOUP

Black beans, like split peas and lentils, make a number of hearty soups. They also are the basis for a traiditional Cuban dish, black beans and yellow rice. This savory dish is usually served with a big handful of chopped onions on top and little pieces of pork, cooked in a savory oil, around the sides. Black beans and yellow rice play as important a role in Cuban cuisine as spaghetti in Italian food—the meal seems incomplete without them.

Like most dried legumes, the cooking time of the beans depends on a number of factors, such as the season in which they were grown and how long they have been on the shelf. Normally they take a bit longer than lentils. We once made a pot, however, which we pressure cooked for 4 hours without success. The beans were almost as hard after four hours as when we began. Having eaten home cooked black bean soup many times, we can vouch that this minor tragedy was most unique and might have been the result of the beans which sat in our galley larder for 3 years.

BLACK BEAN SOUP   Serves Six to Eight

Black bean soup, like lentil and split pea soup, tastes even better the next day. The beans do absorb moisture overnight, however, and it is usually necessary to add a bit of water to the pot before reheating. Black bean soup may actually be kept indefinitely without refrigeration. The method is simple. Serve the soup while it is still bubbling in the pressure cooker pot; replace the lid with the pressure valve still on top. The heat from the soup will kill all bacteria while the pressure lid and valve will act as a stopper. As the soup cools, a partial vacuum will be formed, even further reducing the chances of spoilage.

1. Fry in pressure cooker:
    ½   lb bacon, chopped; or ¼ lb. salt pork, diced; or a large ham bone with a liberal amount of meat still on it (best).
    1   large onion, diced

2. When onions are golden, add:
   5 pepper corns
   1 bay leaf
   10 cups water
   1 cup celery with leaves, well chopped
   1 lb. black beans
   2 chicken bouillon cubes
   5 cloves garlic
3. Pressure cook for 25 minutes. Simmer thereafter until tender and thick. Salt and pepper to taste. Add:

   1 onion, diced
      Cook with lid off for 5 minutes, or until excess water is boiled off.
4. Serve in bowl with handful of well-chopped onions on top and one or more of the following as a garnish:
      Hard-boiled egg quarters
      Carrot slices
      Lemon wedges, salted

BLACK BEANS AND YELLOW RICE   Serves Two

1. Prepare as for Black Bean soup.
2. Simmer briskly for 15 to 20 minutes until the consistency of spaghetti sauce.
3. In a bowl place:
      A cup of cooked yellow rice
      A cup or two of the black beans around the rice
      A handful of well-chopped onions sprinkled on top

This dish is traditionally served with fried plantans or bananas, or pork saute, page 259.

IMPROVED CANNED BLACK BEAN SOUP   Serves Two

Since black beans are such tough customers they usually hold their flavor when canned. The canned product may be improved in any of the following ways.

1. In a pot fry:
      ½ lb. bacon; or chopped ham; or 3 ounces salt pork, chicken, or beef picked off leftover bones
      1 large onion, diced
      1 carrot, finely chopped

2. When onion is golden add:
   Black bean soup, diluted as directed
   Cook for 10 minutes; serve with onion and garnished from scratch recipe.

PRESSURE COOKER LENTIL SOUP

When I first met Rebecca, she was a vegetarian. This taxed my imagination a bit since I was doing most of the cooking and had never faced the necessity of making a completely meatless menu. One of the big early entrees into this scene was lentil soup. But when I tried to make it without any sort or pork meat or stock, it tasted a little bland. So I made it as described below and simply removed the bone prior to serving. May God forgive me.

Lentil soup is one of those hearty meals-in-a-bowl that are inexpensive and, therefore, excellent for large groups. All of the ingredients are long-lasting and the soup is even better the next day. For this reason we have made the recipe for six. After all, if it was so good at dinner, why not have a cup of it for lunch the next day?

LENTIL SOUP   Serves Six
1. Fry in pressure cooker:
   ½ lb. chopped bacon, salt pork, Danish salami, hot dogs, or ham. A ham bone with some meat on it may be substituted.
   1 large onion, diced

2. When onion is golden, add:
   4 cups water
   5 cloves garlic, chopped
   2 chicken bouillon cubes, crumbled
   1 bay leaf
   1 teaspoon pepper, roughly ground

3. When water boils, slowly add:
   2 cups lentils
   Cover and pressure cook 20 minutes after the first jiggle at 15 pounds using low heat.
4. Salt and pepper to taste. (The salt is added last because the meat contributes an uncertain amount of saltiness.) Serve with lots of thinly sliced onions on top.

CURRY LENTIL SOUP   Serves Six
  1. Fry meat according to lentil soup recipe.
  2. Make a curry sauce, page 277. (Make the curry right in with the meat.) Be sure to have enought oil in the pot to keep the curry from burning. When the smell of the cooking curry has disappeared, proceed with the lentil soup recipe. Delicious!

FROZEN PEA AND SPINACH SOUP
1. Boil for 5 minutes or until tender:
     2 pkg. (equal portions) peas and spinach
     1 can chicken consomme
     1 teaspoon lemon juice, sugar, salt, pepper
     1 tablespoon curry powder or fresh mint
     (¼ cup leaves)
     ½ cup grated coconut plus the juice
2. Use a blender or ricer to liquify the soup.
3. Add cream or condensed milk and water to thin.
4. Garnish with grated coconut.

NAVY BEAN SOUP
1. Saute until browned in a pressure cooker:
     6 slices bacon, chopped, or ¼ lb. chopped ham
     2 onions, chopped
2. Add:
     1½ cups washed navy beans
     6 cups water
     3 carrots, diced
     1 bay leaf
     2 teaspoons salt
     1 teaspoon pepper
3. Pressure cook for 20 minutes, then add milk or cream to taste. This soup may be liquified in a blender if desired.

7
eggs

Eggs are the cruising chef's best friend. They store well, often lasting for months without refrigeration. A rich source of protein, vitamins, and fat, eggs provide fresh food when other fresh stores are gone. They can be prepared in rough weather and provide a hot, hearty meal that might otherwise be available only from tins. Perfect for any occasion from delicate snacks to filling, one- course dinners, eggs are used for making sauces, for thickening and enriching soups, and for preparing stews and casseroles. Two eggs per person per day should be sufficient.

As with most foods, the best eggs are the freshest ones. Whites should be clear and firm; yolks should not break when the egg is opened. If fresh eggs are definitely available along your route, purchase just enough to get by; otherwise, stock up. Eggs last much longer when refrigerated, but they may be kept without refrigeration. Supermarket eggs, however, have a shorter shelf life since they have been in the refrigerator for a while and are not super fresh. If you are planning an extended cruise or an ocean passage, get fresh eggs as close to the prime source as possible—if not from under the chicken itself, then at least from the hatchery. If you must buy eggs from a suspicious source, a few of them should be opened on the spot to test for freshness. Several eggs should be opened and dropped, one at a time, into a container held about a foot away. When they land, the egg yolks should not break. The white should be clear, firm and odorless, and the cord should be white, strong and distinct.

blue heron

Country chickens, free to roam an area where there is plenty of food, lay eggs superior to those produced in a hatchery where egg production is chemically accelerated. The country egg shells are thicker and the membrane beneath distinctly tough. The egg is more flavorful because of its higher fat content.

Country eggs are the sailor's choice since the heavy, protective shell increases its shelf life. All eggs, regardless of their source, should be washed in the fruit and vegetable dip, page 28, and thoroughly dried before stowage. If any of the eggs float in the dip water, they are spoiled and should be discarded.

Unrefrigerated eggs will last for at least a month, even in the tropics, if kept cool and handled properly. They will last longer in more temperate areas where the majority of ocean passages are made. We have kept eggs unrefrigerated for seven weeks on an ocean passage before some began to spoil. Some sailors coat eggs with Vaseline, varnish, or paraffin wax, then pack them in a solution of waterglass (sodium silicate, 1 quart per 2 gallons water) or in salt. Each of these processes accomplishes the same purpose, which is to protect the egg from contamination. There is no question that treated eggs last longer, six months if in waterglass.

Physiological changes occur in eggs as the weeks pass. The whites lose their firmness and their ability to keep the yolk in suspension. The membrane surrounding the yolk becomes degenerated and less resistant to outside contamination. The yolks slowly settle to the bottom of the egg; when in contact with the shell, they begin to spoil if not packed in a preservative. The yolks settling process may be postponed for quite a long time simply by turning the eggs every two or three days. This keeps the yolk in the center of the white where it belongs. As the weeks pass, yolk membranes degenerate to the point where the yolks always break when the eggs are opened. The yolk itself becomes pale as the fat within it is utilized. These eggs, though of disappointing appearance, are perfectly acceptable and taste fine. At this point, however, it is advisable to first break the eggs into a glass, one at a time, rather than opening them directly over the food that you are preparing. In this way the occasional bad one can be eliminated. Unlike people, there is absolutely no difficulty in recognizing a bad egg. It is discolored and probably has a bad odor (generally speaking, if you can get the egg past your nose, your stomach will accept it!). When 2 or 3 eggs in a row are found to be rotten, put all of them in a pail of water and discard the floaters, which are rotten. The remainder should be hard-boiled at once. This arrests further contamination and preserves the good eggs for another week. After hard-boiling your only alternative is to pickle the eggs, page 126. Pickling makes them virtually immortal, but seriously reduces their food value. Don't forget, the best egg is a fresh one, even though the shelf life of eggs is long.

SEPARATING THE YOLK FROM THE WHITE

Fresh eggs, whose yolks do not break easily, are treated differently from older ones. Fresh eggs are cracked in the center with a sharp tap of a knife; avoid cutting the yolk. Hold the egg upright over a bowl and open, allowing most of the white to run into the bowl. Pour the remainder into the other half of the egg shell, draining more of the white in the transfer. Repeat the process until the separation is complete.

Separating the yolks of older eggs is definitely classified as a sport; not, perhaps as exciting as baseball or soccer, but far superior to picking figs. Eggs yolks three or more weeks old often break on opening, no matter how careful you are. The method we recommend (having plucked a few old yolks in our time) is the Greenwald Shot Glass Technique, modestly named after the author. The shot glass is first used as originally intended. This gives the wrist a resiliency that might otherwise not exist. Break the egg as closely as possible to the bottom of a flat fry pan. We assume, from our own experience, that the yolk breaks immediately. The shot glass is placed immediately over the yolk while the white is poured quickly into another dish. This separation technique is not precise; therefore, we recommend an omelet somewhere in the menu for the day. But in most cases, the result is acceptable. Since the whites of old eggs will not "stand" when beaten, a small amount of yolk in them makes little difference.

BEATING EGGS

When **whole eggs** are combined for use in omelets or scrambled eggs, they should not be beaten for more than 10 or 15 seconds, never with an egg beater. Egg beaters are used for beating egg whites and other members of the crew, not whole eggs. Beat whole eggs with a whisk or fork, just long enough to combine the white and yolk; otherwise, they will be thin and tough. A little cream helps restore a thick, rich quality to old eggs.

Egg whites must be fresh and free of all traces of yolk if they are to stand when beaten. The mixing bowl must be free of all fat and oil and should be dry. Eggs whites will beat to three or four times their original volume; they can be stiffened by adding ½ teaspoon lemon juice per three egg whites when they are frothy.

Egg yolks should be beaten in a small bowl to minimize loss to the bowl's sides. (We always use a rubber scraper to get every drop out of a bowl.) Beat with a fork or whisk until the yolks are pale yellow.

HARD AND SOFT-BOILED EGGS

The best way to hard or soft-boil an egg is not to boil it. Boiling cooks the egg too rapidly, resulting in toughness and uneven texture.

Place egg in generous amount of boiling water to cover, approximately one pint per egg. Reduce heat so water just simmers (salt water may be used instead of fresh). For best results use stop watch to time egg to your liking.

> 3 minutes: very soft, yolks runny and whites just jelly-like
> 4 minutes: yolk still runny, white just set
> 5 minutes: yolk soft, white set
> 6 minutes: white set, yolk just beginning to set
> 10 minutes: hard-boiled

After cooking, eggs are immediately plunged into cold water to stop further hardening. In rough seas, make eggs by using the pressure cooker with the lid on and pressure gauge off, reduce cooking time by 20 percent.

POACHED EGGS

Poached eggs are definitely a fair weather or in-port dish; any sort of motion tends to make the white and yolk separate. Poached eggs are delicate and a few tricks are needed to ensure good results.

1. To a large, heavy skillet Add:
   1   inch of water
   1   teaspoon salt
   1   tablespoon vinegar
   Bring to boil and reduce heat to simmer.
2. Break eggs, one at a time, into a glass and gently slip into water. Allow, at least, one or two inches around each egg—don't crowd them.
3. Cook for 2 to 6 minutes, as desired.

4. Remove egg from the pan with drainer spoon and dip in fresh, warm water to remove vinegar taste. Edges may be trimmed with a cookie cutter or empty tin can. Serve at once on buttered toast.

EGGS POACHED IN WINE   Serves Six (one egg each)

The basic European way of poaching an egg is to add a bit of vinegar to the poaching water. This makes the white jell quickly and in a more solid mass. In this variation, rich red wine is the poaching liquid; any wine, even champagne, may be used as long as it is very dry. For a flamboyant late Sunday brunch (every day is Sunday on a cruise), why not give it a try?

1. Add to skillet:
   1 cup dry wine
   1 cup water, or enough to make 1½ inches liquid
   1 clove garlic, crushed
   2 tablespoons shallot or onoin, minced or finely chopped
   ¼ teaspoon peppercorns, roughtly crushed
   Pinch of salt
2. Bring to boil; reduce heat and simmer for 3 to 4 mintues.
3. With wine just simmering, slide in eggs from a glass. Allow adequate room around each egg. Six eggs per 8-inch skillet. Poach until whites are firm, about 8 minutes; remove eggs with a drainer spoon and place on fried bread.
4. Thicken ½ cup of wine sauce by adding:
   1 tablespoon corn flour mixed in a little cold wine (no lumps)
   1 tablespoon butter
   Bring wine to fast simmer and stir until sauce thickens. Pour very hot over poached eggs and serve. (For variety, try a marinara sauce topped with one tablespoon of Parmesean instead of the wine sauce.)

POACHED EGGS AND BAKED BEANS ON TOAST

We think this may be one of those recipes only one person can love, like a peanut butter and banana sandwich or watermelon with vinegar. Nevertheless, we seem to have this craving, especially when the first light of dawn is just upon us, the morning fix is in the book, and the decks are still wet with dew. Eggs riding triumphantly on a righteous portion of hot baked beans and generously buttered toast taste like the sun feels as it pops its yolk above the horizon. With the eggs gone, the sun shining, and the bite of the morning breeze in the sails, our watch is finished. We lie back in total contentment and watch the sky turn blue.

FRIED EGGS

If you don't like your fried eggs tough around the eges and runny on top, try our method.

1. Heat in 10-inch skillet:
   3   teaspoons butter, bacon fat, or oil
   Heat until oil runs thin, coating bottom and edges of pan.
2. Break eggs into a glass or dish and slip them gently into the pan. Leave sufficient room to use a spatula.
3. Cover and reduce heat to a minimum. Cook slowly, removing lid to check only once or twice. Cook from 3 to 5 minutes. The slower the egg cooks, the softer and more delicate its texture.

SCRAMBLED EGGS

There are a number of different variations on the theme of scrambled eggs; the one discussed here is merely preference.

1. In a mixing bowl combine;
   eggs, two or three per person
   Salt and pepper to taste
   1   teaspoon cream or milk for every two eggs.
   Beat for 15 seconds.
2. Melt in heavy skillet:
   1   teaspoon butter per serving.
   When butter stops bubbling, give eggs a few swift beats and pour them into skillet; reduce heat.
3. When eggs begin to set, sweep them toward the side of the pan with a spatula in long, even strokes. Scrambled eggs are finished when just set, yielding to the touch, and shiny in appearance.
4. Remove from pan and serve with buttered toast. (If anyone in your crew prefers eggs cooked until dry, turn off the heat and serve his portion last. The heat from the pan will cook the eggs to the desired consistency.)

AH, THE OMELET

Great chefs, like great artists, are judged not by their most elaborate productions but by the simple things in life such as painting the perfect circle, raising a simple chalice, making a delicate French pancake or producing a basic omelet that is light and delicious. The omelet is the sailor's best friend and its mastery is well worth the time. If you do not know how to make a basic omelet, now is the time to learn. Don't worry about ruining the first few. Like riding a bicycle, once you have the technique, it's yours forever.

The pan is of some importance. Omelet freaks use their pan for no other purpose and, in fact, never wash it; they merely wipe it after each use. This preserves the oily coating that is the essence of success. Such a fanatical approach is not really practical on a yacht and is not actually necessary. The pan, however, must be spotlessly clean and the bottom free from scratches. Teflon pans are fine for making omelets, but since they scratch easily, particular care must be taken to avoid flakes of Teflon in your masterful creations. Omelet pans have sloped sides (essential for turning the omelet) and are of extra heavy construction so heat is distributed evenly. A 10" pan makes a 3 egg omelet. It's perfect for two people. We think it's better to make several small omelets than 1 large one and 3 eggs are perfect. An omelet pan should be oily, and brief preparation will go a long way toward success. Therefore, add a few tablespoons of a vegetable oil to the pan, before you place it over high heat. Shake the pan to coat the bottom and sides thoroughly. Remove pan from the heat when oil begins to smoke; discard the oil, and wipe away the excess. When the pan has cooled slightly, melt a generous tablespoon of butter. The pan is now ready.

THE BASIC OMELET   Serves Two

1. Combine in mixing bowl and beat for 15 seconds with fork:

   3 eggs

   3 tablespoons milk, cream, or condensed unsweetened milk

   Pinch of salt and pepper

2. Heat the skillet until tablespoon of butter sizzles; pour in egg mixture. Reduce to low heat. As eggs begin to set, tilt pan, allowing uncooked egg to run over edge of

omelet. Keep pan frequently in motion with short, deft movements. (The shaking should approximate hitting the handle of the pan lightly on the side with a hammer.) This process prevents eggs from sticking to bottom of pan, an essential factor for a successful omelet.

3. When eggs are almost firm but still shiny, remove pan from heat and fold omelet. (Our technique is to shake edge of omelet up over edge of pan, holding omelet with fingers and quickly folding edge of omelet toward center of pan. The other side is done in the same way, resulting in a rectangle. The alternative is to shake it a bit further and fold in half.) Slide omelet onto warm plate and serve at once.

MUSHROOM OMELET   Serves Two

1. Saute in pan over medium heat:
   2 tablespoons butter
   1½ cups mushrooms, sliced
   1 teaspoon parsley, preferably fresh
   Pinch of salt and pepper
   If mushrooms are fresh or reconstituted, saute for 3 to 5 minutes until browned. If tinned, saute over high heat for not more than 60 seconds. Remove mushrooms from pan and reserve.

2. Make a basic egg omelet, page 115. Add to eggs before beating:
   1 tablespoon chopped parsley, chives, scallion ends or grated onion (onion is last choice)
   ½ Teaspoon garlic salt
   ½ teaspoon pepper

3. Pour egg mixture into pan. Thirty seconds later pour mushrooms in a broad band across center of omelet. When surface of omelet is not quite set, fold the edges and serve immediately.

A WORD ON OMELET MUSHROOMS

Like all other basic ingredients, mushrooms and their close relatives, truffles, taste best when fresh. But unlike many other vegetables, we have never found a way to extend the life of fresh mushrooms. They will last longer (as much as week) under refrigeration if washed in the fruit and vegetable dip and spread on a clean towel to dry in the sun. To guarantee a supply of mushrooms for extended cruises, purchase either dried or tinned mushrooms. We believe select dried mushrooms are superior to tinned. Dried mushrooms are available in most markets or you can dry them yourself, page 350. Try phone calls to supply houses specializing in Chinese food. There is, in our opinion, nothing better in an omelet then reconstituted, black Chinese mushrooms. Dried mushrooms are reconstituted by soaking them for an hour in hot water, then use as though fresh.

Tinned mushrooms have the shape and plumpness of the fresh variety, but lack the rich flavor.

TWO DELIGHTFUL LOBSTER OMELETS

If you love steamed lobster as much as we do, you may wonder why we bother with a lobster omelet. There are times when one lovely lobster must feed three or four people. This first recipe was a favorite of King Edward VII. It's easy to see why.

LOBSTER OMELET BARON DE BARANTE   Serves Four

Three pots, two burners, feeds three

1. Saute over high heat, stirring constantly:
   ½   cup sliced mushrooms (drained if tinned)
   1   tablespoon butter
   2   pinches salt and pepper

2. Reduce heat and add to pot:
   2   tablespoons ruby port or sherry
   Simmer for one minute to cook away alcohol.
3. Add:
   ½   teaspoon lemon juice
   ½   cup heavy cream or unsweetened condensed milk blended with 1 teaspoon flour
   1   cup cooked lobster meat or fresh crawfish, sliced
   Pinch of nutmeg (optional)
4. Simmer over low heat until sauce thickens. The lobster filling is now completed. Remove 3 tablespoons of sauce without any lobster and reserve in a pot.

4. To these three tablespoons of sauce add:
   2 tablespoons cream, or unsweetened condensed milk blended with ½ teaspoon flour
   1 tablespoon brandy
   2 tablespoons grated Parmesean cheese
   Simmer over low heat until sauce thickens; remove immediately from flame.
5. Make basic 3-egg omelet. Put lobster filling in center; fold and pour on the sauce. Top may be browned in oven.

LOBSTER OMELET MARINARA   Serves Three

This second lobster omelet fares equally well with shrimp, mussels or scallops.

1. Saute in sauce pan over high heat:
   1 green pepper, sliced
   ½ onion, chopped
   1 teaspoon olive oil
2. When onions turn golden, reduce heat; add:
   ½ cup tomato puree
   1 teaspoon lemon juice
   1 teaspoon sugar
   1 teaspoon oregano
   Pinch of salt and pepper
   Simmer for 5 minutes, stirring occasionally
3. Add:
   1 cup sliced, cooked lobster
   Simmer lobster over low heat for 2 minutes; set aside.
4. Make basic   omelet. Pour in the filling, reserving some of sauce to pour over the top.

CRAB FOR OMELETS

We have a small but dependable crab trap, which automatically goes over the side when we are in port. It has provided many delightul meals, and, on occasion, has come up almost groaning from the weight of crabs. But there are those moments when we have taken our luck for granted, invited guests for lunch, then pulled up our trap to find, alas, only two crabs. That may not be enough to have cracked crab for lunch, but the meat of two crabs is most adequate for creamed crab omelets that are a real delight. Crab is not the only seafood that does well in this omelet. Chopped shrimp, scallop, even flaked fish, such as snapper or sea bass, are also a delight. One of our favorite combinations is crab, shrimp, and crawfish tail in whatever proportions are at hand. A delightful sort of **omelette de la mere**.

CREAMED CRAB OR MIXED SEAFOOD OMELET   Serves Three
1. Combine in sauce pan over moderate heat:
   ¾   cup seafood cooked and flaked
   1   generous tablespoon butter
   4   tablespoons heavy cream mixed with a teaspoon flour (no lumps!)
   1   tablespoon sherry or Madeira
   Pinch of salt, nutmeg, or pepper
   Simmer for 2 minutes, stirring constantly.
2. Set sauce pan aside and make a basic   omelet for two. Pour seafood into center of omelet and fold in sides. Sprinkle lightly with paprika and serve at one.

DEEP SEA TUNA OMELET   Serves Three
   The essence of serving fine food on a long cruise is to use as many fresh ingredients as possible, in this case, onions and eggs. They should be available to you whether you have been at sea a day or a month.

1. Saute in sauce pan over high heat:
   ½   onion, chopped
   1   tablespoon butter
2. When onion begins to turn golden, reduce heat and add:
   1   tin (7 oz) tuna, drained and flaked
   3   tablespoon heavy cream or unsweetened condensed milk
   ½   teaspoon salt
   ½   teaspoon pepper
   Simmer lightly for 5 minutes, stirring regularly to heat fish.
3. Make a basic   omelet, but pour tuna into a broad band in center of omelet while eggs are still quite runny. Fold omelet as soon as you can lift edges. Cover pan; turn up heat and cook for 2 minutes, shaking pan constantly. Serve hot with toast.

ANCHOVY OMELETTE NICOISE   Serves Two

A simple omelet from the Provence region of France.

1. Prepare a basic 3 egg omelet in a bowl that has been thoroughly rubbed with **crushed garlic**.
2. Add to bowl:
   - **6   chopped anchovy fillets**
3. Pour mixture in pan containing:
   - **1   tablespoon olive oil, hot**

ANCHOVY OMELET ITALIAN   Serves Three

1. In omelet pan heat:
   1 tablespoon olive oil
2. Fry:
   6 anchovies, chopped
   ½ cup salami, thickly sliced and chopped
   2 garlic cloves, finely chopped.
   When garlic turns golden, remove contents of pan but do not wipe.
3. Pour basic 3-egg omelet mixture in pan and as it begins to set, pour anchovy and salami mixture over it. Cook a few minutes; pour a **half cup of marinara sauce** over omelet, fold and serve.

HAM AND SWISS CHEESE OMELET   Serves Three

1. Saute for approximately 5 minutes in pan:
   1 tablespoon bacon fat or oil
   1 cup ham, finely diced
   ½ medium onion, diced
2. When onions begin to turn golden add to pan:
   3 Italian tomatoes, skinned, chopped and seeded (as they come from the can)
   1 teaspoon parsley
   3 tablespoons white wine
   Generous pinch of pepper
   Pinch of salt
   Cook until mixture is steaming.
3. Make basic   omelet and add
   ½ teaspoon garlic salt
   3 tablespoons condensed milk
4. When omelet begins to set, sprinkle ham mixture evenly over top of omelet. Immediately sprinkle:
   ½ cup of grated Swiss cheese
5. Cook over low heat until omelet is cooked. **Serve flat.**

MEDITERRANEAN PEASANT OMELET

The omelet Paysanne is one of the most popular **frittatas**, or flat omelets, in the Mediterranean. We learned this recipe not in the Mediterranean, but from a French gypsy who tied up alongside in Miami. He had a big pan, a quick hand, and a fast tongue—essential qualities not only of gypsies but of good chefs as well. He fed us this lovely omelet, helped along the road with large glasses of robust Algerian wine, Camembert cheese, black Spanish olives, and crusty, home-baked French bread. The diversified nature of his background was reflected in his cuisine, but his blood was all gypsy. After the dishes were cleared, the last drop of wine drunk, and the pipes well lit, he pulled out a tray of home-made rings set with the most incredible uncut stones. Rebecca soon found one that just fit her and it instantly became her heart's desire. It was the most expensive peasant omelet I ever ate!

OMELET PAYSANNE—A FRITTATA　　　　　　　Serves Four

1. Parboil for 2 minutes:
   - **1　large potato, diced**
   - .　**carrots, diced**

   Fry until brown:
   - **8　bacon slices**

   Remove bacon and reserve.

2. Saute until brown in bacon fat:
   - **Parboiled carrots and potatoes**
   - **1　medium onion, diced**
   - **1　green pepper, diced**
   - **2　cloves garlic, finely chopped**
   - **1　tablespoon marjoram**

   (An additional cup of precooked vegetables, such as **corn, zucchini, yellow squash, or green beans,** may be added.)

3. Add:
   - **1　tablespoon butter, oil, or bacon fat.**

4. Add:
   - **4　eggs beaten**
   - **1　teaspoon salt**
   - **½　teaspoon pepper**

   Cook over low heat for 10 to 15 minutes.

5. Brown the top in broiler.

THE CAPTAIN'S BLUE WATER SCRAMBLED EGGS

Serves Three

Always a favorite with the crew, this recipe combines the subtle flavors of mushrooms, onions and cheese.

1. Saute over high heat until onions are golden:
   - **4   tablespoons butter**
   - **1   cup medium or small mushrooms, sliced in half**
   - **½   cup chopped onion**
   - **½   teaspoon marjoram**
2. Remove mushrooms and onions with drainer spoon, leaving as much of butter in the pan as possible. Combine and add to pan:
   - **4   eggs**
   - **2   tablespoons cream or condensed milk**
   - **½   teaspoon salt**
   - **½   teaspoon pepper**

3. Cook for 20 seconds without disturbing eggs. Sprinkle over eggs:

> **Generous handful of grated mild cheese (Swiss or Gruyere)**
> As soon as cheese begins to melt, start pushing cooked eggs toward edge of pan in even, sweeping strokes. When eggs are almost done, still shiny and yielding to the touch, turn off heat and distribute eggs evenly; sprinkle on mushrooms and onions. **Do not turn the eggs.** Cover the pan with a lid for 30 seconds to warm everything evenly and serve.
> Ah, delight!

SCOTCHMAN'S DELIGHT—AN UNUSAL APPROACH TO SCRAMBLED EGGS
Serves Two

This unique recipe calls for the egg mixture to be cooked in a double boiler, producing a rich, sauce-like scrambled egg that is then poured over a special toast.

1. Fry in butter until just brown:
   > **2 slices bread**
   > **1 teaspoon Parmesan cheese** (For each slice)
   > Remove pan from heat.

2. Combine by beating for not more than 20 seconds:
   > **4 egg yolks**
   > **½ cup cream**
   > **2 tablespoons Parmesan cheese**
   > **Pinch of salt and pepper**
   > **1 teaspoon dry white wine (optional)**
3. Melt in double boiler:
   > **2 tablespoons butter**
   > Add the egg mixture. Stir frequently, scraping the sides and bottom. The eggs should have the consistency of heavy porridge. If they are too thick, add more cream. Pour over the toast, sprinkle with a dash of paprika and serve.

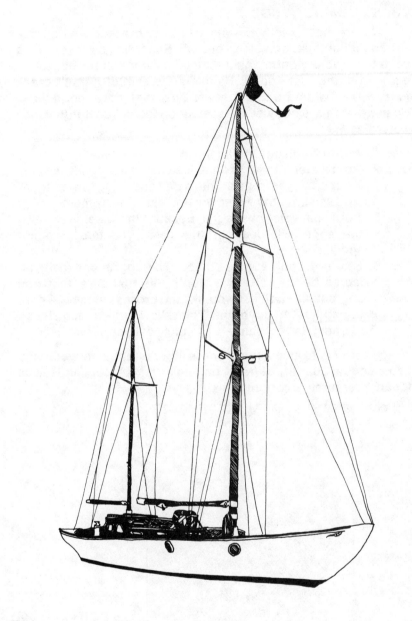

"barcarolle"

CHINESE SALTED EGGS

We are not exactly certain whether this is a recipe, or a storage technique, or a blend of both. Regarding storage, salted eggs last 4 to 6 months. As a recipe, hard or soft boiled, salted eggs look and taste great. Handle eggs carefully; **don't crack them**. (Use wide-mouthed quart jars that have good lids.) Remember this is not just a preservation technique; for that, use waterglass.

1. Add enough eggs to fill the jar.
2. Pour water into jar to fill to measure amount needed.
3. Pour off water from jar into a pan and bring to a boil.
4. Add salt until the water will not dissolve any more.
5. Pour salt water over eggs. Because the water is so salty, the eggs will float. In this case, "floaters" are not spoiled.
6. Store in cool, sunless place. The egg is not really affected by the salt for a month. After 30 days, take one egg out and boil it. If you like the process, it may be continued for 4 to 6 months. The yellow turns a reddish color and gets very salty—absolutely delightful with beer.

If you wish to arrest the process, pour off the salty water and add an equal quantity of fresh, boiling water. Let cool and reseal for another turee or four months.

haj absalem

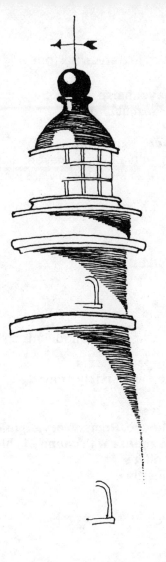

PICKLED EGGS

If you have some end-of-the-package, not so fresh eggs, they can be pickled rather than thrown out.

1. Hard boil all eggs, allow to cool, then shell and discard the bad ones.
2. Pack all the others in a scalded jar and pour over them a steaming hot mixture of the following, enough to cover:
   vinegar and water (50-50)
   mustard seed
   salt
   hot sauce to taste
3. Allow to stand at least 3-4 days before eating. Does not require refrigeration.

DEVILED EGGS

There are many different approaches to making deviled eggs; just select the combination that turns you on. Hard-cook the eggs in either fresh or salt water, then let them stand for a few minutes in cold water to make shelling easier. With a very sharp knife slice them in half, lenghtwise, and carefully remove the yolks.

127

CLASSIC DEVILED EGGS   **Serves Six** (one egg each)
1. Combine thoroughly:
    2 tablespoons mayonnaise
    2 tablespoons dijon mustard
    1 teaspoon salt
    1 teaspoon pepper
2. Add yolks, flaked lightly with a fork, to mayonnaise mixture. Combine the mixture as though you were whipping egg whites with a fork.
3. Stuff whites with the yolk mixture; sprinkle with paprika and serve.

NOVEL DEVILED EGGS

Instead of mustard try:
    catsup
    curry sauce

Add whatever sounds good. Our Favorite additions are:

    Anchovies, chopped or paste
    Chopped chicken liver, finely ground
    Caviar
    Deviled ham spread
    Grated sharp cheese, Romano or Roquefort
    Whipped cream cheese with chopped chives
    Chopped black olives
Serve chilled if possible.

the author

8
sarasota shuffle

When people think of clams they usually have in mind cherry-stones, little necks, or quahogs and, indeed, these are probably the best-known edible clams in the eastern United States. But any experienced clam digger worth his salt knows that literally hundreds of other edible clams exist. They range in size from the tiny, wedge clams that are usually less than half an inch in length, to the surf clam, more than 6-inches long. There are no quahogs in the Mediterranean, but there are many, many other edible mollusks to be taken from sandy beaches and shallow bays. If anything, they are even more popular, and consumed in greater quantities, than the famous quahog. There is no seafood, in my opinion, more delicious than the giant saw-toothed pen shell which, around the Greek Islands, grow more than 12-inches long!

I first learned clamming, not as an amateur, but as an honest-to-goodness professional. It happened one summer during school vacation when I was hitchhiking through the South looking for some adventure and a little work. A friend named Beau and I chanced to be in Sarasota, Florida where we learned that a commercial clam supply house was in need of a few hands. Being a bit broke, the idea of work actually intrigued us. We could dig clams for a month, and, in the critical few days before payday, we could eat and trade the smaller ones for supplies. The clamming procedure in Sarasota Bay consisted of walking along the shallow water, towing a little runabout, and "feeling" for clams in stocking feet. It is amazing how well educated the toes become if given a chance. After all, it's almost a snap to tell the difference between the hard roundness of a half buried clam and, say, a sunken beer can or an old tire. After a short time, Beau and I developed the Sarasota Shuffle, a little dance most likely akin to a cow trying to throw a stone from her hoof. It consisted of standing on one foot while probing in a half circle with the toes of the other. A sort of half step terminated our dance. One moved a little forward, a bit sideways, then repeated the whole act while humming Muskrat Ramble in three-quarter time. Cut feet, or "turtle toe" as we called it, were always a worry, and the old timers at the clam house always warned us, with straight faces, to be sure to get shark insurance from Blue Cross. So, with these stories always somewhere in the back of my mind you can imagine my reaction one day, while doing the Sarasota Shuffle, when I felt something grab my big toe. I let out a scream and vaulted over the transom into the skiff. Quickly, examining the injured member, fully expecting to see it half gone, I discovered my toe squarely in the big, open jaws of a scallop. I ate him in revenge.

Unlike clams, scallops just can't seem to keep their mouths or shells shut, even when you haul them from the water. They'll snap right back at you. But in the process, they lose all their

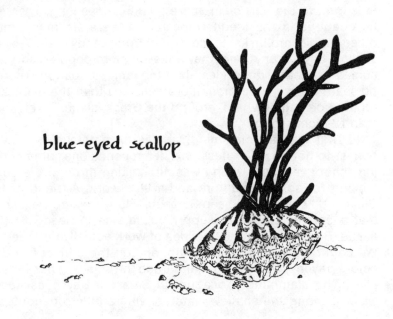

blue-eyed scallop

water and, so, quickly die. That's why 99 percent of the world's scallop lovers buy them frozen or refrigerated. But fresh scallops are as different from frozen or refrigerated scallops as fresh and frozen lobster. Few mollusks are superior in flavor to the fresh scallop. Thus, properly alerted to the delicacy just a toe's length away, Beau and I borrowed diving gear and, in clear patches of bay, chased scallops. Scallops have remarkably sophisticated eyes—considering the primitive nature of the beast. They're good enough to spot toes doing the Sarasota Shuffle and avoid a kick by getting away. This is a type of mollusk locomotion. The scallop gets away by forcefully snapping its shells together to expel water and move backward about a foot at a time. Thus, scallops know well where they have been, but not where they are going. Needless to say, this form of motion does lack navagational sophistication. It sets a very erratic course indeed; it looks something like a novice learning to tack.

THE SCALLOP

The Clam Corporation paid us 3 cents per pound for our labors. This might sound like a losing proposition but the clams were mostly large ones intended for use in canned soups. About 14 clams weighed ten pounds. Beau and I would dig nearly 2000 clams daily to make twenty dollars each, but that was really a lot of money for a couple of high school kids in those days, and we didn't mind the work. In addition, there was an abundance of clams, and we usually had made our "20" by nightfall.

But we started hard. After the second day of reaching down and grabbing clams with our hands, we completely wore off our fingerprints. A bit discouraged, we had already gone through a good set of calluses as well, and the weekend wasn't even in sight. Then, a fellow clammer took us down to the local blacksmith and had him make us a pair of clam forks. A clam fork looks exactly like a huge meat carving fork cut off about 3 inches from the tines. The tines are usually made from ¼-inch rod about 4 inches long and terminate in dull points. At the other end, a length of ¾-inch tubing, long enough to act as a handle, is welded. After a clam was located with the Sarasota Shuffle, we would reach down and, in one motion, slip the fork under it and pry him out of the sand.

A kindly landlady who rented us a room knew so many different ways to cook clams that Beau and I never tired of them. We did become very discriminating, however, especially after payday. From that time on we selected only the very smallest (2 to 3 in.) cherrystones; they are unquestionably sweeter and more tender than the big ones. One of our favorite meals was butter clam nectar drunk from a mug followed by clam fritters which look very much like salmon croquettes and potato pancakes combined. They sure were good! Helped along by a couple mugs of cold beer, Beau and I put away platefuls of this cracker country cuisine.

But quahogs aren't the only clam worth having, and as a sailor it never hurts to go poking around the shallow bays where you drop the hook. After all, it certainly beats playing cards and waiting for bedtime!

RAZOR CLAM

Another delightful clam is the Atlantic Razor found on sandy beaches from northern Canada all the way to Florida's gulf coast. There is a slightly smaller Mediterranean variety so popular on the half shell that no Italian beach-side food stand would be complete without a big bucket of them. Razors are fast movers and are totally immune to the Sarasota Shuffle. We usually find their holes at low tide, particularly the neap and spring tide when unusually large amounts of beach are exposed. They are found where the sand is clean and the surf not too vicious—the same kind of territory perferred by surf clams. Atlantic Razors grow up to a foot long and an inch or more wide. Their Mediterranean cousins are usually less than 5-inches long and about as thick as your little finger. Both are delicious, but both really know how to turn on the speed when you go after them. They do this by thrusting their foot into the sand, then forming a ball at the end of it that reminds me of a mushroom mooring anchor. They finally draw the shell to the ball with a swift jerk. All of this happens in far less time than it takes to describe, so the southern phrase "slow as a clam" certainly didn't come from razor clams! Getting a bucket full of razor clams is really an experience, especially if rum has been used to oil your approach. You must sneak up on the little devils using the walk-on-eggshells technique; they are very sensitive to vibration and can burrow into the sand much faster than you can dig. In addition, a razor clam can swim better than a lot of sailors I know by using the same ball anchor technique through the water. They go through the same procedure as when burrowing, but they can do it so quickly that it is difficult to follow

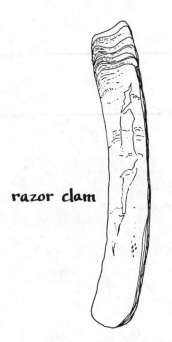

razor clam

their act with the eye. Their course is rather erratic, but they have no eyes at all so, therefore, they have no idea they are going.

Our approach to catching them is extremely unsophisticated. Wearing light cotton gloves (the shell edges are sharp) we creep to within arm's length and then grab them any way we can. They are really fast, so you must not be discouraged by frequent failure. Once you have your fingers around a razor clam you must avoid a temptation to try to pull it from the sand. The razor clam inevitability extends his anchor and is just as interested in winning as you. If you simply keep pulling, you each end up with half a clam which, you must admit, leaves both of you unsatisfied. So, after you grab a razor clam, the best way to win the bout is to dig the sand away from the foot with the other hand. Razor clams have an opening at each end and will die if left out of water. It is, therefore, necessary to have a water-filled pail or canvas bucket to keep them fresh. If you add a little corn meal to the water in the bucket (this is true for all clams) the razors will void the grit in their stomachs and take in the corn meal making them even more tasty.

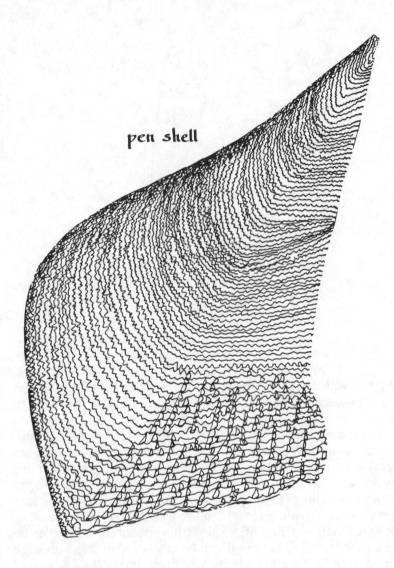

pen shell

PEN SHELLS

Pen shells are scientifically closer to oysters than clams. There were plenty of them in Sarasota Bay, and the sharp lips of their shells were one of the chief reasons we wore heavy socks. Beau and I soon discovered them, then cut our hands getting them out of the mud and broke the delicate shells trying to get at the insides. Finally, we were repulsed by the unappetizing-looking creature inside. Since we weren't exactly hurting for shellfish, we promptly thought no more of them. It's probably a good example of how an animal comes to be known as inedible. It wasn't until fifteen years later that this creature probed the culinary lobes of my mind. It happened when Rebecca and I were living on the hook. Though living surrounded by the gentle sea breeze and blue sky is a habit hard to kick, the City of Miami Police Department does not like hippies, drifters, visiting yachtsmen or any other hook addict "littering" its bay with boats. The police repeatedly urged us to move into the marina (which was full) or haul in our hook and quietly steal away. They threatened to fine us for rowing our six-foot dinghy at night without running lights, and I guess they would have been pretty mad about us stealing pen shells from the bay bottom. Then, a little Tahiti ketch with a Martha's Vineyard registry worked its way under sail into the anchorage near us and dropped the hook. The mud hadn't even settled before the police were there telling the captain to move to the city marina. The skipper said he wouldn't mind moving there "atall" but "seein as how (he) didn't have a motor an' it bein' illegal to sail under a draw bridge (he) wouldn't mind "atall" if they'd give (him) a tow. It was about ten miles to city marina and the police had other things to do that day, so our two little boats were soon alone on the hook. With both my admiration and attention fully aroused, I watched somewhat in amazement as the skipper proceeded to dive up a big bucket full of pen shells. Knowing full well that pen shells do not grow in northern waters, I rowed over in the dinghy to kindly tell this Yankee about how inedible pen shells were.

"You going to eat those pen shells, Mister?" I asked.

"Ah yep," he replied.

"Not many folks around here eat them," I said.

He looked at his overflowing bucket and said "Ah yep."

"Most folks thing they're kind of tough and gritty," I said.

"Mostly," he replied.

I was beginning to realize that he was a man of few words, but while his jaw was a little slow his hands weren't. He was opening the pen shells with a knife, cutting out the huge adductor muscle and throwing the rest back into the bay, thus explaining the "mostly" in answer number three.

"The bay's a bit polluted around here, Mister," I said. "Aren't you worried about catching something?"

For a moment I thought he would actually converse, but when the word finally came, it was "Nope." At this point his wife came on deck and began rolling the fresh muscles in frying crumbs to most eloquently answer my last question. Since our conversation had somehow lacked the stuff of great debate, I rowed off to do a little pen shell fishing on my own.

There are three different species of pen shells in United States waters; all of them are very similar in shape and all taste about the same. They can be found from Cape Hatteras to Florida, including the Gulf Coast, throughout the Bahamas, the upper Caribbean, and on the west coast of Mexico around the Yucatan channel. There are also several species of pen shell in the "Med." The largest are the noble pen, or Nero's pen shell, which refers to the days when they were the pinnacle of fine cuisine. We first discovered the Nero's pen shell in the clear, shallow waters of Western Sardinia. We had not planned to stop there but a vicious norther sent us running under storm sails for the nearest port of opportunity. This turned out to be the Gulf of Oristano—a huge bay with a relatively small opening. It was quite an experience. One moment we were taking aboard green water; then, as we entered, the bay water had just the slightest ripple—not even the hint of a wave. Of course, the wind also moderated, and we were able to hoist the working jib and mainsail to pass in ghostly nighttime fashion along our course. The hills looked as though they were made of living steel in the bright moonlight, and we could still hear the angry sea yammering behind us. With the full moon, with the clear sky and stars, with the hills stretching before us like mountains of the moon and the moonlight blending with the phosphorescence of our wake, we came in incredible silence to an anchorage at the foot of a hill covered with ruins. Greek columns, beautifully preserved, glowed whitely in the moonlight as they marched toward the sea. A Punic tower, misshapen and silent, seemed to watch darkly from the crest of the hill. A short distance away there was a little village with houses made from reeds. The embers of their dying fires made reflections on the walls.

Then in the morning, we found ourselves swinging at anchor in the midst of a tiny fishing port whose inhabitants used gill nets to work the fertile bay. We rowed to the bistro, a little place made from cement block and reed. We were a bit concerned, for Sardinia belongs to Italy, and we spoke no Italian. We needn't have worried. The population didn't speak much

Italian. It was a local dialect of Sardinian, which made no sense to us at all either! But as we entered the bistro, a young lady behind the bar greeted us in faultless English. As it turned out, she was not the only person in the area to speak English. But she was the only one with letters behind her name that spelled Doctor of English Literature. She was helping her parents run the bar during summer. We became fast friends with Maria Manca, and during the course of the day, we asked if there was any good diving in the area. The fish in the bay were a bit small, she said, but there were some "big shells" at the foot of the ruins. We went there that afternoon and found, among the shards of pottery and ruined columns, the largest bed of noble pen shells we have ever seen. There were literally hundreds of them so big that their shells were later to serve as plates big enough to hold a full course meal. The shells themselves were a translucent white covered, on the outside, with a brownish green periostracum. After we worked a patch of these shells free from the bottom, we opened them with a thin filleting knife. The mollusk within was the most awful looking thing we have ever seen. Coils of intestines were woven in unpleasant colors of orange, black, and brown. No wonder the local population disdained them! But the adductor muscle was absolutely huge. It was slightly bigger than a silver dollar and about 1½-inches thick. We ate a goodly number of them right on the spot, flavored with nothing more than sea water in which they lived and a little lemon juice. Later that day we would sprinkle them with celery salt and a little flour and fry them lightly in butter. What a delight! The next day we steamed them for five minutes in dry, white wine and served them with fresh mayonnaise to which we had added a little mustard. Could this have been what drove Nero mad? Thus we spent our days, walking the countryside with our friend, Maria, and eating nature's wonderful gifts from the sea.

Pen shells live in gritty, sandy mud with just the edge of their lips protruding. They do not have any sort of escape locomotion, so once you have found them with either the Sarasota Shuffle technique or flippers and mask, simply pull them up. The huge, single adductor muscle is found near the base, or pointed, end of the shell and is easily severed by slipping a knife between the pen's imperfectly closed lips. The curious thing about pen shells is their interior. It is frequently inhabited by a little, red crustacean which looks so much like a lobster we thought we had discovered something new. But this little beast is, in fact, a shrimp which lives inside the pen shell for protection. It gets its food from debris in the water sucked in by the pen shell's siphons. These little shrimp are hermits and, with the exception of cohabitation for breeding, will readily attack each other. We have tried, on several occasions to save these shrimp when we shuck pen shells. There are usually three or four in a pail after we are through, but in the morning there is inevitability just one and a few other bits and pieces.

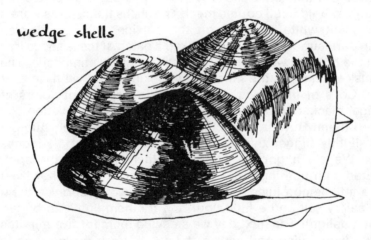

wedge shells

WEDGE SHELLS

Wedge shells are tiny clams not much larger than a penny. They come in all sorts of colors, so many in fact that trying to identify a wedge shell by color would be a futile job. Wedge shells, wherever they are found, look like tiny, smooth, brightly colored cherrystones. Should you turn over a shovel full of wet sand and find it full of shiny little clams, you have probably found wedge shells. Species live from Massachusetts to Florida, throughout the Caribbean and Central America, the Mediterranean, and in great numbers along the west coast of the United States. What these delicious gems lack in size is more than compensated by number. Quite frequently, you can find them filling the bottom of tidal pools and puddles. Empty shells at the tide line also display their presence. They are so small that Americans just don't consider them food, other than for an occasional use in broth. But the Spanish, French, Portuguese and others take these clams quite seriously, and I am certain that literally thousands of tons are sold annually. For example, wedge shells, called Vongola in Italy, are widely esteemed for the making of clam sauce for spaghetti. A handful of these little beauties in wine and garlic sauce, over spaghetti, is a great treat. Many restaurants serve big plates of wedge shells for customers. Wedge shells are so delicious that we ate them three or four times per week when we cruised the coast of Italy.

When we collect wedges we rinse them free of sand in sea water using a colander. They are then left for the rest of the day in a bucket of sea water treated with a little corn meal to free them of their intestinal grit. By dinner time they are ready to go; a better clam chowder is hard to find. Because wedge shells are so small, it is a bit tedious to shell them by hand. There is a simple way. Steam the wedge shells open in one cup of water and ½ cup of dry, white wine per quart of shells. Let the broth cool, then pour half the shells and all of the liquid into a jar. Tightly cap the jar and shake the whole thing hard for a few minutes. This will free quite a few of the clams from their shells. To remove the shells, give the mixture in the jar a vigorous stirring with a spoon. This will cause the free clam meat to swirl up, then you can easily remove the shells on the bottom with a spoon. Repeat the process with the remaining clams.

COCKLES

Cockles of various sizes and species are found all over the east coast of the United States from Maine to Florida, throughout the Gulf Coast, along the shores of the British Isles, in the Med, and along the west coast of Africa. The word cockle actually refers to a relatively large number of different species, and in many areas, various bivalves are called cockles when in fact they are not. Most small bivalves are quite edible and it is only a question of how they get from the sea to your stomach. For simplicity and our culinary purposes, it is merely necessary to classify cockles as large or small, and treat them accordingly. As is generally true, the smaller ones can be eaten whole, in soup or in sauce, while large cockles are usually better when ground.

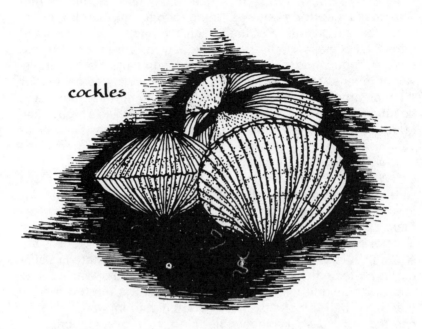

cockles

Cockles seem to prefer estauries or protected bays where the surf is light and the sand not too compact. They have no siphons and are usually found lying about the sand at low tide.

This is our "cockles" story. We spent several weeks on the hook in Portimao, Portugal, a lovely little town on the Algarve coast, not far from Cape Sagres. A river broadens as it runs past the town—actually a sizable fishing port. This grand river continues southward, across numerous sandbanks and spits, until it broadens into a small estuary whose mouth is protected by a breakwater. River currents are accentuated by six-foot tides which when on the ebb, run with a vengence. It is essential to drop an upstream and downstream anchor and be well clear of the port's 50 fishing boats when the tide turns. Despite this natural barrier caused by the current, the sandbanks and bars of the river are just covered with common cockles as much as three miles inland. How they got there against the current is a mystery to me—how they find their way into the mouth of the breakwater against this outward flow is strange enough.

Nevertheless, when the tide is out and miles of sandy beach are exposed, literally thousands of small cockles are to be found lying around. The townspeople are always out there to gather them when the tide is out, but despite their determined efforts, the supply never seems to diminish.

These little cockles are about 1½ to 2½ inches long and their meat has a fine clam flavor. They are numerous enough on some parts of the European coast, mostly south of Biscay, to be gathered commercially and canned. They suffer somewhat by this but do better when used in tinned seafood sauces.

Since our visit to Portimao, I have seen numerous cockle shells on the beaches of Florida, including the Gulf Coast, and in the Bahamas; a slightly different species is found all over the east coast of the United States. Don't let their drab, unassuming shells fool you; the contents within make really fine eating and can be used in any of the recipes for wedge shells or fried clams. Or, you can just steam them in a little white wine for cocktail snacks.

LARGE COCKLES

Considering the unassuming size of the common cockle, the Atlantic cockle, found all over the southeast coast, Bahamas, Caribbean and throughout the Gulf of Mexico, is a real giant. It grows as large as 6 inches, though the median size would be closer to four. It is particularly abundant in Florida and the lower Gulf states, and is abundant from the Yucatan channel as far south as Belize. In some parts of Florida, such as around Marco and Sanibel islands, giant cockles and scallops were particularly abundant in ancient times. Primitive man came from miles around to eat them. These islands, which are both several miles long and solid enough to build houses upon, are actually huge kitchen middens made entirely from the discarded shells of ancient feasts! There are still areas in South Florida where giant cockles can be found in great abundance.

As with their smaller brothers, Atlantic cockles are usually found in protected bays or estuaries where there is relatively light surf. They are not deep burrowers and are usually found either on the sand or just below it. Large cockles, as are many of the shell fish mentioned here, are very popular in France, Italy, Corsica, Sardinia, and Spain. Popular enough, in fact, to be sold in numerous seaside food stands for use in soups or to eat on the half shell. They are a highly flavored clam which make wonderful broths in combination with, or as a replacement for, quahogs in chowders and fritters. The shells of the bigger ones are so nicely hollowed that people have a natural tendency to save them for use as containers or ashtrays. A friend of mine uses them as sugar and flour scoops, and they work just fine.

There are many other types of clams and oysters that are easily obtained by the interested sailor. With your sailboat and dinghy, it is possible to reach deserted islands and sand flats that the landlubber can never reach. These are hunting grounds that can yield rich harvests of food and fun. Clamming is not only a good way to stretch your budget, it is a fine way to idle away a sunny day and, to my mind, it certainly beats sunbathing. Even the complete novice can be an immediate success as a clam hunter and beachcomber extraordinaire: returning to the ship with the makings of a fine meal gives one great sense of independence. A sailor's cookbook is not the place for a complete discussion of all the world's edible bivalves. But I hope that with these few pages we have, at least been able to whet your interest.

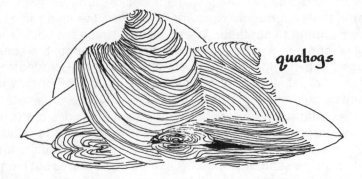

quahogs

9
mollusks

No edible mollusk becomes seasonally poisonous. The problem is created by a microscopic creature called a dinoflagellate. It is similar to but not the same variety which causes the red tide. Bivalves strain water for edible debris and thereby concentrate these creatures in toxic quantities. Cooking does not destroy the poison. However, if the black stomach and guts are cut away, the meat is edible. Northern California is the principal problem area as the toxic variety prefers cool water. The dangerous months are May through October and Federal warnings are posted. Most Old Salts in the affected areas know about it, so just ask. And be sure to gut your shellfish for two weeks after a red tide for, on rare occasions, several species of dinoflagellate proliferate at the same time.

Pollution is another problem. We just don't think that shellfish near heavy population areas should be eaten. Frying kills all living organisms but doesn't rule out chemical, heavy metal and insecticide toxins. So, if you are near a populous area, eat fish or take advantage of the grocery.

Unless the water is sea-clean and the area free even of villages, it is best to cook all seafood.

THE PREPARATION OF BIVALVES

We would be lax in our presentation and duty if we did not begin this introduction with these warnings. Never eat bivalves that are open and do not close to the touch, float when dropped

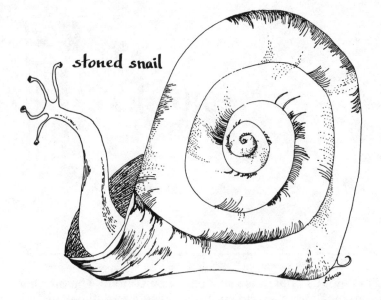

stoned snail

in water, smell foul if purchased canned or refrigerated, have been gathered from an area where the water is polluted, or look or smell bad after cooking.

CLEANING

All bivalves should be scrubbed and made as clean as possible with a stiff brush prior to cooking. Mussels should be debearded by pulling the beard toward the front of the shell. Any barnacles on mollusk shells are disregarded and will not detract from the flavor of the meal.

DEGRITTING

All bivalves taste better if allowed to sit 6 hours or, preferably, overnight in a generous amount of sea water onto which has been sprinkled a half a cup of corn meal. The mollusks will consume the cornmeal and eject their intestinal grit. This is important for all bivalves, but even more so for surf clams, southern oysters, quahogs, and steamers. If you cannot, for some reason, apply the corn meal technique, open shells can be washed after cooking and the liquor strained through cheese cloth.

OPENING

All bivalves open when cooked, so this solves the opening problem 99 percent of the time. If you want mollusks on the half shell, a little stealth may prove more effective than the best hammer. Place the shells, with lips up, in a pan of sea water. (A plastic egg holder will help here.) After an hour or so, the shells will begin to open. Very carefully, so as not to disturb the others, slip a small nail or cotter pin into the opening. Should this technique prove unfeasible, see the sections on individual mollusks for specific instructions about opening them.

STORAGE

Live bivalves will last a long time if placed in a bait bucket, or some other stout container, and hung in the sea. It is a mistake, however, to put them in a cloth or mesh sack since shellfish-eating rays and sharks will make short work of them. If this is not practical, they can be kept in sea water refrigerated at about 50° F or in a dish in the refrigerator at 40° F. In water they will usually last at least a week; this is a technique essential to mollusks that do not retain their water (scallops and razor clams for example). The others, such as oysters and quahogs, will last at least four to five days dry, if maintained at a temperature of 40 to 45°F. Do not store them on ice, however; this can quickly kill them.

Fresh, deshelled mollusks or those such as oysters that come in refrigerator tins may be stored directly on the ice or in a refrigerator at 35 to 40° F for about four days. The important thing to remember is that you store the meat in its own liquor or, in any event, never wash it until you are ready to use it. Regarding the danger of spoilage, let your nose be the guide. If they smell rank, don't eat them.

Regardless of how the mollusk is prepared, whether it is tough or delicate, the liquor inside its shell is invariably tasty and should not be discarded. It can always be used to make fish sauces.

CANNED SHELLFISH

Canned shellfish of any kind suffer a bit from the cooking necessary to sterilize them. They are already wounded in flavor, so treat them gently. Never wash canned shellfish since this reduces the flavor. They are most successfully used in recipes where they do not have to be cooked at all, such as in pate or

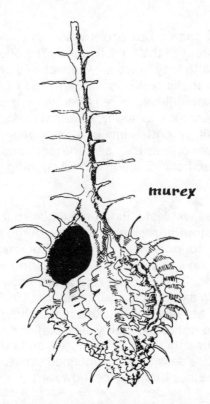

murex

where they can be added at the last moment to soup or sauces. A little additional lemon juice often will improve the flavor. Canned or bottled clam juice, by constrast, holds up quite well and can be added without hesitation wherever clam juice is called for.

INTERCHANGING SHELLFISH SPECIES

Recipes for mussels, oysters, and clams are somewhat interchangeable as are recipes for scallops, surf clams, and pen shell mussels. In addition, excellent variety can be achieved by mixing one or more different species together. Almost invariably each complements the other and everyone compliments the cook.

SHUCKING OYSTERS

We almost invariably break off a piece of the oyster's shell at the lips big enough for the entry of a thin knife. Slip the knife in toward the top of the flat shell and cut the single muscle that holds the oyster togther. Remove the flat shell and sever the muscle holding the body to the lower shell. Be careful not to lose too much of the liquor. Examine the meat for debris caused by your forced entry.

CLEANING
BLUE MUSSELS

Mussles secrete a fine thread called byssus which helps anchor them to the surrounding rocks and other mussels. This golden thread, though fine, is remarkably tough. The ancient Romans actually wove it into a fabric so fine that a dress of it was able to pass through a finger ring! The byssus are secreted from one place and can, therefore, be easily grasped, pulled forward toward the opening end of the shell and torn free. The shell should be scrubbed with a brush. Mussels can be eaten on the half shell with a little lemon juice, but great care should be taken that they come from a non-polluted area should you eat them au natural. A knife blade is easily slipped between the lip and drawn toward the rear or pointed end of the shell where the muscles lie. Some mussel bodies are white, some are orange. Both are perfectly edible. Mussels are very tender mollusks and full of flavor. They are excellent just steamed open and dipped in butter or sauce. Mussel soup and stews are also a delight and the fine meat is a good addition to seafood Newburg.

CLAMS ON THE HALF SHELL

Clam shells should be washed and freed from all loose debris prior to opening. It is highly recommended that they be allowed to sit overnight in a bucket of sea water containing a half cup of corn meal to free them of intestinal grit. Chill them before opening and serve immediately.

If clams are placed in a pan, lips up, then covered with sea water for an hour they usually open a bit. It is then possible to gently slip a knife between the lips, which then immediately close on the blade. The clam is then gently lifted from the pan so as to not disturb its .friends. The blade can then be worked around to cut the muscles.

Clam adductor muscles are located on either side of the shell toward the rear, so don't go hewing around inside the shell with your knife. Open over a bowl to catch the juice.

Should the clam outwit you in this initial approach you can take a stout knife, place the blade across the lip line and tap the **blade into the cavity with a hammer. This always works. Never try to break away the lips of a clam or cockle as the shell usually fractures and leaves fragments in the meat.**

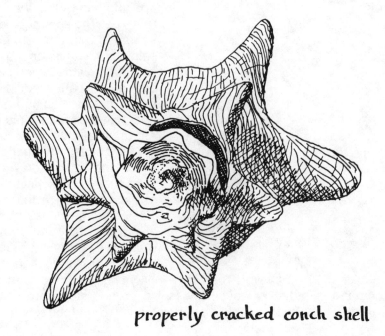

properly cracked conch shell

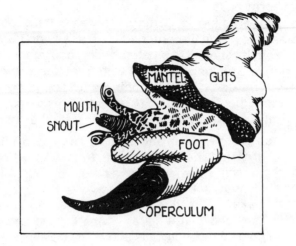

ABOUT CONCH

There are a number of different varieties of this huge, snail-like mollusk, most of them found in the warm Atlantic and Pacific waters and in the Indian Ocean. All are edible except the huge horse conch, really a Grant welk, which may exceed 18 inches in length. Conch are slow moving, bottom feeders that live in shallow water on sand or grass. Their huge shells are easily spotted when snorkling and there is no trick to finding them. When there is one there are a million and where there are none you may not see them for days. Most conch and their relatives, the beautiful helmet shells, are timid and immediately retreat into their shells when handled. But there are several small (3 to 4 inch) varieties that don't know this and will attack you aggressively when you pick them up. You may well wonder how an overgrown snail can move to the attack, and it is best that we tell you before you endeavor to pick them up. All conch have a horny covering on their foot called an opurculum. It is pointed at one end, rather sharp, and covered with mucus. The conch will take one look at your hand and spear you with its opurculum so

149

severely (though fortunately not with lightning speed) that you will immediately forget all about conch fritters and begin thinking about first aid. The best defense is to grab the opurculum or hold the creature in its shell by placing your thumb over the flat part of this horny cover.

Your next problem is getting the damn thing out of its shell—no easy task for the uninitiated. There is no way to pull the conch from its shell; it is a better puller than you and always wins this game. Breaking the shell with a rock is also a loser's game unless you don't mind dropping a 50 pound boulder on your dinner and picking the pieces of shell from the mess. There is, in fact, only one reasonable way to separate the conch from

his home. Grab the operculum and attach a vise grip to it. This will make removal from the shell much easier. Hold the shell in the left hand, with the opening downward. It is better to work away from the boat as shell and slime tend to fly everywhere. Using the claw of a hammer, make a slit in the shell (see illustration on page 148) between the third and fourth spiral. Rinse the slit and cut the tendon which holds the conch in its shell. The tendon is beneath the meat. It is a broad flat sheet which lies against the pink center column, extending several inches into the shell. Slip a knife into the slit beneath the meat and cut the tendon completely. The

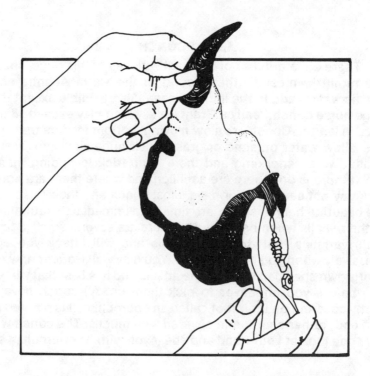

conch can be removed from the shell with a slight pull. If it will not come out, the tendon is not completely cut. Resist the temptation to force the conch free by pulling with the vise grips. The operculum is brittle and easily broken.

Kill the conch with a scooping cut which removes the eye stalks and snout. Do not delay as the conch is now thoroughly aggravated and can secrete an amazing amount of slime. Cut away the guts and the colorful orange-yellow mantle. Feel the mantle for conch pearls before discarding it. Some people save the mantle for fritters but eating it raw is an acquired taste. The clear rubbery "style," looking like a piece of spaghetti, may be eaten raw but doesn't have much flavor. A short digestive tract runs from the snout to the center of the body. Cut it open and wash the meat.

The dark, tough skin must now be removed, a difficult job as it is slimy and doesn't want to come off. Make a series of slits through the skin radiating away from the operculum. Pull the skin off with a butter knife or pliers. Put the meat into a baggie so it won't spatter and pound with a meat hammer 'til it begs for mercy. Wash the meat and your tools in vinegar. The conch is now ready for use.

queen conch

151

STORING LIVE CONCH

Live conch will last all day out of water if kept in a cool, dark spot. The natives collect a bunch of conch, tap a hole in the lip of each shell, tie them together, and throw them over the side at night. The conch all try to go in different directions (like some sailors we know) and therefore go nowhere. But never try to suspend a conch over the side from a string—ironically enough, conch thus treated inevitably drown.

CRACKED CONCH

This popular Bahamian recipe is the West Indies's answer to the hamburger. When one fried conch is served on a hamburger bun, it's called a conchburger. When two fried conchs are served on a plate they are called "cracked conch." Call it what you like, the taste is great!

1. Thoroughly pound until tender:
   1 conch body, cleaned
2. Rinse conch in salt water and sprinkle all over with:
   lemon juice
3. Dust conch thoroughly with:
   flour
4. Pan fry until golden, in:
   ½ inch vegetable oil
5. Serve as hamburger with some garnishes, or on a plate with a side dish of potato salad.

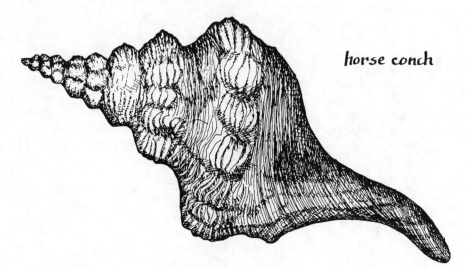

horse conch

CONCH SALAD

Conch salad is similar to gazspacho with less liquid and a lot of chopped or ground conch. It is made spicy with hot sauce after all the ingredients are in the pot. Add the hot sauce slowly and stir. It is better to add a bit less hot sauce and allow each person to season to taste. The hot sauce does not appear in the recipe below.

1. Add to the pot:
   3 cleaned conch, chopped or coarsely ground
   ½ large onion, chopped
   ½ cup chopped celery
   ½ can (28 oz.) crushed Italian tomatoes with juice
   ½ lemon (juice only)
   1 teaspoon salt, pepper, sugar
   1 green pepper, chopped
   ½ cup scallions chopped, green and all
   2 tablespoons garlic, chopped
   ½ cup light oil
2. Stir well and allow to stand several hours before serving. Even better the next day.

OCTOPUS

The octopus is a mollusk as are the clam and squid; a more amazing beast is hard to find. They have eyes similar to humans, resulting from what scientists call convergent evolution. The octopus can change color from a white or pale gray through many shades of brown to an angry red. Their eight legs are used for walking or for opening mollusks (the octopus is a gourmet who loves clams on the half shell). Highly intelligent among sea beasts, the octopus occasionally displays his ability to use tools when building rocky dens. In addition to walking on many tentacles, they can jet backward by filling gill pouches with water, and squirting it out with great force. Like the squid, the octopus has an ink sac for protection. Our theory is that the ink is used not as a false image, but as a scent lure. We say this because there is no better bait for predatory fish, especially moray eels, than octopus ink sacs. We have seen moray eels come boiling out of their rocky dens when octopus ink is nearby.

The boneless octopus spends his time in the most unlikely places. We found one living inside an empty tin can. We have even seen a few carrying cans around with them, a sort of instant armor. While the octopus loves clams and oysters, the mainstay of its diet is crab. It stalks them like a cat, then leaps and drops upon them. We have never been able to understand how the octopus avoids being severely pinched by the crab's vicious claws. The normal, garden variety octopus inhabits shallow water and never exceeds a few feet from tentacle to tentacle. Sailors' fables tell about huge monsters of the deep who suddenly come out of the night to attack whole ships, grappling them with their vicious tentacles, and pulling the vessels down to Davy Jones. The famous giant squid episode in Jules Verne's **Twenty Thousand Leagues Under the Sea** makes even the most sensible of us wonder if the sea harbors these fantastic creatures.

Late one night, alone on deck and deep into the dog watch, I heard a commotion in the sea nearby. I switched on our cockpit torch, a powerful light, to see what was about. Suddenly the water just astern seemed to boil, a huge octopus rose from the sea and seemed to float just above the waves; its arms splayed wildly. It glared balefully into the torch beam, then, with a splash was gone. My hair stood right up on my head as I reached down the companionway for a pistol. With the gun in one hand and my torch in the other, I peered around the ship into the darkness,

author on night watch

expecting to see tentacles come creeping over the toerail. The gleaming .38 stayed in my belt all night ready for action, but then there was only the moonlight, the gentle swell, and the sparkle of the sea. In the morning I realized that the monster I had seen was certainly a deep water octopus, surely not more than four to six feet from tentacle to tentacle, not big enough to suck even a dinghy under. Where it came from and why it was there, I'll never know.

We greatly respect these strange creatures and have spent many an hour watching them beneath the sea. We see them in another light, as quite delicious additions to our table.

KILLING, CLEANING

A hammer blow between the eyes is the most effective method of killing an octopus. Piercing the same area with a knife blade does not provide as swift a death. Do not let them linger on the spear or in the dinghy; they could escape and, in any event, get very tough if allowed to live wounded.

When the octopus is dead, slit the hood, remove the viscera, and pop off the beak. Grab it by the tentacles and beat it on a rock or the gunnel of the dinghy for not less than 5 minutes. If not beaten properly, the octopus provides the toughest meat you have ever tasted. Boil for 10 minutes in enough sea water to cover, plus ½ cup vinegar. Peel the tough skin from the tentacles and hood. The octopus is now ready for use.

USES OF OCTOPUS

Octopus is molluscan in flavor and when ground may be substituted for tender mollusks in any recipe including chowder, fritters, newburgs, or casseroles. But our favorite recipe is the Mediterranean Fruite del Mare, fruit of the sea, a combination of whatever tender mollusks you may find, especially mussels, clams, cockles, and squid. All are simmered in crab boil, for an additional 5 minutes, then drained. They are then allowed to marinate in the same onion, vinegar, spice combination found on page 409. Absolutely delicious.

SQUID

The mysterious squid is a mollusk that carries its vestigal shell in the form of a small sword-shaped plate inside the body. This plate is usually the only part of a squid that most Americans

ever see. Even then they don't realize that "cuttle bone," sold in pet shops for parakeets, is from a squid.

Squid are usually not encountered by the individual in sufficient numbers to make their capture worthwhile; they are usually netted by trawlers. Once, however, when we were in mid-Atlantic, we heard a huge rain squall approaching, yet the sky was clear. Suddenly, with a dull roar, the water churned all around us and hundreds of tiny shapes shot into the air. Some hit the boat, and even the sail. We found, to our astonishment, that they were little squid, so intensely engrossed in mating that they did not resist even when picked up and slipped into a bucket of water. In the mating ritual the pair faced each other and locked their many legs with much petting, rubbing, and changing of color. The male had an extra leg-like appendage which, human fashion, he offered to the female. She not only accepted it but kept it! One would think such behavior would encourage celibacy in male squid.

Becalmed one evening in the middle of a transatlantic passage, I sat in the cockpit watching the stars, occasionally disturbed by an elusive noise. I finally realized that it was the occasional "click" of my fishing reel. I had neglected to reel in the trolling line – the lure was hanging several hundred feet beneath the glowing stern light. The line had some sort of dead weight on it, it offered no struggle as I reeled it in, making me think I had hooked a plastic bag. To my amazement out of the water came an unusual squid, a brilliant, angry red in color, perhaps two feet long and as thick as a man's leg. As I held it at arms length, to study the beast, it took one look at me with enormous eyes and squirted me in the face and chest with a powerful acid. I screamed in pain and rushed to the sink to wash my face. By the time the pain was gone my woolen sweater had burned away where the acid had hit it. I returned to the deck and cut the line, then pushed the beast over the side with a broom. He was the winner, not the dinner.

Squid vary tremendously in size. Tiny but delicious sepia fit comfortably in a tablespoon. But the giant, deep sea squid is the favorite food of sperm whales. We have seen tentacle marks on whales that measured 20 feet long. Imagine how large the whole beast must have been!

The most commonly found squid, usually sold frozen in the United States as fish bait, are six to eight inches long. Not a popular food in the United States, squid, in our opinion, ranks right up at the top of the list of fine seafoods; it is easier to prepare than most and is worthy of consideration by any cruising gourmet. The Europeans, who treat squid with much reverence, have a variety of fancy recipes, including cooking the squid in its own ink. We limit its use to fish chowders or bouillabaisse and to frying.

CLEANING SQUID

1. Pull off the semitransparent membrane that serves as the skin.
2. Separate the head and legs from the body by gently pulling and twisting.
3. Separate the legs from the head by cutting just below the eyes. Pop off the beak at the center of the tentacles.
4. Pull the cuttle bone out from the body; rinse everything. If the squid is bigger than 12 inches, it should be beaten to make it tender.

COOKING SQUID (FRIED)

1. Slice the hood-like body into rings.
2. Pat dry and shake rings and tentacles in a bag with seasoned flour.
3. Saute in vegetable oil for about 5 minutes or until golden. Do not overcook as it toughens the meat.

STEAMERS, LONGNECK OR SOFT-SHELLED CLAMS

Longneck clams are an American favorite without which no New England seafood restaurant would be complete. They are found in abundance north of Cape Cod while there are lesser numbers as far south as Cape Hatteras. The leathery neck actually contains both of the clam's siphons; while this odd appendage seems long for a neck, it is short as siphons go. The longnecks live just below the sand surface in the intertidal zone. They are gathered commercially by the millions while many more are collected by amateurs for home consumption. Nevertheless, the demand is greater than the natural supply; for this reason commercial farms raise longnecks by the ton.

Since the longneck clam lives so close to the surface, it is easy game for the amateur clammer. Longnecks are hunted at low tide by watching for the telltale squirt as the longneck, detecting your advance, hastily withdraws his siphon. When a relatively larger number of squirts indicate a concentration of clams, the sand is turned back and the mollusks collected at leisure. When plentiful, they may be collected by the quart or the bushel basket; the largest, four to five inches long, is just as sweet and delicious as the smallest.

Longnecks are sandy clams, and should be washed several times in a bucket. Change the water a few times, and agitate the clams to loosen clinging sand. They should then be soaked for a day in the sea water/corn meal mixture, page 144. Last but not least, a small cup of clam juice should be served with each portion of longnecks. The diner may then swirl each clam in the juice to free it of the last possible bits of sand.

Longnecks may be eaten raw, by slitting the rubbery "skin" along the edge of the shell, shucking off the tough neck, and dipping in cocktail sauce. We have always preferred them steamed, page 159, allowing about 1 quart or more per person. Serve them with a cup of clam nectar, some melted butter, a few seafood fritters, page 164, on the side, and cold beer or a big jug of lemonade. This is a seaside treat that seems completely in keeping with your vacation afloat.

After longnecks have been degritted, they may be used in all of the recipes for sweet, tender clams. Longnecks, of course, like all sweet, tender bivalves, are great for clambakes.

STEAMED CLAMS

Any clam can be served steamed, but the guide to good eating is to use only the smallest ones, such as cherrystones, or the most tender species, such as razor clams. Nothing tastes worse than a nice, big, steamed quahog or surf clam; they are as tough as shoe leather. If your steamed clams do turn out to be made of old golf balls, don't throw them out. Grind and use them for fritters, page 163. Clams can be steamed in any pot or container with a lid.

QUANTITIES

It is a hard to give explicit serving quantities when dealing with clams since they vary in size and shell thickness from species to species. About 1 cup of cooked meat is an ample portion for one person. If there is any doubt in your mind as to quantity, it is best to open a clam or two and make your estimates from what you see inside. About a dozen cherrystones, for example, make a generous main course serving for one. Steamers, as usually found in New England restaurants, are served by the bowl. A big, heaping bowl of them makes a fine main course. If you don't have quite enough clams to go around, consider adding some other shellfish, such as shrimp or crab. These can be sauteed while everyone is busy with the clams.

STEAMING

1. Place one-half inch of water or wine in the bottom of the pot and dump in the clams.
2. Close the lid and steam for about 15 minutes, or until all of the clams are open. Do not overcook since this toughens the meat. Serve with **hot melted butter** or shellfish dip, page 165. Bon Appetite!

CLAM HASH KNICKERBOCKER   Serves Four
2   **cups chopped clams, fresh or canned**
½   **cup clam juice**
2   **cups potatoes, cooked and well chopped**
1   **tablespoon parsley, chives, grated onion and chopped mushroom**
1   **tablespoon chives**
1   **tablespoon onion, grated**
1   **tablespoon mushrooms, chopped**
3   **tablespoons butter**
2   **tablespoons sherry**
3   **eggs, beaten**
1   **teaspoon salt**
1   **teaspoon pepper**

1. Combine everything but clams and butter.
2. Melt half of butter, 1½ tablespoons, in a skillet; saute the mixture over low heat for 20 minutes, stirring two or three times, sparingly, to keep from burning.
3. Add fresh or tinned clams and fold into mixture.
4. In a second skillet, melt the remaining butter, 1½ tablespoons. Add the hash mixture to the new skillet; press the hash flat in the skillet.
5. Brown hash using high heat, for about 10 minutes; be careful not to burn.
6. Cut hash into four wedges and turn; brown the other side. Serve steaming hot with a side dish of fried bacon.

CLAMKABOB—FIRE WITCH STYLE   Serves Four

1 **quart clams or scallops, cut into bite-sized pieces**
6 **medium onions, quartered**
6 **green peppers, cut in 1½-inch squares**
6 **tomatoes, skinned, seeded, and thickly sliced**
½ **cup olive oil**
4 **cloves garlic, minced or ½ teaspoon garlic powder**
1 **tablespoon celery seed, crushed**

1. Combine and let stand overnight:
2. Tightly pack on skewers, in following order,
    green pepper
    clam wrapped in a piece of bacon
    another green pepper
    an onion quarter
    a tomato slice
3 Repeat as many times as will fit on the skewer; brush thoroughly with the oil, garlic mixture. Tuck everything firmly together.
4. Cook over glowing coals, basting frequently with oil mixture until bacon is brown; serve on big beds of fluffy, steamed rice.

MRS. KELLY'S SOUTHERN CLAM PANCAKES   Serves Four

The landlady from my Sarasota clamming days called these clam fritters, but they resemble the potato pancake that is often found in a Jewish Deli.

1. Combine:
   4 **medium, mature potatoes, grated**
   2 **eggs, beaten**
   1 **medium onion, grated**
   2½ **teaspoons flour**
   2 **teaspoons salt**
   1 **teaspoon baking powder**
   1½ **cups ground clams (razors, chrrystones, quahogs, softshells, or steamers)**

2. Make into patties about 2 inches in diameter and no more than ½-inch thick. Deep fry in vegetable oil until golden, then turn and fry until crisp.
3. Drain or blot excess oil and serve immediately.

CLAMBAKE

Some of the best seafood we have eaten was cooked, primitive style, at a clambake. Traditionally, a shallow pit is dug in the sand and lined with flat rocks. If the rocks are not available, skip them. Build the fire and let it burn for at least an hour, adding fuel steadily to make a good supply of coals. After the hour, stop adding fuel; allow the wood to burn down. If you have lined the pit with rocks, sweep the fire toward the edges of the pit to expose the hot rocks. If not, lay several layers of aluminum foil directly over the coals and weight it down with pebbles or shells.

Next, cover the stones or foil with a one-inch layer of clean, freshly washed seaweed. If you cannot find enough seaweed, use lettuce that has been chopped and beaten, then soaked for an hour in the sea; but, try to mix some seaweed with the lettuce. The briny steam from seaweed enhances the flavor of the food.

If potatoes are on the menu, add them to the coals first. Brush them with oil or butter, wrap in foil, pierce, and place on the coals. Now, add the seafood. Work quickly to minimize the loss of heat. Put the juiciest items, such clams, on the bottom; as they cook, their juice will steam flavor up over the other food. Soak the clams the night before in a large pail of sea water with some corn meal in it (a half-cup per pail). The clams will eat this and discharge their intestinal grit in the process.

Next, add crabs, if you have them. (Kill them first with a hammer blow between the eyes, or they will immediately make every

possible effort to vacate the area). Then, place whole fish, which have been gutted and scaled, directly on the clams or crabs. Next come the lobsters, noble creatures that may be added whole. Shrimp, as large as possible, may be substituted for the lobster. Cook the shrimp in their shells then enclose them in an old stocking and dump them right on top of everything.

After all the ingredients have been added to the pit, cover it with a clean cloth that has been dipped in the sea; add more seaweed, if possible. The pit is traditionally closed with wet canvas, but we never seem to have any. We usually use coconut fronds or newspaper that has been soaked in the sea. Whatever you use, the object is to seal in the steam.

Corn is an excellent and traditional clambake ingredient. Pull the husks back, but not off; remove the silk. Brush the ears with melted butter or vegetable oil, then pull the husks back over the corn. Shove the ears into the coals, butt end first, when the seafood is half cooked. Cook everything for approximately 45 minutes. Open the corner of the pit after 30 minutes and pull out a clam with tongs. It should be cooked but not dried out. Cooking time varies from 30 to 50 minutes depending on the heat of the coals.

As soon as the pit is opened and the food removed, sweep the coals over all and throw on more wood. You will need heat to toast those marshmallows and to burn the used plates.

When everything is cooked, sit down and enjoy the feast. Be sure to have a big pot of melted butter, coleslaw, and lots of cold drinks on hand. Have fun!

SHELLFISH FRITTERS

Any type of shellfish can be used for fritters, but it is particularly useful for tough mollusks. Toughies, such as surf clam bodies (the muscles should be saved and used separately since they are tender and delicious), welks, periwinkles, conch, and limpets may be used; these animals are often available when all else fails. If you are a lover of fried clams, this recipe is an ace up your sleeve. Other seafoods, such as chopped shrimp, little pieces of fish, crab meat, or even vegetables, such as bits of pan-boiled broccoli, asparagus, or green beans may be added. This not only adds to the interest of the fritter, but also helps to stretch a short supply of clams.

Mollusks, regardless of the species, should first be removed from their shells. They may be steamed or broiled open and rinsed in water to remove any clinging grit. They must be chopped or ground for fritters. The tougher they are, the finer should be the pieces. Thus, succulent oysters need only be roughly chopped, while welks or limpets should be ground until they beg for mercy. The chopped or ground seafood should be drained as much as possible; otherwise, the batter will not cling. If using a variety of seafood, mix it throughly before adding to the batter. It is essential to the fritter texture that stirring be kept at a minimum.

In the South, seafood fritters are extremely popular and often served on the side with lobster and steamed crab. They are also tasty and nourishing as a main course, served with a vegetable and cold applesauce.

SEAFOOD FRITTERS   Serves Four to Six

Remember, the secret of a successful seafood fritter is to go heavy on the seafood and light on the batter. The batter is simply used to bind the pieces of fish together and to cover them with a pleasing, crispy coat.

1. Make 2 to 3 cups of prepared seafood into 16 little mounds. The mounds must cling together; a small amount of flour may be dusted over seafood to assist in this process.
2. With large drainer spoon or your hand, immerse seafood in batter, page 377, coating thoroughly.
3. In one smooth motion, transfer coated seafood to small skillet containing 1 to 1½ inches of hot vegetable oil. Let the excess batter on the spoon or your fingers run onto the fritter. Take care that the bubbling oil does not burn you.
4. Fry until golden brown, turning occasionally. Do not permit the fritter to stick to the bottom.

PERIWINKLES AND TURBAN SHELLS

Periwinkles are another of those animals that are disdained in the United States, but eagerly sought in Europe. There are about a dozen different varieties of winkles, the largest not much more than 1¼ inches long. Don't let their humble appearance fool you; they are as tasty as the best French snails. Since they are usually free for the taking along any rocky shore, the price is certainly right! Another strong inducement to become a winkle gourmet is the ease of preparation.

periwinkle

1. Simply rinse clean and simmer 10 minutes in salted water (about 1 tablespoon per quart with a generous pinch of bouquet garni). The salt helps shrivel the meat enough to facilitate its removal from the shell.
2. The next step is your choice. You may put the shells in a pan, brush with garlic butter, sprinkle with fine herbs, and broil. Or if you prefer, just add to a quarter pound of melted butter:

2   cloves garlic, minced
1   teaspoon bouquet garni
¼   teaspoon pepper

Heat until it bubbles, then use as a dip for the "winks." To be perfectly honest, snails in general don't have a decisive taste; it's the fine butter and herbs that make them a gourmet treat.

wentletrap

10

crustaceans

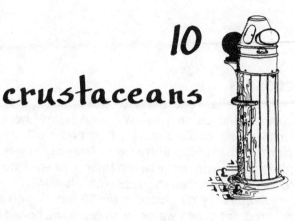

One delight of a cruising chef is enjoying crab, shrimp, and lobster fresh from the sea. These crustaceans are definitely worth the time spent catching and preparing them.

CRABS

Crabs are an extremely widespread and greatly varied marine invertebrate. Various species are found in the deepest ocean trenches, while their cousins are found in brackish inlets miles from the sea. All are edible, even hermit crabs, which occasionally grow to astonishing proportions. We usually don't bother with crabs smaller than four to six inches across since the only easy pickings are in the claws. But if you should find yourself in an area with many small, easily caught crabs, catch them and collect the claws. Most species of crab have one claw much larger than the other; this is the one to take. If both claws are removed, the animal is defenseless and will probably not survive. Be sure to remove the arm along with the claw; it also is full of meat. And don't feel sorry for the crabs; they grow new claws very quickly.

Soft-shell crabs, often fried and served on toast, are small crabs which have just molted. The new shell is quite soft but hardens after several days. During this interim, the "softie" is completely edible and quite delicious.

COOKING

All crabs, regardless of the species, may be cooked and cleaned the same way. We usually kill them before cooking since crabs cooked alive often break off their own legs and claws as the temperature rises. The easiest way to kill crabs is to force a screwdriver between their eyes until the shell crushes, or to hit them between the eyes with a hammer.

Crabs may be steamed for 30 minutes on a trivet in a large covered pot of sea water, or they may be boiled for 20 minutes in sea water. If the crab is very large, such as king crab or large spider crab, 30 minutes is necessary. After cooking is completed, pour the water down the drain and let the crab cool in the sink. Now comes the big job, cleaning.

CLEANING

Blue crabs, dungeness, and rock crabs have large quantities of body meat. Spider crabs, king crabs, Jonah crabs, and

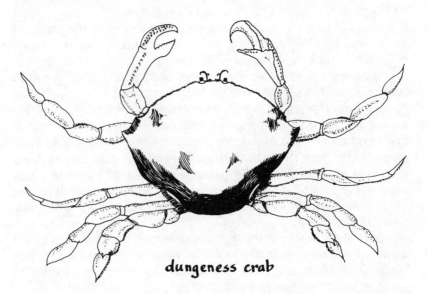

dungeness crab

several other species have most of their meat in the legs and claws; but, even these crabs have a large lump of meat where the leg joins the body. The only way to get it is to clean the crab as follows:

1. Remove the upper shell. If you pry the shell forward from the rear, it will lift like the hood of a sports car. Don't be discouraged by your first glimpse of the insides; remember, it's well worth the trouble for that superb flavor.
2. Scrape the crab butter from the top of the shell. Crab butter is a yellow paste that adheres to the upper shell. It is delicious and may be made into all kinds of pates.
3. Tear off all loose, spongy material. This includes the thin cover tissue, the gills, and all viscera. Rinse the remainder in sea water.
4. If the crab is a female with eggs under the tail, carefully snip off the tail and save; crab roe is delicious steamed.
5. Break the crab in half along its mid-line.
6. Pick out any body meat that is accessible.
7. Use a hammer or mallet to break protective membranes; then using a knife or cleaver, separate the legs by cutting between them. The legs and claws may be cracked with a hammer or winch handle and the meat extracted.

All of this is a messy, time-consuming, delicious job, and we heartily recommend that only good friends be invited to the food orgy. Cleaned crab meat may also be used in all mixed seafood recipes, Newburg dishes, fritters, devil sauces or just chilled and eaten with cocktail sauce.

CANNED CRAB MEAT

Fresh crab in cans must be kept under refrigeration or eaten before it reaches room temperature. The meat has been cooked but not sterilized. There is usually a refrigeration warning on the lid. Fresh canned crab may be used the same as fresh crab; it is quite delicious.

Crab in unrefrigerated tins has been cooked until sterile and is as immortal as tinned tuna. It has been somewhat wounded in flavor, and must be treated with great love and understanding. Use it in recipes where other ingredients dominate the flavor, or where other fresh seafood is added. Always add the crab at the last minute to prevent further flavor loss.

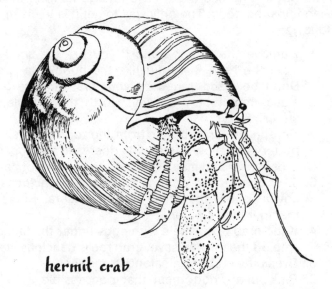

hermit crab

HERMIT CRABS

Marine hermit crabs often grow to great size and inhabit conch or other large shells. In some cases they have found the shells abandoned, but crabs in general are extremely aggressive and the hermit crab is no exception. They are capable of killing and eating the conch, then appropriating its shell. These large crabs are extremely delicious and taste more like lobster than crab. They may be steamed in the shell with the opening toward the top of the pot. As the heat penetrates the shell the beast will usually abandon it, making your work easier. If the crab remains inside the shell pull it out gently as the best eating is in the tail. Large hermit crabs should be steamed in a small amount of water for about 15 minutes. The cooking time varies depending on the size of the shell but it is better to initially undercook the crab which can then be removed from its shell and steamed to completion.

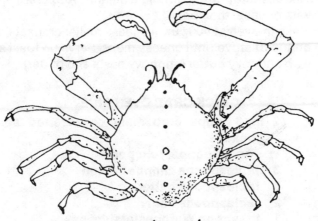

spider crab

CRAB DELIGHT ON TOAST Serves Four

As with most of our crab recipes, fresh, precooked shrimp, lobster, or fish may be added either to expand the crab, or to create a mixed seafood delight.

1   lb. crab meat, fresh or frozen or 2 cans (ap-proximately 6½ oz. each) crab
1   teaspoon butter
2   tablespoons flour
1   cup milk
2   slices stale bread, diced
1   cup mushrooms, sliced
½   teaspoon crushed celery seed or salt (op-tional)
1   teaspoon lemon juice
½   cup dry white wine
½   cup Gruyere or Swiss cheese
    Paprika, salt, pepper

1. Melt butter in pan. Mix flour and milk together; add to pan. Stir over low heat until sauce thickens.
2. Add all other ingredeints except crab, cheese, and paprika. Simmer for 10 minutes over low heat, stirring frequently to avoid burning.

3. Reduce heat until liquid just steams. Add crab; sprinkle with cheese, then paprika.
4. Bake in oven at 400° until cheese melts; or, heat covered on top of stove until cheese melts. Serve on toast spread with anchovy butter (anchovy paste and butter).

QUICK CRAB OVER RICE

2 to 3 cups crab meat or assorted seafood, cooked
½ green pepper, chopped
3 tablespoons chopped onion
3 tablespoons butter
2 tablespoons flour
1 teaspoon Worchestershire sauce
1½ cups milk
½ cup condensed tomato soup
½ cup Gruyere or Swiss cheese, shredded

1. Melt butter in pan; saute onions and pepper until onions are translucent.
2. Add flour, dissolved in milk; stir until mixture thickens.
3. Add Worchestershire sauce and soup; heat until steaming.
4. Fold crab in lightly; sprinkle with cheese. Simmer over low heat for 5 to 8 minutes.
5 Serve over white rice.

SHRIMP

Shrimp, like most seafood, tastes much better fresh than canned; and there are none fresher than those you catch yourself. We spent some very pleasant evenings in Coconut Grove, Florida, catching shrimp that were running on the incoming tide. The air was cool and balmy and full of the pungent smells of the sea. The tide made delicate sucking sounds around the piers, and silver full moonlight flecked the bay. As though on cue, everyone aboard the sailboats would fire up their pressure lanterns, pull their shrimp nets from under the dinghy, and jump onto the pier. They usually came well prepared to make a night of it. The lanterns were placed at the edge of the pier or tied to oars and hung over the water. The dock looked like a Japanese garden party twinkling with lights and alive with laughter. Soon

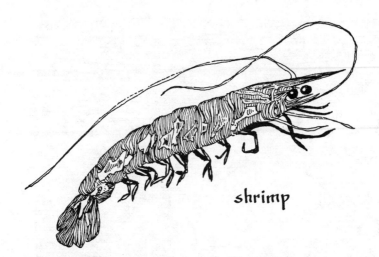

shrimp

the experts were arguing about holding qualities of the Danforth anchor versus the plow, and the virtues of nylon anchor rope versus chain. The shrimp would come chugging by in the tide to be captured by a gentle sweep of the net. But in the midst of the festivities, I'm afraid many escaped unnoticed.

Shrimp caught this way always taste better than those bought in a store; first, because you caught them, and, second, because they are as fresh as they can be. I'm not an expert at shrimping, but I do know that they seem to be stimulated by the full moon, particularly in the summer when they run on the surface with the incoming tide. Fresh shrimp are treasured jewels to us, as are the memories of those fine evenings in Florida. We have hung our lantern over the side in many strange corners of the earth during the week of the full moon, hoping for a Florida-size catch. Many times we have been disappointed. Occasionally, the harvest has been bountiful, like the night in the Caicos Islands, off Haiti, when we netted eight pounds of shrimp in two hours. If you have never tried shrimping, you should consider it. A net can be purchased for only a few dollars, or it can be made by sewing plastic screening over bent electrical conduit. If the shrimp are not running with the tide, another excellent method of netting them is to wade through shallow weed beds at slack, low tide, sweeping the grass with a net. The net used for this method has a flattened side to make the sweep more effective.

Put your catch in a bait bucket until cooking time the following day. The intestinal grit will be excreted making deveining unnecessary for all but the large shrimp.

shrimping in coconut grove

Shrimp come in all sizes and colors. The smallest we ever saw came from Argentina. These tiny canned shrimp would fit, curled up, on a thumbnail; we wondered who had the patience to clean them. Denmark and the West Coast of the United States produce another small variety, often sold canned as hors d'oeuvres. Medium-sized shrimp are found throughout the United States and Europe. Large shrimps, called langoustines, turn up everywhere. Jumbo shrimp, as hefty as small lobsters, come from India. Two or three of them make a full meal. Although there are differences in flavor, the recipes in this book may be used with any variety of shrimp. Remember, when you buy, the bigger the size, the higher the cost.

The flavor of any variety is enhanced if the shrimp are cooked in their shells. When cooking them in a sauce, remove the legs and slit the shell at the top. This facilitates deveining in large shrimp (unnecessary with the very small ones) and creates an entrance for the sauce. Crustacean heads, tails, legs, and shells make a fine clear broth, tasty as is, or as a base for soup. They also make terrific fish bait. Do not throw them away too hastily.

BOILED SHRIMP

1. Shrimp are delicate little beasts, and great care must be exercised when boiling them. Use plenty of water, stock, or shrimp boil (water with prepared spices) to prevent a significant drop in water temperature when shrimp are added. Bring liquid to a rolling boil; add shrimp; immediately reduce the flame.
2. Simmer shrimp for 3 to 5 minutes, no more.
3. Drain liquid; allow shrimp to cool. If you are in a hurry and have boiled the shrimp without seasonings, you may rinse them in cold water immediately after cooking. This speeds the process and makes the shells easier to remove.
4. To clean shrimp, twist off heads, pull off legs, then remove shell, prying from underside with your fingers. Do not remove last shell segment and tail. If shelling seems difficult, slit shells with small pair of scissors; slit top of shell down to tail segment, then pull shell off.

The cleaning operation reduces the weight of the shrimp by almost half; two pounds uncleaned, uncooked shrimp yield one pound cooked and cleaned. Half a pound of cooked shrimp is a generous portion as a main course.

FROZEN SHRIMP

Frozen shrimp come either "green" with heads, tails, and shells, or cleaned and deveined. The latter are usually quite expensive, but the weight loss from cleaning should be considered.

To boil frozen shrimp:

1. Put the frozen block of shrimp in a bucket of sea water for a few minutes; break the block into small chunks or, better yet, individual shrimp.
2. Drop them into boiling water; keep over high heat until water boils.
3. Simmer for 3 to 5 minutes, counting one half of interval before water boiled toward cooking time.

CANNED SHRIMP

Canned shrimp require no boiling, but should be rinsed in cold water to reduce saltiness. Do not soak them; soaking will reduce their flavor and make them soggy.

FRIED SHRIMP   Serves Two

    1   lb   raw shrimp, cleaned
    1   tablespoon cognac
    1   teaspoon Worchestershire sauce
    ½   cup seasoned flour
    2   eggs, beaten
    2   tablespoons melted butter
    ½   cup beer

1. Toss shrimp in cognac and Worchestershire sauce.
2. Combine all remaining ingredients to make batter. It should be thick and sticky.
3. Dip shrimp in batter; fry in almost enough hot oil (375°) to cover. Cook just until batter begins to brown, 2 to 3 minutes. Serve with sweet and sour sauce.

SHRIMP IN DILL SAUCE   Serves Two

    5   tablespoons butter
    1   tablespoons chopped onion

1 lb. raw shrimp
1 cup dry white wine
3 tablespoons flour
1 cup milk
2 tablespoons fresh dill

1. Cook shelled shrimp and onions in wine for 5 minutes.
2. Melt butter; stir in flour until blended.
3. Add milk; bring to a boil, stirring constantly.
4. Reduce heat; stir until sauce thickens.
5. Add sauce and dill to shrimp; simmer for 5 minutes.

SEAFOOD AU GRATIN   Serves Two

Au gratin seafood is traditionally baked and served in individual ramekins, but neither are necessary on board. The whole thing may be quickly cooked over low heat and served over toast. Any delicately flavored seafood blends well with an au gratin sauce, except mollusks.

¼ cup butter
1 lb. cooked seafood, shelled if shrimp or lobster
2 tbls. flour
½ cup white wine
1 cup cream or condensed milk
2 tablespoons sherry
1 cup mild, grated cheese
salt, pepper, paprika

1. Melt butter in large pan; stir in flour. Let flour bubble for a minute; stir constantly to remove lumps.
2. Add cream and wine; stir over medium heat until thickened.
3. Add seafood and cheese; cook over low heat; stir constantly until cheese melts.
4. Serve on toast; sprinkle with salt, pepper and paprika.

SHRIMP PATE   Serves Two

This delicate, tasty little nothing is actually quite rich and filling. Mounded into a hollowed tomato or avocado, it makes an exotic and easy dockside appetizer. Underway, served on crackers with pieces of cheese, it makes a fine warm weather lunch.

½ lb. fresh boiled or canned shrimp, drained and completely dry
1 onion, minced and dried in a paper towel
½ cup mayonnaise
¼ cup canned black olive pieces or sliced Greek olives
2 teaspoons lemon juice
3 tablespoons condensed milk
salt, if needed (Canned shrimp is often salty.)

1. Finely chop shrimp; fold in other ingredients.
2. Let stand for a few hours. Serve chilled, if possible, or at room temperature; sprinkle with parsley or chives.

shrimp pate

PICKLED SHRIMP WITH ONIONS   Serves Four

This is one of the most delightful shrimp appetizers I have ever tasted. It's so good that it brings pangs of sweet remembrance, even as I write these words. The shrimp must be fresh or raw frozen, and should be cooked in the shells. It makes a fine warm weather lunch. Squid, octopus, and shellfish may be added for an extra delight.

¾ lb. small or medium shrimp, deveined
1½ cups onion, chopped
½ cup white vinegar
2 cloves garlic, finely chopped
¼ cup celery leaf tops, chopped (optional)

½ cup corn oil
1½ ounces of crab and shrimp boil
1 teaspoon salt

1. Wrap shrimp boil mixture in piece of cloth to confine it in the pot. Boil it for 10 minutes in 1½ quarts of water
2. Add shrimp; simmer over low heat for 2 minutes.
3. Remove from flame; let stand for 1 to 2 hours.
4. Remove boil spices; shell shrimp, drain water thoroughly; add other ingredients. Cover pot and let stand for at least one day before eating. Serve with crackers. Pickled shrimp keep for about a week with refrigeration, four or five days, in moderate temperatures, without refrigeration.

SHRIMP ACAPULCO   Serves Four

This excellent, but quite simple recipe is found not only in Acapulco; it is the speciality of the esteemed Embers restaurant in Miami Beach. The Mexicans serve it on big, colorful ceramic plates. At the Embers, a tuxedoed waiter delivers it to your table on a domed silver tray. Regardless of how it arrives at the table, Shrimp Acapulco is an exceptional treat.

24 to 30 large shrimp, shelled but not detailed
½ cup lime juice, fresh, if possible
½ cup vegetable oil (coconut oil is best)
6 cloves garlic, finely chopped
4 chillies, sliced, or ½ sliced green pepper and a pinch of cayenne pepper
Salt, pepper, butter

1. Combine all ingredients; let stand overnight. Toss occasionally.
2. Drain ingredients thoroughly; pan broil over high heat for 4 minutes, tossing constantly.
3. Brush with butter and sprinkle with fresh chopped parsley.

SEAFOOD NEWBURG   Serves Four

This recipe, popular with lobster, shrimp, or crab, is also excellent with any mild flavored, cooked fish. Seafood leftovers, if not originally cooked in a strong sauce, blend well in newburg. Combined seafood is particularly excellent. Small, succulent shellfish, steamed open and drained, make a nice addition, but they should not be the dominant fish.

1. Melt in pan:
   3 tablespoons butter
2. Saute for 3 minutes:
   2¼ cups seafood
3. Add to pan:
   ¼   cup cream sherry. Saute 2 minutes.
4. Add to pan:
   ½   teaspoon paprika
5. Combine and add:
   3   egg yolks
   1   cup condensed milk

crab newburg

6. Lightly simmer until thickened; do not boil. (If consistency needs improving, thicken with corn flour or arrowroot mixed in a little milk.) Serve over toast or rice.

For variety, try adding celery seed, or sprinkling a mild cheese, such as Gruyere, over all. Another favorite is sliced mushrooms added to step 2.

KEDGEREE OF SHRIMP—NEW ORLEANS STYLE
Serves Four

1 **lb. medium shrimp, shelled but not detailed**
2 **cups Italian tomatoes, drained and chopped**
1 **onion, chopped**
1 **cup cooked rice**
2 **hard-boiled eggs, grated**
¼ **teaspoon celery seed**
4 **slices bacon**
  Salt and pepper

1. Fry bacon and reserve.
2. Brown onion in bacon drippings. Add tomatoes; simmer 5 minutes.
3. Add shrimp; simmer another 3 minutes, covered.
4. Add all remaining ingredients including bacon, crumbled; simmer another 3 minutes, stirring frequently.

THE NOBLE LOBSTER

The various species of lobster differ greatly in appearance, but their delicious flavor is always the same. The early Greeks considered them so delicious that only the high priests and the gods were fit to eat them. The American lobster, occasionally exceeding 20 pounds, is known for its heavy claws. Most commonly found in the ¾ to 2 pound range, this size lobster makes a fine meal for one. American lobsters are cold water inhabitants; meaner, more aggressive and voracious creatures are hard to find. They will fight to the death with other members of their species and will eat any meat, dead or alive, they can lay their claws on. Normally lobsters reach the market with pegs in their claws, not only to prevent mayhem in the fish shop, but also to keep them from destroying each other. Should you chance to meet an unpegged lobster, grab it by its claws, which close easily, and wrap a rubberband around them.

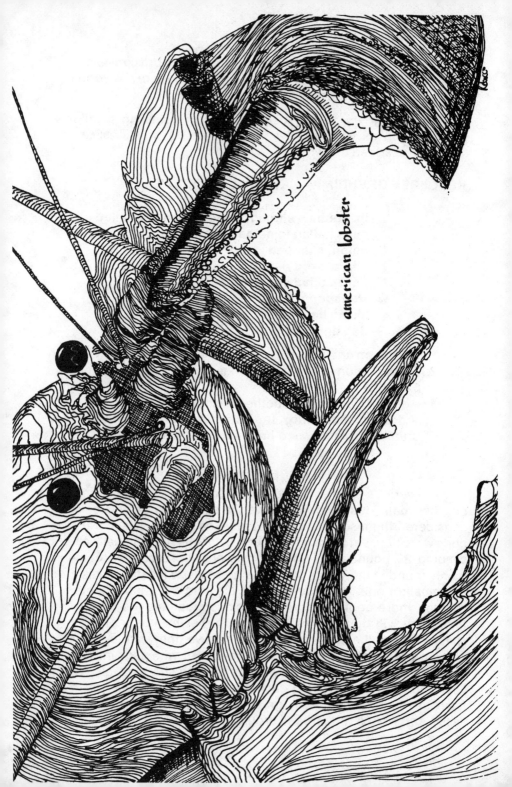

american lobster

There are several species of spiny or rock lobsters, also called crawfish. Do not confuse crawfish with crayfish, which are a smaller, fresh water species. Spiny lobsters lack claws and are usually timid and retiring; occasionally, especially at night, they seem to lose their instinctive fear, often crossing shallow grass beds in great numbers—boldly advancing en masse, antennae waving.

Spiny lobsters grow about the same size as American lobsters, but are inhabitants of warm water; they can be found in tropic seas all over the world. It has been suggested that spiny lobsters are less flavorful than the American lobster. Spiny lobsters are normally sold precooked or frozen; it's hardly fair to compare American lobster dropped live on the steam with a defrosted crawfish tail.

The mole lobster, a clawless relative of the American lobster, is a cold water species found on or around weed beds, usually near isolated islands. Many are found in the Azores, while some have been netted off the Shetlands, Greenland, and Iceland. Mole lobsters seem almost as broad as they are long since up to 60 percent of the creature's weight is a huge hunk of tail meat.

The Mediterranean Sea and the Indian Ocean are home to several species of clawed, lobster-like crustaceans similar in flavor and appearance to the spiny lobster. Their size, however,

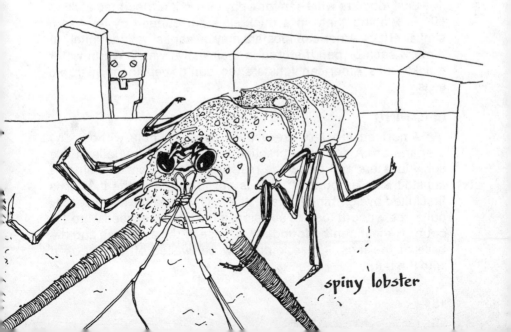

spiny lobster

never exceeds one pound; normally they are only 4 to 6 ounces. They are tasty like shrimp, but do not share the absolute gastronomic pinnacle with American and spiny lobster.

Most countries have a closed season on lobster coinciding with the lobster's reproductive cycle. The demand for this delicious creature far exceeds the supply.

Many fisherman disobey the limit on quantities and the closed season. This greediness could easily cause the extinction of this noble lobster; if the rules are followed, enough will be available for all to enjoy.

PRECOOKED LOBSTER

When buying precooked lobsters, use two methods for determining freshness. First, make sure the meat has the briny odor of the sea. Second, pull the tails back; they should recurl when released.

FROZEN SPINY LOBSTERS

Frozen spiny lobsters are sometimes tough and often have an iodine taste if the tail is over 10 ounces. It's expensive and generally has little of its distinctive flavor. Who needs it, especially when frozen shrimp taste better and are cheaper.

STORAGE

Live lobsters will keep for a day or two if refrigerated at 45 to 50° F. Placing them in a thick sack surrounded by ice has a similar effect. American lobsters may be kept alive indefinitely in a mesh sack or pen if stored in their native water. Warm water quickly kills American lobsters, so don't keep them in tropic seas.

CLEANING

American lobsters are usually cooked whole without any preparation. A common practice is to twist off the tails of live spiny lobsters and throw the rest away. This is wasteful since a considerable amount of meat is not torn free. If the lobster is first killed by crushing its head, the tail muscle relaxes and easily pulls free without loss. In addition, if the lobster exceeds 1 to 1½ pounds, meat can be found at the base of the antennae and the base of the legs. These joints may be twisted off and cooked with the tail.

night hunting for spiny lobster

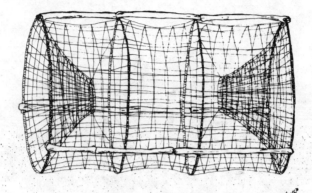

azorian lobster trap

A 4 to 6-inch piece of antenna is usually broken off, and the broken end is slipped into the anal vent. With a good jerk the antenna is pulled out, effectively eviscerating the beast. Now it is ready for cooking.

STEAMED LOBSTER
1. Add about 1 inch of sea water to large pot. Insert a trivet or, if you don't have one, a generous handful of bolts or screws.
2. Cover; bring water to fast boil. Add lobster and recover.
3. When steam begins escaping from under lid, reduce flame and cook for 20 minutes. Boiled lobster are similarly cooked, but in boiling water.

OPENING COOKED LOBSTERS
Spiny lobster tails are usually cut open on the bottom with heavy scissors, then the shell is pried back. If you have quite a few to open, wear gloves as protection from the heat.

American lobsters are messy to open; a large towel should be used. Insert a heavy, sharp knife into the bottom at the joint between body and tail with the blade toward the head. Protecting the other hand with a folded towel, lever the blade back toward the head. Be very careful of hot splatters. Snip the tail open at the bottom with scissors. Cover the claws with a towel; give the claw and each joint a smart rap with a hammer. Allow the hot liquid to drain at bit; serve with hot melted butter.

BROILED LOBSTER
1. Split lobster in half from head to tail; discard the dark stomach, a hard sack near the head.
2. Squeeze lemon all over; let stand for a few minutes.
3. Brush with melted butter; slip under broiler for 7 minutes, checking frequently and basting with more butter to prevent drying.

DEEP FAT FRIED LOBSTER

We disdained this Caribbean specialty until we tried it. However, we did find it to be trouble on board since it requires close to a half gallon of very hot oil. The lobster must be killed by severing the main nerve at the joint between the body and tail. If this is not done, the beast will struggle for a moment in the oil, splattering everything. The oil does not penetrate the lobster, but seals in the moisture, which cooks the meat. Spiny lobster tails may also be cooked in deep fat. The ends are usually dipped in bread or cracker crumbs prior to cooking.

Deep fat fry lobster, whole or tails, for four minutes; three minutes if the lobster weighs less than ½ pound.

AMERICAN LOBSTER STUFFING

Lobster stuffing is usually made from the green liver and red coral, or premature roe, mixed with:
    1   tablespoon fried bread crumbs
    1   teaspoon lemon juice
    1   teaspoon dry sherry
We personally prefer the lobster au natural. If you decide to make the stuffing, have the ingredients mixed and ready for instant use; this way there will be no delay in getting the lobster to the table.

ll
fish

One of the great joys of cruising is dropping the hook in some isolated little bay, rowing ashore, and touring the local markets. Throughout the Mediterranean, along the west coast of Africa, and along the French Brittany coast, the fish markets are a gourmet's curious delight, so richly stocked with varied wonders from the sea. The smaller fish, attractively arranged in boxes of ice, are often stacked to the ceiling. Large fish, eels of several species weighing as much as a hundred pounds, squid of every size and shape from the tiny sepia to the huge deep sea monster 10 feet long, baskets of urchins much esteemed for their fine roe, mussels, snails, rays, sharks, shrimp, limpets, and oysters, all are there, each with its culinary contribution to make. Most of these creatures are fresh from the sea, still gleaming and supple. Each day, however, some fish are leftover for the next day; the rule, as everywhere, is "let the buyer beware." In the United States there is a growing tendency to freeze all seafood before it reaches the supermarket. This is not really the fault of either the fisherman or the wholesaler, but of the supermarkets who dislike the thought of losing merchandise due to spoilage. The difference between the taste of fresh and frozen fish is like that between fresh and canned fruit. Always choose fresh fish, if offered the choice, and follow these simple rules to be sure it is fresh:

1. Does it smell right, especially the gills and body cavity?
2. Are the eyes bulging, glistening, and supple?
3. Are the scales glistening and slippery?

bahamian cat boat

If the fish passes all three tests, especially the nose test, it is a safe buy. If not, don't let the assurances of the fishmonger sway you.

CLEANING FISH OVER SIX INCHES

1. Remove the fins, snip off the spines. We never do and invariably stick ourselves.
2. Scaling is next; it is most easily effected with a scaler, but a supple knife will do the job. Scaling is easier when the fish is wet; it is helpful to have a crewman stand by with a bucket of sea water to assist you. Scaling should always be done before gutting, filleting, or steaking the fish, because the guts fill out the abdominal cavity and make the job easier. Hold the fish down by its tail and slide the knife or scaler, in short strokes, toward the head. Be sure to get those not-too-accessible areas, such as the base of the tail, around the fin bases, and under the head. Wash the fish thoroughly in sea water, then feel it all over to be sure all the scales are removed.

3. Gut the fish by slipping a very sharp knife ½ inch into the anal vent, then sliding the blade toward the head until it is stopped by the pectoral (fin) bones. Cut the fin bones away by sliding the knife under them at right angles to the fish. The fish is then simultaneously gutted and decapitated by bending the head back and twisting it off after the backbone snaps. Remove any clinging viscera, and be sure to remove the blood lines under the backbone. Rinse thoroughly and you're all set.

CLEANING FISH UNDER SIX INCHES

1. Finely scaled fish of less than six inches need not be scaled, such as all pilchards, including sardines and all small herring. But heavily scaled fish, such as white fish or bass, must be scaled.
2. Evisceration of small fish often is effected most easily by first cutting through the backbone and behind the pectoral fins; then pulling off the head with gills and guts attached. A finger thrust into the abdominal cavity cleans out blood lines beneath the backbone and removes any clinging viscera.

FILLETING

Filleting separates the fish from its guts and bones prior to cooking. If done properly, the result is two long slabs of meat without bones or ragged edges. If done wrong, the result is a terrible mess of hacked meat with little bone ends sticking out here and there. We recommend filleting only large, 2 pounds or more, big-boned fish. This simplifies the magical art of filleting, letting the cook breathe a little easier. The leftover skeleton may be poached and made into a pate, page 206.

Some cookbooks recommend skinning fillets, but we believe the skin, even if not eaten, adds to the flavor of the meat. Tough-skinned fish, such as sole, should have the skin pulled off. Pull the skin off with pliers if necessary.

1. To fillet, use a thin, very sharp, and supple knife. Make cuts from the top of the head to the tail, with the knife point firmly bumping along the spine.
2. Then make a cut just behind the gills to the depth of the spine. Turn the fish around having the belly facing you.

3. Slip the knife into the gill cut and cut backward in the same plane as the backbone, modifying this angle as necessary to avoid the ribs. With your other hand, lift the fillet away from the cutting area as you slice.

The leftover head, tail, fins, and bones may be used for making either soup or a sauce; once cooked, the meat clinging to these scraps slips off easily.

CUTTING STEAKS

Any heavily fleshed, thick-boned fish, such as tuna, mackerel, sea bass, or grouper, may be cut into steaks. Gut and scale the fish, then make slices of even thickness through the fish, at right angles to the body line.

FISH FINGERS OR STICKS

The essence of burner top fish cookery is being sure the pieces of fish are not too thick. If the fish slice is more than ¾ inch thick, the result is almost always overcooked fish on the outside and undercooked fish on the inside. Reducing the cooking temperature does nothing except dry out the fish. The Bahamians' favorite fish is grouper, a heavily fleshed sea bass whose fillets are generally too large to cook in two pieces. The Bahamians solve this problem by steaking the fillets, cutting ¾ inch thick slices at right angles to the body line. The resulting strips of meat, held together by a thin strip of skin, are called fingers. They may be rolled in crumbs and fried, or poached/steamed.

GENERAL HINTS ON COOKING FISH

Unlike meat, fish does not indicate its "doneness" by color change, but is just as sensitive to overcooking as beef. Why bother preparing fresh fish if you cook it until it is dry and tasteless, or poach it until the meat disintegrates from the bone. Fish is so often overcooked because it requires a much lower cooking temperature than meat—140° to 150°F. Another frequent cause of overcooking is that fish will continue to cook from its own internal heat and the heat of the pan, even after the fire beneath it is out. Cooked fish must be taken from the stove and eaten immediately. Fish should never be kept "warming" during a meal since the result will be overcooked leftovers, fit only for pate use or for Davy Jones. There are a number of specific tests for doneness, which will be discussed with each of the different

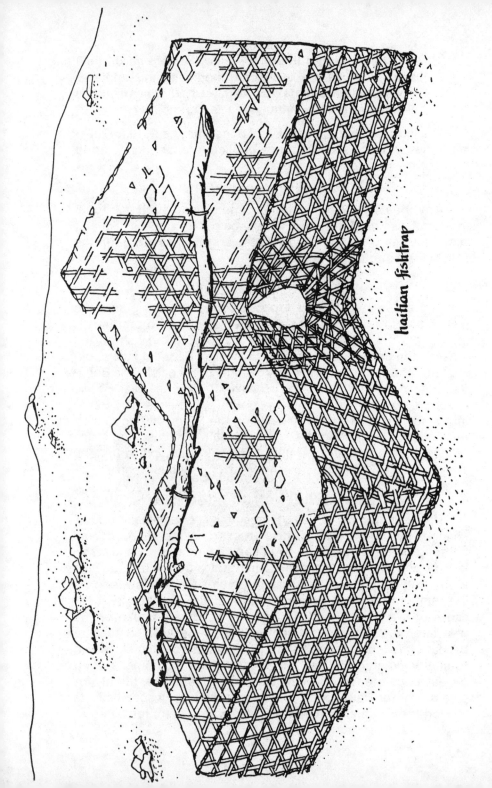

haitian fishtrap

fish cooking techniques, but the best test of all is to taste a sample, right in the pan. The finest flavored, most perfectly cooked fish may occasionally taste dry. Should this be the case, a liberal dotting with butter usually helps; or, if time allows, a Hollandaise or rich white sauce can save the day.

Marinating, soaking fish in various mixtures of wine, garlic, vinegar, and onions for a few hours prior to cooking, accomplishes several purposes. It helps reduce the fishy odor and taste of some species, and if a little heavy on the vinegar, makes a delicately fleshed fish more firm, reducing its tendency to disintegrate. A good marinade also imparts some of its flavor to the fish.

To remove the fish smell from pots, utensils, and counter tops, scrub them with baking soda or a mixture of salt, lemon juice, and water. Lemon juice also works well in removing the fish smell from the cook's hands.

If you have a freezer, or find it impossible to purchase fresh fish, frozen fish is a good second choice, and is frequently cheaper. Frozen fish must be used soon after it is thawed, and should never be refrozen. Do not be tempted into cooking fish while it is still frozen. Rumor has it that frozen fish may be Dutch baked by wrapping it in foil with butter and spices. Our experience in this department is rather limited; limited, in fact, to one trial. The result was a fillet curled and leathery on the edges, and stone cold within.

When cooking any fish, fresh or frozen, remember that it is surprisingly filling. One-half pound per person is a generous serving, if the weight does not include the head; an even smaller portion is sufficient for fillets.

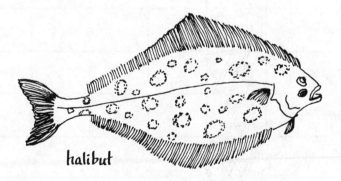

halibut

FISH COOKERY

NAME OF FISH	FOIL BAKE	SOUP	SAUTE OR FRY	POACH	STEW
Bass, Sea	√	√	*		√
Bluefish	*		√		
Boxfish or Puffer	√		√	√	
Cowfish	√			√	
Cod	√	√	√		√
Cunner			√		
Dolphin	√		√	*	
Eel, fresh	*		*		√
Eel, Moray			√	√	
Flatfish, General	√		*	*	
Flying Fish			*	√	
Grouper	*	√	√	√	*
Grunt			*		

KEY: √ Accepted method
      * Recommended by the cruising chef
      f Fritters

NAME OF FISH	FOIL BAKE	SOUP	SAUTE OR FRY	POACH	STEW
Haddock			✓		✓
Hake	✓	✓	✓		✓
Halibut	*	✓	✓		✓
Jacks			*		
Mackerel	✓		*		
Mullet	*				✓
Pollock	✓		✓	✓	
Pompano	*	✓	✓	*	✓
Porgy or Sheepshead			*		
Rays & Skates			✓		✓
Salmon or Bonito	✓		*		*
Shad	✓	✓	*		
Shark			*		
Smelt			✓		
Snapper	*		✓	✓	

NAME OF FISH	FOIL BAKE	SOUP	SAUTE OR FRY	POACH	STEW
Swordfish	*		√		
Trout, sea	*	√			√
Tuna	*		f√		
Whitefish			√		√
Whiting	√	√			

POACHING AND STEAMING

Both poaching and steaming are excellent cooking methods for delicately flavored and textured fish. The basic difference between these two techniques is that steamed fish is cooked above the liquid while poached fish is cooked right in it. Steaming is a bit of a problem on a boat since it requires either a steamer pot, lid, and tray, or a tray with feet that will fit one of the ship's pots.

Fish can be steamed or poached in plain salted water, 1 tablespoon per quart, but a combination of water, wine, herbs, onions, and fish stock is usually preferred. An excellent stock made from the fish heads, bones, and tails, as well as wine, herbs, and water, may be found on page 213. The poaching liquid may be thickened into an elegant sauce for the fish.

When poaching or steaming, be sure the fish is not too thick. Steamed or poached fish cannot be turned over without the whole piece falling apart. If the portions are more than ¾ to 1-inch thick, it is better to steak, fillet, or divide the fish otherwise to make it thinner. Poached fish is never completely covered by the poaching liquid. A good description, straight from the nautical chart, might be "uncovers and is awash at low tide." We almost always use a frying pan with a lid for poaching. With this flat pan, it is easier to slide the very delicate, cooked

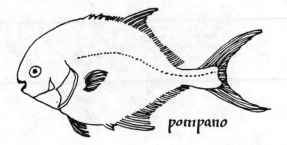

pompano

fish onto the plate; a frying pan also eliminates the need for a special poaching tray.

Follow these easy directions for poaching fish.

1. Thoroughly butter bottom of large fry pan. Place fish flat on bottom of pan. Pour on poaching liquid; sprinkle salt and pepper on fish.
2. Heat until liquid is steaming; never exceed a simmer. Cook 5 to 8 minutes.
3. Test for doneness after 5 minutes by opening fish with a fork, extracting a flake, and tasting it. Do this once each minute until fish is cooked. The flesh should be steaming and have lost all of its translucence, but it should not be dry, crumbly and unresilient. The meat should slip easily from the bones.

A poached fish may be served as is, dotted with butter and lemon juice, or covered with a sauce.

ABOUT URCHINS

It's hard to believe that something which looks as unappetizing and formidable as an urchin could be delicious, but delicious is the only way to describe this Caribbean specialty. The edible part of the urchin is its eggs. Urchins are echinoderms, like starfish, and this becomes evident when you have snipped off its spines and

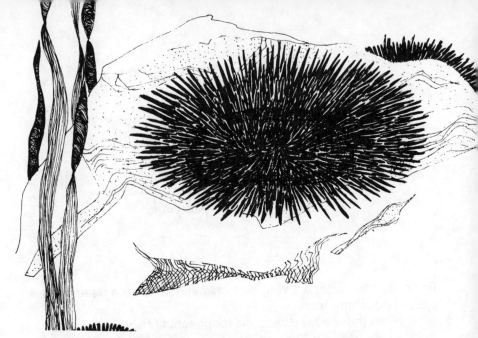

opened its bottom like a tin can with a spoon (wear gloves). Inside on the top of the shell are five radial arms of orange roe which may be scooped out and used in this recipe. Look closely at the roe to be sure you see tiny eggs. Reject the smooth looking sacks of milt found in male urchins. Urchins reproduce by ejecting eggs and milt into the surrounding water with fertilization left to chance. So, if you open a few urhcins and find no roe, wait a few weeks and try again.

URCHINS SERVED IN THEIR OWN SHELL   Serves Two

1. Clean enough urchins to provide 1 cup of eggs. Wash and parboil them in salted water, then drain and chop.
2. Fry until browned:
> **1 chopped onio.ı**
> **3 slices chopped bacon**

Add:
> **1 cup bread crumbs**
> **½ cup choped celery and green pepper**
> **½ cup cooked rice (optional)**
> **½ teaspoon pepper, salt to taste**
> **the urchin roe**

4. Saute until the bread browns slightly. If too dry, add butter and little chicken stock.
5. Stuff into the urchin shell and serve.

PAN FRYING FISH

Fish to be pan fried may be dusted with flour or corn meal before being cooked in butter or oil over high heat. If the fish is more than 1-inch thick, it must be filleted, steaked, or in some way made thinner. Thick, meaty fish may also be partially pan fried on both sides until slightly brown, then baked in a 350° oven for 10 to 15 minutes.

Butter is good for frying small fish, but has a tendency to get too hot and burn when cooking larger fish. We love coconut oil, most of all but it's hard to find, except in Jamaica and the Caribbean. Our next choice is corn oil, then vegetable oil. Olive oil usually flavors the fish; unless a specific recipe calls for it, it should be avoided. Dusting fish with seasoned (salt and pepper) flour, corn meal, corn muffin mix, prepared frying mixtures, bread, or cracker crumbs adds a crispy flavor to the fish and acts as a color indicator of doneness; the flour or meal turns a nice golden brown when the fish is cooked.

Follow these easy directions for pan frying fish.

1. Cover bottom of large fry pan with about ⅛ inch of butter or oil.
2. Heat butter until it begins to bubble, oil until it runs like water.
3. Slip fish into pan; be sure the fish is free from water, which causes spattering.
4. Immediately reduce heat; cook until done, about 5 minutes.

GRILLED FISH

Any fish can be grilled, but the smaller ones, particularly pilchards (sardines included), smelts, small mackerel, herring, and chubs (fresh water) are to us the most delectable. One of the very best grilled fish are small rock moray eels, whose meat is fatty but flavorful. Small fish do not need to be scaled since the scales char away or drop off as the fish cooks. But all fish, even the small ones, must be gutted. Marinating for an hour in the fish marinade, page 215, is a beneficial addition. But if you have just caught a pile of fresh sardines or other little fellows, nothing more than their own saltiness or, perhaps, a few drops of olive oil is necessary.

We learned a fine trick for spitting small fish from the Spanish fishermen. Instead of running the spit through each fish lengthwise, run two spits (cut coat hangers work fine) through four of five fish at right angles to the body line, behind the head, and in front of the tail. This makes them easier to turn over the coals. Four or five small, grilled fish make a portion for one.

A French technique is to spit the fish in a similar manner, but then to stake them on the down wind side of the fire while savory fennel and thyme sprigs are thrown onto the flames. The fish, once aromatically smoked, are then grilled in the normal fashion.

Grilled fish are usually cooked until crusty on the outside; the high heat is usually sufficient to make the bones brittle and crunchy. Perhaps you will find them as pleasant to eat as we do; if you prefer, of course, the bones may be removed.

FISH BAKED IN FOIL

This simple technique must have been made for cruises. We think of it as the first line of defense in our beach bum's arsenal, for what could be more fun after a long day of fishing than to spend the sunset around a beach campfire. And what campfire could be more friendly than one about to deliver some fine cooked fish, grilled on a spit if they are small, or baked in foil on the embers if large. Spiny lobster tails may also be cooked in foil. Individual portions may be prepared using the foil as a plate. This makes the clean-up easier for the chef, who, alas, is often the chief bottle washer as well.

Foiled fish does not require a campfire. The packages can be laid flat in a fry pan, covered, and cooked over low heat for 10

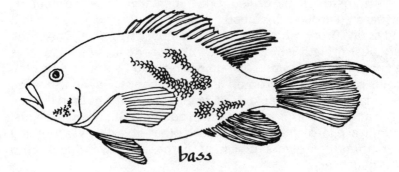

bass

minutes. The result is a steamed or stewed fish; better results are achieved if this is kept in mind. If sliced onions are added to the foil packages; they must be pan fried to a golden brown before being sprinkled on the fish; otherwise the result is steamed, stringy, soggy onions.

Follow these easy directions for foil baking fish.

1. Thoroughly butter shiny side of a foil square, approximately 14 inches on a side.
2. Place individual portions of fish flat on foil.
3. Add any or all of following spices:
   chervil
   dill (just a pinch, but a very nice addition)
   thyme
   marjoram
   crushed peppercorns
   salt
4. If desired, place on top of spices:
   tomato slices
   crisscrossed anchovies
   bacon fried to a light golden color
   chopped olives and green peppers
5. Fold edges of package together so that they form a tight seal, but be sure to puncture the top with a fork to prevent bursting.
6. If cooking over a campfire, let the fire burn down a bit since the fish is best when prepared on hot coals. If cooking in the galley, lightly grease pan bottom with oil to prevent any escaped juices from sticking.

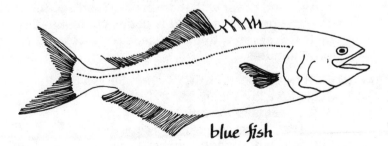

blue fish

7. Cook 5 to 7 minutes directly on the coals, or 8 to 10 minutes in fry pan over low heat.

This main course goes well with a green salad or a big tub of potato salad.

BAKED FISH

Baking offers the most creative and numerous possibilities for cooking fish, particularly the larger ones. But many yachts do not have an oven, or, they have one too small for serious cooking. If you have an oven big enough to be useful, most of these recipes bake the fish 7 to 10 minutes per pound at 350° F. If you do not have an oven, these same recipes can be cooked in a heavy casserole dish on a burner flame diffuser at medium heat for the same period of time. Frequently, a fork should be slipped around and beneath the fish, covering the bottom of the pan with liquid to prevent burning.

QUICK BAKED FISH   Serves Four

This is a fast recipe using cream of mushroom soup as a base. It's convenience is doubled since canned tuna may be used to stretch the fish fillets.

1. Heavily butter bottom and sides of casserole dish.
2. In a separate pot, heat and stir until combined:
    - 1 **cup cream of mushroom soup**
    - 1½ **cup condensed milk**
    - 3 **tablespoons dry, white wine (optional)**
    - 1 **teaspoon celery salt**
    - ½ **teaspoon pepper**
3. Pour thin layer of sauce in casserole. Add layer of tuna, if used, and cover with more sauce. Then add fillets of a fine flavored fish (salt cod is good), cut in 4 to 6 pieces each. Cover top with the sauce; bake uncovered at 350° for 15 minutes.

BAKED FISH IN CAPER SAUCE   Serves Two Per Pound

1. Saute for a few minutes:
    - 4 **tablespoons butter**
    - 1½ **teaspoon crushed celery seed**

Tilt pan; with spoon remove as much of white butter scum as possible.

202

2. Brush seasoned, clarified butter over both sides and body cavity of:

    1 fresh fish, such as pompano, sole, or fresh water trout

3. Place fish on platter; cover with mixture of:

    3 tablespoons butter
    2 tablespoons capers
    1 teaspoon chopped chives or green onion ends
    2 teaspoons lemon juice
    Salt and pepper

4. Cook 8 minutes per pound at 350°, basting with sauce once or twice. If you don't have an oven, this recipe may be pan fried 6 minutes per pound over low heat.

FRESH FISH ROE

Fresh roe, considered a delicacy in many places, is far superior to the canned variety. Shad roe is commonly known, but most any fish roe can be used. Here are two quick recipes, one simple, one elegant.

QUICK FRIED FISH ROE

Fish size determines the number of servings.

1. Fry:

    4 to 6 pieces bacon

2. Fry in bacon fat until golden on outside:

    roe sack of 1 fish

3. Split roe sack in pan, allowing bacon fat to penetrate.

4. Crumble bacon strips and sprinkle inside roe; add a few drops of lemon juice and serve.

ROE WITH A FINE HERBS SAUCE

1. Fry in butter until golden:

    roe sack of 1 fish

2. Remove roe and set aside; add to pan:

    ¼ to ½ stick of butter
    ½ teaspoon chopped chives or green onion ends
    ½ teaspoon chopped parsley
    ½ teaspoon chopped tarragon
    ½ small onion, minced or finely chopped
    ½ teaspoon wine vinegar

3. Simmer sauce for 2 to 3 minutes until onion turns golden.

4. Remove from flame; add 1 teaspoon lemon juice and pour over roe.

EELS MARINATED IN COGNAC　　　　　Serves Six to Eight

　　Old New York salts, sailin' down Boston, used to say with disgust, "All a New Englander wants from life is an eel and a jug of rum." If you have ever had well prepared eel, you might appreciate this attitude.

- 3 lbs. eel (4 medium, fresh water eels)
- ½ cup water
- 2 tablespoons lemon juice
- 2 cups flour
- 4 tablespoons cognac
- ½ teaspoon baking powder
- 2 eggs, beaten
- ½ cup milk, fresh or tinned
- ½ teaspoon salt and pepper

1. Skin eels; cut into 3 or 4 pieces each. Marinate 4 to 6 hours in lemon, cognac, salt, pepper and water.
   Turn about every 2 hours

italian eel fishermen

2. Mix flour, baking powder, ¼ teaspoon pepper, ¼ teaspoon salt. Beat egg and milk together; blend with dry ingredients.
3. Dip eels in batter; pan fry in corn oil until browned.

The best way we know to skin an eel is to tie a string around the eel's neck and hang it from the mast. The skin is then cut below the string and pulled in one piece with the help of pliers. The meat is best filleted below the ribs, thus avoiding tiny bones.

FISH PATE
Makes 1¾ to 2 Cups

The pate is the cruising chef's delicious solution to the problem of leftover fish. Regardless of how the fish was originally cooked, the leftovers, scraped free of sauce, will make a fine pate. In addition, the head, tail, and skeleton left from a filleted fish contain meat that can make a pate. Simply poach these leftover parts in a little chicken bouillon for 15 minutes. The meat will slip easily from the bones. Don't throw the cooking liquid away; it makes a good stock. Breaded, fried fish may be used in this recipe without removing the breading. Fish pate may be used as a sandwich spread, or stuffed into cold artichokes, avocados, or tomatoes.

Mix and let stand overnight:
- 1 cup fish (no bones)
- 1 tablespoon mayonnaise
- 1½ teaspoons dijon mustard
- ½ cup celery, finely chopped (if available)
- 1 small onion, finely diced
- ½ teaspoon celery seed or ¼ teaspoon dill
- 1 teaspoon lemon juice
- salt and pepper to taste
- ¼ cup toasted cracker crumbs, if the fish had not been previously breaded

flounder

FISH FILLETS AMANDINE   Serves Two Per Pound

Dover sole is often served this way as the grand entree of fine restaurants; yet, the recipe is quite simple, and any fine flavored fish fillet may be used.

1. Dip fillets in:
    milk
   Dust in:
    seasoned flour
2. Pan fry both sides until golden brown in:
    butter
   Remove fish and any pieces of cooking debris that you can.
3. Add to pan:
    ¼ stick of butter (approximate)
   When butter is melted add:
    1¼ to ½ cup shredded or chopped almonds, skinned.*
   Saute until light brown over low heat, occassionally rubbing bottom of pan with a wooden spatula. The nuts should take just a few minutes, not enough time for the fish to cool off.
4. Pour butter and nuts over fish; garnish with parsley, if desired, and a pinch of paprika.
   * Whole almonds may be skinned by first boiling them for a few minutes in water, then slipping off the skins.

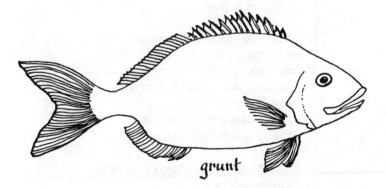

grunt

nassau grouper

BAHAMAS GROUPER STEW

Make this simple, two-pot, one-burner recipe with any firm fleshed, delicate flavored fish. Do not use mullet, mackerel, or hake.

1½   lbs. fish, varieties may be mixed
1   medium onion
5   pieces bacon
1   small (6 oz.) can tomato paste, or 6 fresh tomatoes, skinned and chopped
3   medium potatoes, diced and blanched
4   carrots, diced and blanched
½   teaspoon thyme
½   teaspoon marjoram
½   teaspoon paprika
1   bay leaf
8   peppercorns, coarsely crushed
1   tablespoon salt
    water

1. Blanch (parboil) potatoes and carrots for 5 minutes.
2. Fry bacon until crispy in large pot.
3. Add potatoes, carrots, and onions; fry until onions are golden, stirring frequently.
4. Add just enough water to cover ingredients.
5. Add all spices and tomato paste; put fish   on top of all. Simmer for 10 minutes.

6. Simmer until potatoes are just soft. Add bacon, crumbled.
   Don't overcook the chowder, or the fish will crumble.

BAKED GROUPER OF THE CONCH INN Serves Two Per Pound

There is no question in our minds—the best restaurant in the Bahamas is the Conch Inn at Marsh Harbor. And there is no question that their baked grouper is the best dish on the menu. Any fine flavored fillet may be used, but grouper is a great delight.

grouper fillets, approximately 3″ × 3″ × ½″
lemon juice
milk
seasoned Flour
butter

1. Soak fillets in lemon juice for 1 hour.
2. Pat fillets dry; dip in milk, then in seasoned flour.
3. Fry in butter until brown on both sides, about 4 minutes total.
4. Wrap in buttered aluminum foil, bake for 10 minutes at 325°; or pan bake, covered, for 7 minutes over low heat Fantastic!

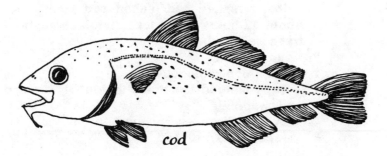

cod

SALTED FISH

In the days before refrigeration, salted fish commanded higher prices than fresh fish of the same species. The cruising chef also values salted fish for its convenience. Since it stores well without refrigeration, is resistant to mold, and provides tasty everyday fare, salted fish should be considered by yachtsmen for cruises where provisions are hard to find. The only negative aspect is that salt fish must be soaked, skin side down, in several changes of fresh water before cooking. However, it is easier to collect water at sea (from rain) than to buy provisions.

SMOKED FISH

The smoked fish sold in various supermarkets and delicatessens is usually cooked and ready to eat. It does, however require some degree of refrigeration or coolness since smoking fish does not preserve it as well as salting does. A few varieties of fish are cold smoked, which means they must be cooked prior to serving. We have omitted them from this book since they are relatively rare, and not really the yachtsman's concern. Some smoked fish are available canned and are frequently quite good. Within this category are smoked herring and smoked salmon, an expensive treat in the deli, but more reasonable and fairly good when canned. There are so many different varieties and brand names of canned fish, smoked or otherwise, that the only way to get what you want is to open a can at the store and taste it. Don't let the assurances of the grocer sway you; nothing is more annoying at sea than having a dozen cans of something that no one will eat.

BLUE WATER COD IN TOMATO SAUCE   Serves Four

This deep water dish uses salted cod and other longlasting ingredients for a one pot, one burner meal.

> 1½   lbs. desalted cod (salted cod soaked for about 12 hours in not less than 3 changes of fresh water)
> ½   cup olive oil
> 1   large onion, chopped
> 1½   cups canned tomatoes, thoroughly drained and chopped
> 4   cloves garlic, finely chopped
> 6   peppercorns, crushed
>   flour

1. Shake small cod pieces in plastic bag with flour, pepper.
2. Heat olive oil in large fry pan until very hot; oil should run like water.
3. Fry cod until it just begins to brown.
4. Reduce flame, remove cod; fry onions until golden.
5. Add tomatoes and peppercorns; simmer over low heat until sauce thickens, approximately 20 minutes.
6. Add cod; heat for about 5 minutes and serve. Boiled potatoes complement this dish.

SPANISH SALT COD CROQUETTES   Serves Three to Four

The fish should be cut into 2 to 3-inch square pieces, then soaked in three or four changes of fresh water for not more than 12, or less than 8 hours, then squeezed dry in a cloth.

> 1   cup desalted cod, chopped
> ¾   cup olive oil
> ½   cup minced or finely grated onion
> 2 to 4   tablespoons corn flour
> 1½ cups milk
> 2   eggs
> ½   cup bread or cracker crumbs mixed with
> ½   cup flour

1. Saute onion in 1 tablespoon olive oil until golden.
2. Add cod; fry until cod is dry, about 5 to 8 minutes.
3. Mix 1 tablespoon corn flour with milk; pour over fish.
4. Cook over low heat for 20 to 30 minutes until mixture thickens to a heavy paste. Add more corn flour, if necessary.
5. Turn off flame, stir in two egg yolks, reserving whites.
6. When paste is cool, wet hands, then shape paste into patties; dip first in egg white, then in equal mixture of bread or cracker crumbs and flour.
7. Fry in ¼ inch of olive oil until golden brown.

SWEET AND SOUR (SALT COD) FISH

Serves Two to Three Per Pound

This traditional Cantonese recipe uses sweet and sour sauce, page 257, which can be made in advance and stored for months. The sauce recipe yields enough for several meals. Salt cod is not necessarily the fish of choice, any big-boned fish, not only cod, may be used for this recipe; pan-sized varieties may be cooked whole. If salt cod, or any other salt fish is used, omit the salt and reconstitute by soaking in water, page 210.

1. Dip the pieces, fillets or whole fish in:
   egg
   seasoned flour (1 cup flour, 1 teaspoon salt, ½ teaspoon pepper)
2. Fry over high heat until crispy brown in:
   2 tablespoons oil
3. Remove fish from pan; add:
   ½ onion, chopped
   Fry until brown.
4. Add:
   ¾ to 1 cup sweet and sour sauce
   Cook for 1 minute over high heat.
5. Add fish; baste thoroughly with sauce.
   Cook for 1 minute over high heat.

BAKED COD, POLLOCK OR HADDOCK IN CREAM SAUCE
Serves Three to Four

4 medium fish fillets
4 tablespoons bottled clam juice
¼ cup dry white wine
1 tablespoon butter
1 cup cream or condensed milk
2 tablespoons sherry
½ teaspoon fennel seed
chopped parsley
nutmeg

1. Add flour to melted butter; saute until light golden.
2. Gradually add clam juice, white wine, then cream, stirring constantly until sauce thickens.

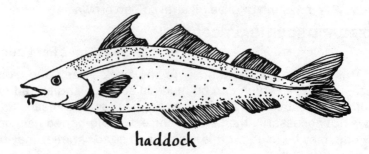

haddock

3. Cook over low heat for 3 minutes, then add sherry and fennel. Cook for another 5 minutes.
4. Place fillets in greased baking dish; cover with sauce.
5. Bake 30 minutes at 325° F. Sprinkle with parsley before serving.

PAN BROILED MACKEREL, WAHOO, OR KINGFISH
Serves Two Per Pound

These fish are strongly flavored and generally unsuitable for boiling, steaming, or stewing. But if properly prepared, they are delicious pan broiled.

1. Cut:
   ¾-inch thick fish steaks
2. Marinate for 20 minutes, or until the flesh begins to turn white in:
   lemon juice
   Do not refrigerate.
3. Pan broil in:
   2   tablespoons butter
   2 minutes per side, using moderate heat.
4. Sprinkle with:
   pan drippings
   lemon juice
   salt
   pepper
   paprika
   Delicious!

THE CAPTAIN'S FISH POACHING STOCK (COURT BOUILLON)
Prepares several meals

1. Saute in pot for 5 minutes over high heat until onions are golden:
   3   tablespoons butter
   ½   cup onions, chopped
   1½ cup carrots, finely chopped
   ½   cup celery with leaves, chopped, or
   ½   teaspoon celery salt
2. Add:
   6   peppercorns, crushed
   ½   cup dry white wine
   2   cups water

> **1 to 2 lbs. fish heads, tails, bones, lobster or crab shells**
> **½ teaspoon thyme**
> **½ bay leaf**
> **1½ teaspoons salt**

3. Simmer over low heat for 20 minutes with lid off; do not allow liquid to reach a rolling boil. Strain and use liquid for poaching.

After poaching the fish, use the poaching stock to make a fine sauce.

1. Melt in pan:
   > **3 tablespoons butter**
2. Add and fry until light golden:
   > **1 tablespoon flour**
3. Thoroughly mix this roux with a little cold wine; slowly add poaching liquid over low heat, stirring constantly, until desired thickness is achieved.

We must confess to using this simplified technique:

1. Mix thoroughly in small pot:
   > **1 tablespoon corn flour**
2. Add:
   > **½ to 1 cup poaching liquid**

   Simmer until sauce thickens. If not thick enough, add more corn flour in a little wine.

The above sauce may be varied by any of the following methods:

1. Add 1 to 2 teaspoons of dijon mustard.
2. Add 1 tablespoon curry paste, page 277.
3. Squeeze a handful of white, seedless grapes over the sauce, then chop and add the remains.
4. Add a small handful of grated, mild cheese, until cheese melts.

A QUICK FISH POACHING STOCK   Prepares One Meal
1. Saute for 5 minutes in poaching pan:
   > **1 small onion, chopped**
   > **1 to 2 carrots, well chopped**
   > **½ teaspoon celery seed, or ½ teaspoon celery salt**

2. Add:
   ½   **cup dry white wine**
   ½   **cup water mixed with 1 chicken bouillon cube,**
        crumbled
   ½   **teaspoon salt**
   ½   **teaspoon pepper**
   ½   **teaspoon thyme**
   ½   **teaspoon marjoram**
   1   **teaspoon butter**
Simmer over low heat for 10 minutes; do not stir.
3. Strain the liquid.
4. Put strained liquid back in pan; rub bottom of pan thoroughly with wooden scraper. Add fish and poach. Thicken poaching liquid following previous recipe.

cow fish

SEVERAL FISH MARINADES

Use this marinade when poaching delicately flavored fish.

1. Thoroughly combine in large bowl:
   ½   **cup white wine**
   3   **tablespoons vinegar**
   1   **teaspoon salt, pepper**
   1   **tablespoon corn flour**
   2   **egg whites**
2. Add fish. Be sure to thoroughly cover each piece with marinade. Allow to stand several hours, if possible, at room temperature.

Use this marinade when grilling small fish, such as sardines and herring, or larger fish, such as mackerel, mullet, ray wings, and moray eel.

1. Thoroughly combine in large bowl:
   ½ cup red wine
   ¼ cup vinegar
   1½ cup corn oil
   2 teaspoons salt
   1 teaspoon pepper
   4 cloves garlic, minced or finely chopped
2. Add fish. Thoroughly cover each fish with marinade. Allow to stand at least 30 minutes. Be sure plenty of marinade is on the fish when placed on the grill.

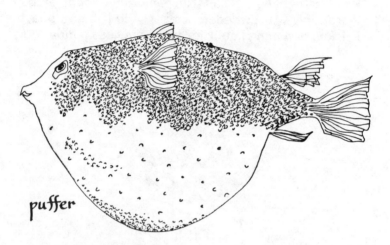

puffer

THE PUFFER, THE WORLD'S DEADLIEST DELIGHT

The puffer is an inflatable fish which further discourages its enemies by poisoning them. The internal organs of some varities contain a toxin twenty-five times more deadly than curare, enough to poison 40-50 people! The puffer is so poisonous that the Japanese government licenses puffer chefs to prevent mass poisoning. Nevertheless many a puffer gourmet has died, fork in hand.

One night logically ask why a fish so deadly is consumed with so much delight by so many. The answer is simple; the puffer is exceedingly delicious. Served raw in thin, translucent strips as sushi it is sweet, gelatenous and mild flavored. Steamed it melts in the mouth. It is a joy in any stew and a cut above Pompano served poached. Perhaps the puffer's flavor is further enhanced by the risk one takes.

216

Fortunately the North Atlantic puffer is not poisonous and is commonly sold in markets as "sea squab". The fish is nearly boneless and the drumstick-like fillets contain only the backbone. They may be cooked like any delicate white fish. We have eaten many a Florida puffer and its cousin the spiny boxfish. Some now say that these are among the dangerous varieties. Had we known, perhaps we might have forgone the feast.

Catching blowfish is definitely not the angler's idea of high drama. Considering their tiny fins and comical vestige of a tail, it's easy to understand why they don't put up much of a fight. I sometimes wonder how they manage to swim at all. The blowfish's idea of resistance is to take water or air into its body until it looks just like a balloon. When inflated, they offer about as much sport as hauling in a soggy tennis ball. But more frequently than not, they get so excited when hooked, they forget to inflate until they are landed. Then they are more comical than ever, puffing away, getting larger and larger in your hand. If fish have any sort of personality, the blowfish is the most friendly clown of all. They would cluster around us when we waded the Florida sand flats at night, looking for lobster. They seemed to be attracted to the light, and would nibble at the hair on my legs. When I shooed them away, they would run in a circle and come right back. They were a snap to spear, and it seemed almost unfair to do so. Anglers fishing for sheepshead and snapper hate blowfish. They have tiny mouths that easily nibble away the bait. This tactic drives most sportsmen away, but if they knew how delicious blowfish are, they might decide to stay. Since they have tiny mouths, blowfish require a very small hook with appropriately sized bait. They bite with vigor, and you can pull them in one after another since they seem to travel in schools. Blowfish will take any bait, but seem to enjoy shrimp tails or tiny beach crabs most of all.

dolphin

217

RAYS AND SKATES

While ignored by the American public, Europeans consider rays and skates exceptionally tasty fish of delicate flavor. European supermarkets sell them at fancy prices, but the cruising yachtsman has the advantage of frequently finding these creatures on sand and grass flats, especially at night. Fishermen often catch rays when bottom fishing, and it is almost inevitable to see a few when diving. They are hardly sport for the man with a spear gun or a gig since they offer an easy target as they lie on the bottom.

Rays, once landed, should be killed with a blow between the eyes. This is more than just a humane act; rays have a sharp spine in the base, not the end, of their tails. Although the spine is not poisonous, it is covered with a mucous membrane that causes great pain and infection. The ray's sting, while worth considering, is really not very dangerous, and, to corrupt the old saying, is much worse than its bite since rays have no teeth. Skates have neither teeth nor sting.

The edible portion of skates and rays is in the wings, which should be cut away close to the body. The wings may be skinned and used as any fine flavored fish, but they are also quite delicious as a substitute for scallops. They may, therefore, be cut into bite-sized pieces and used in any of the scallop recipes in this book. Finally, rays are excellent for stretching a thin supply of crab, shrimp, or lobster meat in recipes where the flaked meat is mixed together, such as fritters and pates.

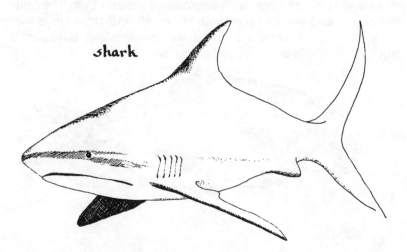

shark

THE WITCHES' CAULDRON

Rebecca and I don't usually invite sharks to dinner, but strangers do drop in uninvited. If a shark takes our bait, he is guilty and must pay the price. The recipe for shark hash was given to us by Ivan Outerbridge, a Bermuda tugboat operator and mechanic who loves good food. Ivanovitch, as his friends call him, warned us that sharks, even small ones, don't appreciate being caught. We found this to be a slight understatement. These mean creatures are fond of thrashing around on deck like a runaway lawnmower. A blow on the top of their head slows them down. However, they persist in staying alive for surprisingly long periods of time. Anyway, if you are fishing for snapper but get shark, just remember the story about the princess who kissed a frog and got a prince. Culinary delights are sometimes hidden in unappetizing packages.

SHARK HASH BERMUDIANA   Serves Four

The following recipe is for a small shark, about 4½ pounds. Any size shark may be used; but if it is over 5 or 6 pounds, use only the body meat close to the spine. The belly meat on larger sharks is tough and requires longer cooking.

1. Remove head and gut shark.
2. Fillet and boil body meat until tender and flakes easily, about 30 minutes.
3. Drain the meat and dry in a towel. The finished product should be light and fluffy; drying is important.
4. Hash meat thoroughly with a fork, or put it through a meat grinder.
5. Blend together:
   - 1½ lbs. shark meat
   - 1 medium onion, grated
   - 2 hot peppers, finely chopped (optional)
   - 2 bell peppers, diced (optional)
   - ½ cup vegetable oil
   - 2 cups bread crumbs
   - 1 tablespoon thyme
   - 1 tablespoon grated or dried parsley
   - salt and pepper to taste

Serve hot or cold with baked sweet potatoes. Tastes similar to cold crabmeat. Serve as a main dish, hot or cold, or mixed with a little mayonnaise as a sandwich spread.

SHARK CAKES A LA FIRE WITCH   Serves Six

Cook shark according to the previous recipe for shark hash. A small shark, about 4 pounds, provides more meat than is needed for the hash. Use 4 cups of hashed meat to make these delicious cakes.

1. Heat in pan:
   4 tablespoons vegetable oil
2. Simmer until golden:
   1 medium onion, minced
   1 cup bread crumbs
   Remove from heat.
3. Combine and add:
   3 eggs, well beaten
   1 small can condensed milk (½ cup)
   1 cup carrots, finely minced
   2 teaspoons lemon juice
   1½ teaspoons salt
   2 teaspoons paprika
4. Mix thoroughly with
   4 cups shark meat, cooked, dried, and hashed
5. Shape into cakes; dip in bread crumbs, crushed corn flakes, or flour.
6. Fry in vegetable oil at high heat until browned on both sides. Then continue frying at low heat for about 8 minutes. Serve with a salad in fair weather, or hash browns when it's cold.

KEDGEREE OF SHARK   Serves Four

Combine:

2 cups cooked rice
1 lb. shark meat, cooked, dried, and hashed
4 hard-boiled eggs, forced through a sieve or grated
½ cup butter or margarine
½ cup canned condensed milk
1 tablespoon lemon juice
1 teaspoon paprika
1 cup cooked celery, finely chopped (optional)
1 cup cooked carrots, finely diced

Serve steaming hot. Inviting a shark to dinner may be fun afterall!

SHARK 'N CHIPS   Serves Two to Three Per Pound

This is not the best recipe for a yacht since it calls for deep frying, and since the oil, once used for shark 'n chips, can only be used for future generations of shark 'n chips. But if you have a calm sea and a shark lying about, give this a try. Perhaps this is the best way to eat a shark.

For this recipe small sharks are best, but any can be used. This is particularly good with dogfish. Use the fillets from around the spine. The other parts can be used for shark bait.

1. In a large pot, bring to high heat:
   1 pint, or more, corn or vegetable oil.
2. Slice lengthwise into ½-inch pieces:
   1 potato per portion
   Cook to golden brown.
3. Dip bite-sized pieces of shark fillet in mixture of:
   1 cup flour
   1 teaspoon baking powder
   ½ cup water
   ½ teaspoon salt and pepper
   2 beaten eggs
4. Fry shark to golden brown in hot oil.

hake

TUNA

All species of tuna are fine food, and a real thrill to catch. They are basically deep water fish, sleek torpedoes of solid meat. When schools of tuna are running, they will strike savagely and fight to complete exhaustion. We have seen little fishing boats from isolated Azore islands return loaded to the rails with small tuna, which were then frozen and stored for the winter in the community freezer.

Fresh tuna tastes surprisingly similar to lean veal and can be treated as such. It can be braised, or roasted with tomatoes, onion, and paprika, or served in a stew with potatoes, carrots, and chicken stock, or just pan fried in a little butter and served with a white sauce.

Canned tuna comes in several different colors, juices, and cuts. The most flavorful packaging liquid is olive, corn, or peanut oil and natural juices, rather than water. Color seems to make no difference at all, but solid chunk tuna is usually a finer texture than tuna flakes. The body meat usually comes in squat cans, the tail meat in tall cans. We consider canned tuna excellent in flavor and nutrition—a basic staple for the cruising yacht. It can be prepared in any number of ways as though it were freshly poached. It makes a fine tuna salad for sandwiches, or a hot casserole when mixed with a white cream, tomato, or mayonnaise sauce and some peas. Canned tuna does just fine in tuna fritters, and can be mixed with other fresh fish for use in fish cakes. Last, but certainly not least, canned tuna makes a warm weather meal when added to a salad topped with a few sliced, hard-boiled eggs.

tuna casserole

MID-OCEAN TUNA CASSEROLE   Serves Four

This favorite recipe is a stovetop casserole, handy when the fresh stores are running out.

1. Combine and mix thoroughly:
   12   oz. tuna, thoroughly drained
   ¾   cup mayonnaise
   1   cup canned or prepared freeze dried peas
   1   cup celery, diced, or ½ teaspoon celery seed
   1   teaspoon garlic salt
   ½   teaspoon pepper
2. Chop:
   1   medium onion
3. Lightly brown in:
   2   tablespoons oil
4. Add fish mixture to onion; cook for 15 minutes over low heat, turning sparingly to avoid breaking the peas. Set aside when hot.
5. Boil in lightly salted water until done:
   a generous handful of noodles or spaghetti per person
6. Drain noodles and add:
   1   heaping teaspoon of sour cream for each portion
   1   tablespoon butter per portion
7. Serve generous portions of tuna mixture over noodles.

SERENITY TUNA SALAD   Serves Four

We rafted next to the Yacht Serenity one night in Lisbon and were invited for a drink. As the dinner hour approached we prepared to leave; but Julia Wheeler, Serenity's first mate, was never one to panic in the face of numbers. She whipped up this tasty, informal dish in no time at all, and made it in generous enough portions to feed about 20 guests. Three cheers for the chef!

   6   oz. macaroni, boiled and drained
   1   can cream of mushroom soup
   1   onion, chopped
   1   green pepper, chopped
   1   large can tuna (12 oz. or more), thoroughly drained

2 tablespoons lemon juice
1 tablespoon Worchestershire sauce
3 tablespoons dry sherry (optional)
  salt and pepper to taste

1. Saute onions and pepper in oil until just soft.
2. Add other ingredients; mix thoroughly. That's all! Serve with bowls of fruit salad, if available.

ONE POT TUNA KEDGEREE   Serves Three or Four

Fast, easy, and really delicious, this recipe may also be used for other seafood, such as lobster, crab, or delicately flavored, flaked fish. The beauty of this fine tasting dish is it requires one pot for the total operation.

3 eggs
1 cup rice
1 cup peas
6 to 8 oz. (1 can) tuna, drained, and/or other seafood, cooked
2 tablespoons butter
1 teaspoon lemon juice
½ cup condensed milk
  salt and pepper to taste

1. To one quart of boiling water add:
   3 eggs
   1 cup rice (15 minute variety)
   Remove eggs, hard-boiled, after 10 minutes. Chop them.
2. If you plan to use fresh peas, add them now. Cook rice and peas until the rice is just done; drain.
3. Add all other ingredients, mix together lightly. Serve over toast.

TUNA FRITTERS   Serves Two or Three

1. Combine:
   6 oz. tuna, drained, dried, and well-flaked
   3 eggs, beaten
   6 tablespoons flour (¼ cup plus 2 tablespoons)
   ½ teaspoon baking powder
   ½ teaspoon pepper
   ½ onion, chopped
2. Shape into patties about 3 inches wide and ½ inch thick; dust with flour.
3. Drop patties into hot oiled pan, fry over high heat until a brown crust forms, about 2 to 3 minutes per side.

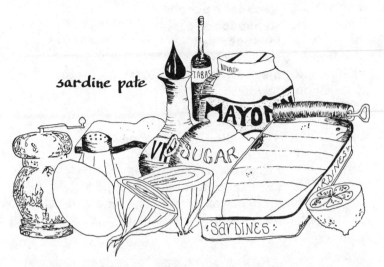

sardine pate

CANNED SARDINES—PATES AND SPREADS

Sardine actually refers to a number of different species of small fish, such as pilchards or anchovies. These fish vary in size, the smaller ones usually having a better flavor. In addition to the size of the sardine, the packing liquid is also important. Olive oil is best, with tuna fish. After olive oil, we prefer several different kinds of vegetable oil, including peanut oil. Last, and least tempting are several nonoily sauces. These sauces are often quite good on other fish, such as herring, but their use on the sardine usually indicates cheap quality.

SARDINE SANDWICH SPREAD (Quick)

> 1   **can sardines packed in oil, mashed into rough paste**
> 1   **teaspoon lemon juice**
> ½   **teaspoon mustard**
> ¼   **teaspoon pepper**
> ½   **medium onion, chopped**

Mix all ingredients together and spread on buttered toast.

SARDINE PATE

1. Combine:
> 2   **tablespoons white vinegar**
> 2   **dashes tobasco sauce or 1 teaspoon prepared mustard**

½   teaspoon pepper
¼   teaspoon sugar
1   teaspoon salt
Pour mixture over:
2   pieces dried melba toast
Chop finely.
2. Combine:
1   can sardines, drained
2   hard-boiled eggs chopped
1   medium onion, chopped
1   tablespoon mayonnaise
2   tablespoons parsley, chopped
3. Combine melba toast with fish mixture, let stand overnight, if possible. Serve in tomato halves as a cold salad.

12
tap dance
on the lifelines

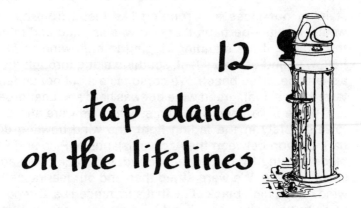

It isn't the taste of fear that we mind, it's not knowing the cause. Fear is a part of the ship's equipment, like the lifelines or the standing rigging, an essential ingredient that keeps you alive and brings you safely through the storm. You thump the standing rigging with your hand to test its tension. Like kicking the tires of a car. The clean, stainless wire gleams as it quivers, muttering to itself. The fine strands within it, strung so gracefully, twist upward, away from you, humming a bit from your blow but mostly keeping their own counsel. The wire is silent and terribly strong. Our lives depend on it. Our rigging has withstood many storms, moaning occasionally in high wind with a voice both anguished and confused. It is strong and silent but fails without warning and when it fails there is a pop, almost like the breaking of a light bulb; an unusual sound, so gentle for such a disastrous event.

We test the strength of our lifelines by dancing upon them as we danced one sunny, windless day in Port Sollar, Majorca. The turquoise of the sea and the green of the hills ran in our blood and we felt very grand standing on the thin wire in the sunshine. The lifeline stanchions, rising like fingers from the deck, did not seem to notice us. They were silent and did not move, concealing their strength and we were not sure that we had found their measure.

Perhaps the fear which we felt that same night, pounding along beside the high dark cliffs of Majorca with the salt spray

227

staining our faces and running like blood from our red foul weather suits—perhaps that fear was as blind and mindless as the moans of the standing rigging in high wind or fear of the hollow sound of crab's feet, scuttling along through the sand of a silent, deserted beach. We could taste it but not understand. It tasted like a cool, green wine but was hard and unapproachable.

There have been other times when we were afraid, beating toward safety in the fading light, the wind howling down the dark canyon between the Azorian islands of Pico and Fayal like blood pulsing from an open wound, the black rocks around us silent, waiting. We were afraid then and our fear rasped like the wind off the high black cliffs that surrounded us. Our course was good but our chart small and the time soon approaching to decide whether to run or risk, in the growing darkness, a last tack past the rocks to safety. The fear which we felt then and that which we experienced beneath the friendly Majorcan moon were strangely the same, bonded by something deeper and more complex which we could not understand. The wind was light and the Majorcan sea calm, but in the silence we could

hear the wind on high rock and the moans of the standing rigging. It gleamed in the moonlight, a luminous thread connecting us with our past. Yes, perhaps it was just the standing rigging.

We had been waiting in Port Sollar for days, waiting for wind, watching the sunsets bloom from the windows of old men in shirt sleeves whose eyes were as bright and gleaming as the sunset in their window panes. We had seen women throw pans of water into the morning heat where it vanished while running down the cobblestones. We reached out and tried to touch the heat; it felt like a kitten but also like a snake and we did not know whether to caress it or withdraw. We watched the flags in the harbor hang limply and whistled for wind, threw pennies for the I Ching and occasionally looked at the sad remnants of our long dead motor.

Our crewman, John, tall and bearded, had met a girl the other day. Justine was a fine girl, very clever and lithe as a young animal with her Levis on. Her long, dark hair hanging in braids and up-turned nose made her look like a little girl, but her fine breasts, loose beneath a green blouse danced when she laughed. The sharp contrasts in her, like the different tastes in a good wine, blended delightfully. She and John had spent the night together on the foredeck, wrapped in a sail with the stars blazing down upon them. They looked good together, two shapes in the darkness and I was sure that if there was no sailing wind for several days, they would not mind.

We walked the paeso maritemo at the setting of the sun, the trees casting long shadows on the cobblestones and the leaves crunching beneath our feet. The little tram from Palma clanged in the distance and the first smells of evening were in the air. Then, on a whim we turned inland, into the growing dusk and stopped at a small cafe beneath the trees and drank a bottle of Monopole. It was so good and cold, woody and tart, tasting like the sea feels on a fine day when the rail is down, the rigging quivering and the sun lapping at your brain. We drank the wine, ate little dishes of peppery snails and watched the pigeons patrol the door.

The gas lights of the octopus fishermen dotted the bay as we walked the cobbled streets. It was the hour of evening when old men in black berets play dominoes by the light of street lamps or in the corners of small cafes whose smoky light oozed across the sidewalks. The slap of the cubes upon the table and the smack of their lips as they drank sharp red wine gave rhythm to the night.

The fine smell of garlic and tomato sauce threaded with laughter slid from half-shut windows on ribbons of light. We pushed through fallen leaves toward the bay, thinking about dinner and thinking about wind.

We found the restaurant full of sardine fishermen eating huge slabs of bread covered with tomato paste and anchovies, drinking strong brandy and wine. Their voices and the fine smell of roast lamb pushed back the night.

We ate bread with garlic and oil, drank rich red wine and waited for the lamb. The little boats of the octopus fishermen had reached the mouth of the bay and solemnly, in single file, they disappeared from sight.

The moon cast its whiteness into the air. The diesel heart of a fishing boat pulsed somewhere in the darkness. Here we were, surrounded by friends in the most beautiful sheltered bay, eating and drinking, warmed by the liquid passion of love, a scene, a place —for this frozen moment most men would gladly sell their souls. Yet we, in our silent madness, waited only for wind.

The wind came that night, tumbling down the mountainside. We stood, high on the hill and watched the moon fracture the sea into a sheet of sparkling white. Rebecca and I, Justine and John stood in the breeze, smelled the pureness of the sea and knew that our frozen moment had passed.

With a fond goodby to Justine we cast off at once. The high rock walls as we passed the mouth of the bay looked like living steel in the moonlight. We glided between them with only the mainsail drawing, hardly breaking the tranquility of this dark, silent, sheltered place with the murmur of our wake. The lighthouse swung its bright arms high above us. We looked at it again as we stood away from the bay. It was red and white like a candy stripe—our last sweet taste of the land as we seeped our fingers with the cold fingers of the sea.

We passed the octopus fishermen as we worked our small sloop, Fire Witch, out of the channel. We passed them, one by one—small, dark men, unshaven and in old clothes with spears in one hand, nets in the other. They were trapped in pools of light, their downcast eyes did not notice us, their minds were lost in the endless depths. We set the working jib, sheeted the mainsail ramrod tight, and set our course into the darkness. The wind was light, the moon huge and white. We waited for the joy of the moment to overwhelm us, rushing into our brains like the first taste of a cold white wine.

But the wind was against us and the rush did not come. Soon we were pounding along, close hauled, with the working jib occasionally flapping in protest. John was at the helm, dressed for foul weather, woolen cap, safety line and rubber

"the light was like a candy stripe"

boots. He played a Dylan tune on his harmonica, and made happy noises. We hated him for leaving so easily when he and Justine could have slept together once more wrapped in a sail, whispering the secret things that lovers say to each other late at night when the flags are dipped in sleep.

Rebecca and I were below, lying on the bunk, watching the moon race back and forth across the companionway. We were afraid but could not explain it, could not understand it. We savored the taste of our fear like wine, trying to find its component parts but it was green and hard and impenetrable like a stone and we could not probe its darkness. We lay in each other's arms and talked of our fear, smiled at each other as we listened to John making his happy noises and playing the blues. We hear the rigging muttering its quiet melody of stress and know that somehow this night is connected to other nights spent clawing off a yammering lee shore or sailing by high rock looking at a lighthouse far above us, distant and unreal, with the wind, as on this night, howling against us as though down a canyon mouth. Perhaps the wind, the rigging, and the moon make us think back to all those other nights when we felt fragile and alone, listening to the wind moan among broken rocks and the waves smashing on the shore. We thought, at those times, of human flesh with its miles of nerves strung so incredibly; about how it quivers, sometimes to the touch of love and of how different it is when it is not alive.

In the end we turned back, as much because of the wind as the fear. We ghosted beneath the lighthouse just as the sun touched the hill, dropped the hook in Port Sollar and watched the waiters sweep the empty streets. We thought that day of our fear, of how simple life had been ages ago when we had nothing to do but drink cold Majorcan wine and dance upon the lifelines. We sat at a little cafe beneath the trees, watched the sun climb higher, drank coffee and double cognacs and laughed with the breeze. The sea, fickle mistress, had reminded us of the courage she demands, her ticket of admission to the green islands that lie beneath the wind. How much courage must we pay? Do we have the means to pay it? We think of courage as part of the ship's equipment, like the standing rigging, water shimmering down the slim steel wire which is ramrod tight and humming a bit in the wind. Will it fail us as it has on occasion in the past? We patch our rigging with curses and bulldog clips, our courage with cognac and laughter.

13
meat

The cruising chef often must purchase meat in out-of-the-way ports. Be wary when selecting meat; insist on giving it the ultimate sniff test. If in doubt, don't buy it.

HAMBURGER OR GROUND CHUCK

Hamburger ranks very high on our list of excellent cruising foods. It is almost as available as chicken, it's cheap, it can be cooked in many different ways, and, ironically, it is usually lower in calories than a good steak. More important to the cruising chef are the many quick, one-pot recipes for hamburger meat that are not only easy and delicious, but elegant as well.

SELECTING HAMBURGER MEAT

We use the term "hamburger" or "ground chuck" because U.S. Federal law has placed a number of restrictions on its fat, filler, and chemical content. Hamburger is, by law, at least, 70 percent meat and 30 percent fat. It must be completely free of meat by-products, such as offal and entrails, and unadulterated by the addition of sodium sulphide, which unscrupulous butchers add to ground meat to preserve its color. Unfortunately, the law is not always observed, and many countries have no restrictions at all when purchasing ground meat, consider the following:

1. If ground meat is pale and greasy looking, it is probably very fatty.
2. If rich, red, ground meat does not change to a darker hue in the sun, it is full of sodium sulphide or paprika.

233

3. If the texture is mushy or dull colored, either the meat has been frozen and defrosted, or has filler added to it.
4. Regardless of its color, take a small piece and smell it. Reject ground meat that smells at all suspicious.
5. Never attempt to preserve ground meat or store it, unfrozen, for more than a few days.
6. Carefully check the surface of frozen hamburger for ice crystals, a sure sign that the meat has been watered to increase its weight.
7. Price is usually, but not always, a good indicator of quality. Never buy the cheapest ground beef; the shrinkage, due to excess water and fat, usually proves your bargain to be a loss.

MAKING HAMBURGERS

1. Hamburgers must be dense.
2. They must be thin, not more than ½ inch; thick 'burgers usually cook dry on the outside before the inside is done.
3. They must be broiled, or pan broiled like a steak.
4. Pan drippings should be poured off as the meat cooks or, the 'burger will be stewed rather than broiled.
5. Hamburgers are traditionally unseasoned before they are cooked. The seasonings, such as salt, pepper, garlic, sauce, are added after the meat is cooked. Never season the surface of a 'burger until the meat is cooked on that side; seasonings usually burn or break down to a bitter taste when subjected to high heat. Never salt the surface of an uncooked hamburger, or the pan, since the salt leaches out tasty meat juice. Should your taste differ from ours, here are some flavorings that may be added to the raw meat:

  1 teaspoon chopped or grated onion per patty (we prefer the onions sauted first)
  garlic, minced (one clove per pound), or
  ¼ teaspoon garlic powder per pound
  ¼ teaspoon chili powder per burger
  Worcestershire sauce
  mustard
  thyme
  chives
  pepper

SLOPPY JOES   Makes 8 Sandwiches

Traditionally served in a 'burger bun, sloppy joes are also good on toast, or inside pan fried bread.

> 1½ **lbs. ground hamburger**
> ½   **onion, finely chopped**
> 3   **teaspoons butter or oil**
> 1   **cup catsup**
> ½   **cup celery and/or green pepper, well chopped**
> or ½ **teaspoon celery salt**
> 2   **tablespoons lemon juice**
> 1   **teaspoon brown sugar**
> 1   **teaspoon Worcestershire sauce**
> 1   **teaspoon dijon mustard**

1. Saute onions in butter or oil until golden.
2. Add and brown hamburger.
3. Add all other ingredients; simmer for 5 minutes.

For variety, add a teaspoon of Parmesan cheese on top.

atria beef

YACHT ATRIA SPICY BEEF CASSEROLE   Serves Four

This easy-to-make delight is an especially good way to prepare an interesting meal from canned ground beef; however, it is much better with fresh meat. All the ingredients, including the noodles, are pressure cooked together in the same pot at the same time. This recipe is easy to make, always turns out well, and brings compliments to the chef.

1. Add to pressure cooker, but do not stir:

   1   **lb. canned or lightly brown fresh beef (add first)**
   1   **green pepper, chopped (optional)**
   2   **cloves garlic, chopped**
   2   **cups broad noodles or macaroni**
   1   **large onion, thinly sliced**
   1   **teaspoon Worcestershire sauce**
   1   **tsp. mustard (more, if desired)**
   6   **tablespoons catsup (more, if desired)**
   1   **can tomato sauce 10 oz.**

2. Mix thoroughly; pressure cook for 5 minutes after jiggle. Bon appetit!

QUICK MEATBALLS AND TWO SAUCES   Serves Four or Five

1   **lb. ground beef, fresh or frozen**
12 **crackers, crushed into crumbs**
1   **large onion, well chopped**
½   **teaspoon pepper**
2   **eggs, beaten**
3   **tablespoons vegetable oil, no more**
½ to ¾   **teaspoon garlic salt, or 3 cloves garlic, minced**
1   **tablespoon Worcestershire sauce**
½   **cup flour**

The Meatballs

1. Combine meat, cracker crumbs, onion, pepper, garlic salt, and Worcestershire sauce.
2. Make into small meat balls, 1 to 1½ inches in diameter.
3. Roll in flour.
4. Saute in vegetable oil over high heat until brown, 3 to 5 minutes.

fairy tern

Sour Cream Sauce
   Try to make this a few hours before dinner.

   1. Combine:
       ¾   cup sour cream
       ½   teaspoon garlic salt (optional)
       ¼   teaspoon nutmeg (optional)
       ¼   teaspoon dill
       ¼   onion, chopped
   2. Pour over the meatballs; do not boil.

Curry Tomato Sauce

   1. Prepare a curry; page 277, with 1 onion in it.
   2. Add:
       1   cup tomato puree
       ½   teaspoon sugar or more, if the tomatoes are
           bitter
       1   teaspoon lemon juice
   3. Heat and simmer 5 minutes. Pour over meatballs.

KIMA   Serves Four

   Curried ground beef and potatoes in one pot

           curry, page 277
       2   large potatoes, diced and parboiled for 3
           minutes
       1   lb. ground beef
       1   cup peas, cooked, preferably fresh
       1   cup canned tomatoes, coarsely chopped and
           drained
       2   beef bouillon cubes mixed in a little red wine,
           or ½ cup beef consomme
       ½   teaspoon salt
       ½   teaspoon pepper
       1   bay leaf, broken up into small pieces
       ½   teaspoon cumin
           butter or oil
           corn flour

   1. Make curry in a large fry pan. (See page 277.)
   2. Add the potatoes and spices; saute until potatoes begin
      to brown. Add butter or oil, if necessary, to prevent dry-
      ing.
   3. Add beef and brown, stirring frequently.

4. Add tomatoes and bouillon mixture. Simmer 15 minutes over low heat, lid off.
5. Add cooked peas, simmer 5 minutes. Thicken with one teaspoon flour dissolved in a little red wine. Serve over noodles or rice.

BRAISED HAMBURGER MEAT A LA CRUISING CHEF
Serves Six

1. In pressure cooker, fry in bacon fat until golden:
   1   onion, chopped
2. Add to cooker and brown:
   1½   lbs. ground beef
   1   teaspoon garlic salt
   ½   teaspoon pepper
3. Then add:
   ½   cup sliced green pepper
   ½   cup celery, well chopped
   2   cups rice, white 15 to 20 minute variety
   1   cup light beer mixed with a beef bouillon cube
4. Simmer for 20 minutes, lid off. Do not let the pan dry out. Add more beer, if necessary, or add an additional ½ cup water and pressure cook for 5 minutes.

The following quick sauces may be served with the braised hamburger:

1. Hot condensed tomato soup with a dash of Worcestershire sauce. Place on table for individual use.
2. ¼ lb. melted butter with ½ cup Parmesan cheese added. Do not cook. Spoon over each serving.

CHILI CON CARNE
Serves Four to Six

1. In a pot, saute until golden:
   1   medium onion
   2   cloves garlic, quartered
2. Add and brown:
   1   lb. ground beef
3. Add and simmer for 45 minutes:
   1   cup canned Italian tomatoes
   2   cups kidney beans, cooked or canned
   ½   teaspoon salt
   1   bay leaf, broken into pieces
   1½   tablespoons chili powder

Serve with crackers. This is one of the few dishes suitable for canned ground beef. Drain it in a colander, then add it with two crumbled beef bouillon cubes, and a pinch of MSG. Simmer for 5 minutes before serving.

HAMBURGER RAREBIT   Serves Four

1. Saute in pressure cooker until meat is gray:
   2   tablespoons butter
   1   lb. ground chuck
   1   cup celery, finely chopped
   1   medium onion, diced
   ½   lb. mushrooms, caps whole, stems chopped
2. Drain off juice; add:
   2   tablespoons butter
   Toss into the meat.
3. Add to pot:
   ½   cup red wine
   1   teaspoon pepper
   1   teaspoon salt
   1   teaspoon Worcestershire sauce
4. Pour over all:
   1   can condensed tomato soup
5. Pressure cook for 5 minutes. Serve over toast.

PIGS IN THE BLANKET—GROUND BEEF IN CABBAGE

Serves Four

1   cup cooked rice
1   lb. ground beef, or 50 % pork or veal
½   medium onion
1   egg
1   teaspoon thyme
1   teaspoon garlic salt
1   teaspoon capers (optional)
2   tablespoons vinegar
2   tablespoons brown sugar
1½   cup catsup
¼   cup water
½   large head cabbage

1. Blanch 1 large cabbage leaf for each "pig."
2. Combine ground beef, onion, beaten egg, thyme, garlic rice salt, capers, vinegar, and brown sugar.
3. Roll into 12 patties.

4. Panbroil over high heat until just brown all over.
5. Add catsup and water to pan; reduce to medium heat.
6. Simmer 20 minutes. Baste occasionally until sauce thickens.
7. Roll each "pig" into a cabbage leaf; pour sauce over all.

PICADILLO   Serves Four

A meat sauce for tacos, rice, or pasta.

 1   lb. ground beef
 1   cup chopped onion
 3   tablespoons oil
 2   tomatoes
 2   tablespoons vinegar
 1   teaspoon sugar
 1   teaspoon cinnamon
 ¼   teaspoon cumin
 1   teaspoon salt
 ½   cup raisins
 ½   cup almond slivers
     pinch cloves
     chili powder to taste

1. Brown meat in oil.
2. Add all ingredients, except almonds; stir.
3. Bring to boil; simmer 30 minutes.
4. Stir in almonds.

BEEF BRAISED IN BEER   Serves Four to Five

1. Brown over high heat in pressure cooker:
   1½ lbs. cubed stew beef, well beaten
    1   teaspoon garlic powder
    2   tablespoons oil
2. When meat is brown, add:
    3   potatoes in walnut-sized pieces
    3   carrots in four slices each
    1   onion, chopped
    1   can beer
    1   bay leaf, crumbled
    4   cloves garlic

1   teaspoon salt
½   teaspoon pepper
1   teaspoon marjoram
1   teaspoon Worcestershire sauce
4. Pressure cook for 8 minutes. Needs no thickening.

BEEF STROGANOFF   Serves Four

Beef Stroganoff is traditionally made from fillet of beef cut into ½-inch slices, pounded until thin, and cut into inch-wide slices. It can also be made from cheaper lean cuts, such as flank steak or stew meat. Slice as for fillet, but pound "con mucho gusto" to tenderize. There are many variations of this fine dish. We have divided our approach into two sections. First, the cooking of the meat, then several versions of the sauce, which is poured over the meat at the last moment. Beef Stroganoff is traditionally served over buttered noodles.

The Meat

1½   lbs. lean beef, or hamburger
2   medium onions, sliced thin
½   teaspoon salt
½   teaspoon thyme
12   large mushrooms, caps whole, stems chopped coarsely
     butter

1. Saute onions in butter until golden.
2. Add beef, mushrooms, and seasonings; saute until meat is browned, being careful not to break the mushrooms.

The Sauce

1   tablespoon flour
3   tablespoons butter
2   beef bouillon cubes dissolved in 1 cup red wine
½   cup sour cream
2 to 3   tablespoons tomato paste
1   teaspoon lemon juice
1   teaspoon sugar

1. Heat butter in small pot; add flour (no lumps). Saute over low heat, stirring often until flour browns. Be careful, don't let it burn. The color of the flour should be golden

brown.
2. Add bouillon cubes and wine; simmer until thickened, about 5 minutes.
3. Add remaining ingredients.

The Sauce, Quick Version

1 can condensed tomato soup
2 beef bouillon cubes dissolved in ¾ cup dry red wine
1½ teaspoons lemon juice
1 teaspoon sugar
Combine and simmer 10 minutes over low heat

Combining the Meat and Sauce

The traditional method is to pour the sauce in with the cooked meat and simmer over low heat for 10 to 15 minutes.

We prefer to place the meat, onions, and mushrooms on the noodles using a slotted spoon, then to pour the sauce over all.

Stroganoff With Ground Chuck

We aren't sure if it's Stroganoff, but it tastes good. Cook meat according to recipe, but pour the sauce on last; don't cook sauce and meat together.

BACHELOR STEW   Serves Two

1 lb. stew meat, cubed
2 boiling potatoes, diced
2 small onions, quartered
1 green pepper, sliced
1 zucchini, ½ inch rounds
1 can (8 oz) Italian tomatoes
1 teaspoon lemon juice
10 fresh mushrooms
½ quart red wine
salt and pepper

Pressure cook above ingredients for 15 minutes. Sprinkle with Parmesan cheese before serving.

castle lookout

BEEF STEW

Serves Six

2 lbs. stew meat, cut into ½ to ¾ cubes and beaten
3 tablespoons vegetable oil
1 tablespoon flour or corn flour
2 cups red wine
2 beef bouillon cubes dissolved in the wine
3 cloves garlic, coarsely chopped
1 large bay leaf, crumbled
1 teaspoon thyme
1 teaspoon salt
½ teaspoon pepper
5 medium carrots, sliced
8 small onions, whole, or 3 medium onions quartered
4 medium potatoes, each in 6 pieces
1 cup canned corn, drained

1. In pressure cooker, brown meat, onions, and potatoes thoroughly in oil.
2. Add remaining ingredients, except flour; pressure cook for 8 minutes after first jiggle.
3. Mix 1 tablespoon flour in a little wine; add to pot. Simmer over low heat until thickened. Correct the seasoning.

Caution! Never open a pressure cooker while steam is coming from the pressure hole. Serious injury can result.

BRITTANY TRAWLER HASH

We made the Portimao, Portugal, breakwater late one night just wishing to give peace a chance. It had been one of those long, miserable days full of squalls, head winds at deadly Cape Vincente, broken halyards in the night, and an engine that ran more at its choosing than ours. We had looked hopefully at the little cove just around the corner; but the waves at the mouth were breaking heavily against the sheer rock cliffs sending spray high into the air with a dull, booming sound. We were afraid, but we pressed on. The spare jib halyard, in some horrendous way, held up a reefed mainsail, while the engine made uncertain, gasping sounds as it searched hungrily ahead in the darkness for the feeble Portimao breakwater light. We mistook some street lights for the breakwater, but realized our mistake, at the last moment, when the sounding lead showed shoal water. We finally found the light and the breakwater range markers. As we slipped through the surf-wracked, breaking inlet, we suddenly found ourselves in a calm pool of perfect silence, broken only occasionally by the hiss of a wave as it sluiced over the low sea wall. Never was an anchor more gratefully lowered, taking our burden of fear with it as it slipped into the depths.

We slept the sleep of the grateful alive, but the instincts of the sea prevailed. Awakening at first light with a feeling that the tide had turned, I peered out the companionway to be sure that all was well. A fishing boat had moved into the anchorage nearby. When the tide had swung us, he had moved into an upwind position. What lovely smells came from the galley! Mixed with the spice smell of the sea and the first cries of early gulls was an irresistible aroma. Seizing a bottle of wine (knowing that fishermen will drink wine at any hour), I jumped into the dingy and rowed over to find out what was in the pot.

Sitting around the main hatch were six hungry fishermen, indifferently clad against the chill morning air, smoking their roughly rolled cigarettes, and drinking coffee from old cans. They were a tired and unshaven crew; their cuts were wrapped with pieces of rag, their hip boots roughly rolled and patched. They thought the wine was just fine. The galley competed for space in the wheel house with the steering assembly and the skipper's birth. It consisted, in fact, of a two-burner propane range and a big pot that was used as a sink.

The cook, Charlie, was an Englishman who had lived most of his life in Portugal, and owned a share of the boat. He gave me these recipes for Trawler Hash, a one-burner dish hefty enough to feed seven hungry fishermen, who had nothing to eat for their long night's work but a slice of bread with tomato paste and anchovies, and a big bowl of coffee. We have reduced the ingredients, which orginally called for 10 potatoes, to feed four hungry sailors.

BRITTANY TRAWLER HASH   Serves Four

1 lb. canned corn beef, coarsely diced
3 large potatoes, diced into ½-inch cubes
1 large onion, diced
1 clove garlic, well minced
½ teaspoon celery salt
1 teaspoon Worchestershire sauce
4 tablespoons butter or oil

1. Boil potatoes in salt water until firm; drain thoroughly.
2. Saute butter, garlic and onions until golden, turning often; add to potatoes.
3. Remove ⅔ of mixture from pot; cover remainder with a layer of corn beef. Sprinkle with ¼ teaspoon celery salt and ½ teaspoon Worchestershire sauce.
4. Repeat with another layer of potatoes and beef.
5. Cook over low heat, stirring lightly. If hash seems too dry, add a little red wine, beef stock, or water (½ to ⅔ cup. Serve when hash is piping hot.

Most everyone enjoys a fried egg or two on top of their hash. With a slice or two of bread, and a good mug of coffee, you have a meal that keeps the cold out for the whole day. If the eggs are not your style, try a generous covering of mild, soft cheese, lightly browned in the oven. It's much easier than eggs, especially when the seas are rough, and is quite good.

BRITTANY TRAWLER HASH PATTIES   Serves Four

> 1   lb. corn beef
> 2   large potatoes, grated
> ½   onion, finely chopped
> 8   slices bacon
> 2   tablespoons horseradish powder
> 1   teaspoon thyme

1. Fry bacon and set aside, reserving drippings.
2. Boil potatoes until firm; drain thoroughly.
3. Add onions and 4 teaspoons bacon drippings.
4. Saute over low heat until onions are clear.
5. Combine and mix thoroughly all remaining ingredients, except bacon and remaining drippings.
6. Form mixture into 8 patties. Dust with flour; saute until lightly brown in bacon drippings.
7. Drain; top with a slice of bacon.

A can of cream of mushroom soup, thinned with a little water, and seasoned with pepper and paprika, makes a fine sauce. Serve hash patties with hot apple sauce flavored with a touch of honey and cinnamon.

YACHT CORINA EASY HASH   Serves Four

> 1½ lbs. canned corn beef
> 1   can beef soup
> 1   large onion, diced
> 2   large potatoes, diced ½-inch square
>   salt and pepper to taste

1. Make layers of beef, potatoes, and onion in a casserole.
2. Heat beef soup, thinned with water to consistency of light gravy.
3. Pour gravy over casserole ingredients; cook in hot oven for ¾ hour. If casserole becomes dry, add a little water.
4. Serve with buttered carrots or hot apple sauce.

SAILOR'S MASH   Serves Three or Four

This pressure cooker meal is quite tasty foul weather fare. Since it cooks down to the consistency of lumpy mashed potatoes, it sticks to the plate as well as the ribs. It stays hot when the day is cold, and tastes better with some salt spray on it.

1   lb. stewing beef, diced not more than ½-inch
    square
8   slices bacon
2   medium onions, well chopped
1   teaspoon each: dill, sage, salt, thyme
½   teaspoon peppercorns, crushed
½   teaspoon fennel, crushed
1   bay leaf
1½ cups water
3   potatoes, well chopped
4   carrots, sliced

1. Fry bacon in pressure cooker, lid off.
2. Remove and reserve bacon.
3. Add onions and meat; fry until meat browns.
4. Add remaining ingredients on top of meat, including the
   bacon, crumbled.
5. Pressure cook for 8 minutes after first jiggle.
6. Stir together and serve.

If it's cold as well as foul, Sailor's Mash goes well with hot grog:

¾   cup strong tea
¼   cup rum
1 to 2   teaspoons brown sugar
       a dot of butter

STEAK

If properly chosen, steak is one of the most popular dinner
treats. We say properly chosen because nothing is less popular
than a tough, dry, or stringy cut; there is no simple way to
salvage such meat after it has been cooked. U.S. meats are
graded, making the consumer's choice easier. But most other
countries do not have such rigid standards. This does not mean
that their meat is of poor quality. It just means that the consumer
must know what to look for when purchasing steak. The best
cuts of steak have plenty of fat everywhere, which makes the
meat taste succulent.

TENDERIZING

It is better to avoid pre-tenderized meats, which contain
questionable substances, and tenderize cheaper steaks
yourself. We have found no better way of doing this than to

pound the meat lustily on both sides for a few minutes with the edge of a winch handle. Garlic, salt, and pepper may be sprinkled on before the pounding begins, forcing these fine flavors into the meat. Pounding has a tendency to flatten and stretch meat just as though you were pounding a piece of clay. If the meat you plan to buy is of questionable tenderness, buy the thickest cut available, and pound it until thin.

Another age-old method of tenderizing meat is to dust it with a commercial tenderizer containing papain, a derivative of the papaya plant. The usual quantity is 1 teaspoon per pound of meat. While we admit that this procedure is much easier on the cook's muscles than pounding, the papain imparts a flabby, vaguely suspicious texture to the meat that we find unappetizing.

CORRECTING EXCESSIVE LEANNESS

If a steak has good texture, but is excessively lean, there are several methods to correct this deficiency and insure a juicy steak. The Europeans, particularly the French, lard meat with a larding needle. The larding needle is used to force precut, drinking straw-sized strips of fat into the meat, thus adding what nature failed to produce. The fat used is usually salt pork, enhanced with garlic and fine herbs. If you are armed with a larding needle and a block of salt pork, by all means, use them. If not, try this other technique.

Cut the fatty part of some bacon into strips about ½ inch longer than the thickness of the meat, about 2 slices per steak. Punch holes in the meat with a marlin spike, then force the bacon through the cuts with something blunt; a bolt works well. Hold the bacon when it emerges from the other side of the meat, and pull out the bolt. An additional strip or two of bacon may be wound around the outside of the cut, and held in place with toothpicks.

STORAGE WITHOUT REFRIGERATION

Steaks may be lightly seared on both sides to kill surface bacteria, painted heavily with a molasses-like mixture of vegetable oil and salt, then wrapped in clean cloth and stored in a wooden box surrounded on all sides by salt. The vegetable oil tends to reduce the juice loss, which makes the meat hard and dry. Prepared in this way, meat will last at least three weeks (by our own test). We have heard of meat successfully preserved for months. But, never try this technique on ground meat. It doesn't work.

A second method, successfully preserving the meat for about a week, is to sear it in 3 to 4 tablespoons oil, coat it with pepper, and hang it inside a paper bag, being sure the meat does not touch the sides of the bag. The steak is then scrubbed before used to rid it of excess pepper. In cool, nothern climates, such preserving will be effective for months. When handling the seared meat, be sure your hands are surgically clean, and scald the plate that is used. Preserved meat that is free from mold and a foul smell is prefectly good to eat.

CHOOSING CUTS

The following steaks are the most tender and taste best when broiled or pan broiled: tenderloins or fillets, strip sirloin, sirloin, porterhouse, and T-bone.

These cuts are often tough, but frequently of good flavor: cube steak, club steak, and rib steak.

Flank steak and London broil are very lean cuts. They can be very good if cooked rare or medium rare over high heat for 3 to 5 minutes per side. Longer or slower cooking, medium or well-done, results in a tough, dry steak.

Swiss steak, usually round steak, is tough and does not broil well, but it has excellent flavor. It should be pounded then braised; it responds well to this slow cooking technique.

Chopped steak can be delicious broiled or pan broiled, but we suggest that you buy the meat unground and watch it go into the grinder. Be sure to have the butcher weigh the meat after it comes out of the grinder; what goes in is often not what comes out.

PAN BROILING

Broiling means to cook by direct heat, so it is really impossible to pan broil meat. But frying is cooking in oil and that is exactly what you don't want. So pan frying is a bad term for meat and should be avoided. A properly pan-broiled steak is just as tasty as an oven-broiled one.

Searing

Searing seals in tasty juices and gives the meat its pleasing brown color. Use a fry pan with a lid; use the lid only during the brief searing process to contain spatters. If the lid is left on during cooking, the meat will be stewed instead of pan broiled.

1. Wipe fry pan with a little vegetable oil. Bring to high heat until oil is on the verge of smoking.
2. Slip in meat; instantly cover it.
3. Cook for 30 seconds or more, each side; ignore smoke and commotion in pan.

Cooking

1. After meat is seared, remove pan from flame; pour off any excess juices. Examine pan and remove any burn marks since they give the cooking juices a bad taste.
2. Cook over medium-low heat for 2 minutes per side, turning several times until correct cooking is achieved, usually 6 to 8 minutes. Pour off excess liquid frequently; save in a small cup, spoon off fat, and pour over meat when served. As steak is cooking, cut it open in the center to at least half the thickness of the meat; check cut frequently for desired doneness.
3. Sprinkle with pepper and salt, or garlic salt.

SALVAGING A MISERABLE STEAK

As we mentioned before, once a steak has been ruined—too dry or too tough to be palatable—there is no real cure for it as a steak. But the meat mixed with half-cooked bacon can be ground the next day, and made into seasoned sausage patties. This sausage recipe adds missing fat, breaks down tough fiber, and adds a seasoning that will somewhat conceal the taste of the previously cooked meat. There is another secret, this one psychological: don't tell the crew they are eating last night's miserable steak until after they tell you how much they like the sausages.

MACHIAVELLI MISERABLE STEAK SAUSAGES
Makes 12 Medium Patties

1. Combine thoroughly:
   1 lb. miserable, cooked steak, ground as fine as possible
   ½ lb. bacon, cooked until fat is clear, then ground fine
   ½ teaspoon marjoram
   ½ teaspoon sage
   ½ teaspoon thyme

½   teaspoon savory
1   teaspoon pepper
¼   teaspoon grated nutmeg (optional)
2. Now comes the delicate part. If the steak was dry, the bacon may or may not add sufficient fat. The combined ingredients above should look as fatty as fat hamburger meat. If they do not, add a bit of bacon fat, not more than ¼ cup. Combine thoroughly.
3. Form mixture into 12 patties.
4. Pan fry in bacon fat over medium heat for 3 to 5 minutes. If the crew asks the name of this dish, just tell them "Sausage Machiavelli."

PORK

Domestic pork is usually of good quality; we have never had any that was truly bad. Since pork is not graded, selection must be made according to the cut. Pork is very fatty and never needs larding or basting, yet it can be cooked until it is insufferably dry. In order to kill the several pork parasites harmful to man, pork is always cooked until the juice runs clear, without any trace of blood, when the meat is pricked. Don't cook pork until it is stringy and dry; it is totally unnecessary, and ruins the taste. When cooking raw pork, including fresh ham, just be sure the juice is clear and the meat is white, with no traces of pink. Processed ham, not fresh ham, cooks to a bright pink, the juice clear. The meat should steam when sliced.

Fresh pork is extremely perishable, and should be eaten within 24 hours, if unrefrigerated. Bacon, which is naturally salty, may be salted further, wrapped in a clean cloth, and stored in a cool place. It will last for several months this way. Country ham, which is aged for at least two years, does not contain live parasites. Aged ham, such as Spanish ham or Italian Proseiutto are similarly safe; they can be eaten without any cooking, and need no refrigeration, just coolness.

Pork does not respond well to pressure cooking; it gets very dry. Baked pork recipes usually take a rather long time, and the crew does get very tired of fried pork chops. For these reasons, we prefer Chinese fried pork cookery. This technique fries small pieces of pork in a scant amount of hot oil for not more than 4 minutes. The wok is the pan of choice, but is certainly not necessary.

TRES REYES MEXICAN PORK CHOPS

Serves Four

- **4** pork chops, center cut preferred
- **½** teaspoon chili powder
- **5** tablespoons salad oil
- **2 to 3** teaspoons bacon fat
- **2** cloves garlic
- **1** cup onion, chopped
- **8** sausages
- **1** can (16 oz.) tomato sauce
- **1** can condensed beef consomme
- **1** sliced green pepper

1. Sprinkle chili powder on pork chops and brown in bacon drippings; remove from pan.
2. Add to pan remaining ingredients; simmer 5 minutes.
3. Add chops; simmer for 30 to 40 minutes covered.

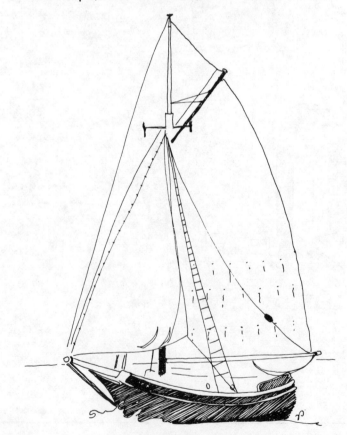

the "spray"

SEVERAL VARIATIONS FOR CANNED HAM

This is one of the very few whole meat products that is delicious canned, and easy to prepare in a variety of ways. We stock plenty of canned ham, and eat it several times a week on a deep water cruise. There are many sauces that garnish and enhance ham's taste; you probably have your own favorites. These are merely suggestions.

Without an oven, baked ham is made in foil that is set on a trivet in a fry pan, then covered and cooked over medium heat for 20 minutes. The surface of the ham is traditionally studded with cloves. Any one of the follow glazes adds variety:

Cover the top with mustard; spoon orange marmalade over all.

Cover with a mixture of raisins, honey, and cinnamon.

Cover with a mixture of canned, crushed pineapple, honey, and lemon juice.

Cover with cranberry sauce and raisins.

Cover with canned peaches, drained, chopped, and fried with raisins in butter.

BEANS 'N BACON DINNER   Serves Three or Four

One-pot blue-water meal

1. In large pot, fry until bacon is done:

    ½ to ¾ lb. bacon, chopped into bite sizes
    1 small onion, chopped

    When bacon is just brown, drain half the fat.
2. Add to pot:

    1 cup corn, cooked or canned
    1 cup navy beans, cooked or canned
    1 cup tomatoes, canned, with excess liquid poured off
    ½ teaspoon paprika
    ½ teaspoon brown sugar
    1 teaspoon chili powder
3. Simmer 5 minutes, stirring occasionally. Stir in:

    ½ cup catsup (optional)

PORK CHOPS IN SAUERKRAUT   Serves Four

This one-pot meal takes less than 20 minutes.

8 pork chops, center cut
4 teaspoons bacon fat

2 potatoes, quartered lengthwise
3 carrots, whole but peeled
1 lb. sauerkraut
½ teaspoon caraway seed
1½ oz. brandy
   salt
   sage (optional)
   pepper

1. Dust chops with flour; brown in bacon fat for 6 minutes, each side, or until juice runs clear when meat is pricked.
2. While meat browns, peel and par-boil potatoes and carrots for 3 minutes.
3. Remove chops from pan; deglaze pan with some of the kraut juice. Sprinkle chops with sage, if desired.
4. Add kraut; toss with caraway seed.
5. Add cooked chops like slices of bread, with a whole carrot or piece of potato between each slice.
6. Pour a good shot of brandy over all; steam for 10 minutes. Salt and pepper to taste.

SWEET AND SOUR PORK—CHINESE STYLE   Serves Four

In this traditional Cantonese recipe, crispy fried pork is covered with a rich sweet and sour sauce. The sauce can be made in advance, and will keep without refrigeration for months. This recipe makes more than twice the volume necessary for sweet and sour pork. Try the sauce with pork ribs, page 258, with salt cod, page 211.

Cantonese Sweet and Sour Sauce
> 1   cup white vinegar
> 1   cup sugar
> ½   cup orange juice
> ½   cup pineapple juice
> 1½   tablespoons salt
> ½   cup tomato paste
>   corn flour

1. Combine all ingredients, except corn flour; simmer 10 minutes.
2. Add corn flour slowly; thicken to consistency of honey.
3. Add more sugar or vinegar to balance the taste as desired. While still hot, pour into a jar; keep lid loose to allow gas to escape. Store in a dark and cool place; it will last months.

The Pork
Any lean cut of pork may be used, except bacon or processed ham.

1. Cut into bite-sized cubes:
> 1½   lbs. lean pork
2. Sprinkle with:
> 4   teaspoons light soy sauce.
3. Shake in:
> seasoned flour.
4. In a plastic bag put:
> 4   egg yolks.
Add pork and shake.
5. Put pork back into the flour and reshake.
6. Fry until brown, not more than 3 minutes, in:
> 1 to 2   tablespoons very hot oil
7. Add to pan and cook over high heat for 1 minute:
> 2   onions, coarsely chopped
> 2   green peppers, sliced (optional)

8. Add to pot and cook for 30 seconds over high heat:
   2   tomatoes, chopped large
   1   cup crushed pineapple, canned
   1   cup sweet and sour sauce
Serve with rice.

SWEET AND SOUR PORK RIBS—SHANGHAI STYLE
Serves Two Per Pound

1. Cut ribs apart, allowing ½ to ¾ pound per person.
2. Dust the ribs in:
   Flour
3. Fry until brown in:
   1   tablespoon very hot oil
4. Remove ribs from pan; add to pan:
   ¾ to 1   cup sweet and sour sauce
5. Bring to fast simmer; add browned ribs.
6. Simmer for 1 minute over high heat; serve with rice.

CHINESE FRIED PORK WITH MUSHROOMS   Serves Four

Fresh mushrooms do well here, but the Chinese are particularly fond of dried, reconstituted mushrooms; the original version of this recipe specified them. To reconstitute dried mushrooms, soak them in warm water, then proceed as with fresh.

1½ lbs. lean pork, sliced into bite-sized pieces about ⅛ to ¼-inch thick
3   cups celery, leaves and stalks, well chopped
1 to 1½   cups fresh or reconstituted mushrooms, large
½   cup red wine
½   teaspoon sugar
soy sauce
corn flour
salt and pepper
vegetable oil

1. Toss sliced mushrooms with:
   2   teaspoons soy sauce
   ½   teaspoon sugar
2. Add to large pan:
   1   tablespoon oil
Add the mushrooms; bring to high heat.

3. Saute for 3 minutes, stirring constantly.
4. Add the celery and:
   3 tablespoons water.
   Cook until water is gone.
5. Remove and reserve the contents of pan. Add:
   1 tablespoon oil
   Add pork; bring to high heat.
6. Brown pork all over; add cooked mushrooms and celery. Saute for another minute, tossing constantly.
7. Mix red wine with:
   1 teaspoon corn flour
   Pour over all. Cook about a minute until sauce thickens, tossing constantly.

SHANGHAI PORK WITH (TURNIPS) VEGETABLES
Serves Three or Four

Vegetables, such as carrots, green beans, broccoli, peas, any or all, may be substituted for turnips. But if mixed, start long-cooking vegetables first.

1 lb. lean pork, sliced thin and cut into bite size
1 lb. turnips (about 4 medium), peeled and sliced thin
1 teaspoon garlic salt
1 tablespoon soy sauce
½ teaspoon sugar
2 tablespoons vegetable oil

1. Add 1 tablespoon oil to fry pan; bring to high heat.
2. Add all ingredients, except pork; cook until turnips are almost soft.
3. Remove turnips. Add 1 tablespoon oil; brown pork all over using high heat and stirring frequently.
4. Add turnips; cook, tossing constantly, until turnips are soft.

CUBAN PORK SAUTE WITH BLACK BEANS AND YELLOW RICE
Serves Three or Four
1. Mix and let stand, unrefrigerated, overnight:
   ¼ cup vegetable oil
   4 cloves garlic, minced
   1 tablespoon Worchestershire sauce
   1 teaspoon thyme
   ½ teaspoon sage

The ingredients settle to the bottom; do not shake before use.

2. Add **3 tablespoons of seasoned oil** to pan and:

   1 lb. lean pork ¼″ thick and about silver dollar size
   1 onion, sliced
   1 bay leaf, broken into pieces

3. Cook over high heat for 6 minutes or until browned. Season with salt and pepper. Serve with black beans and yellow rice, page 105.

COUNTRY STYLE PORK RIBS — Serves Two Per Pound

This is a good recipe for fatty pork ribs.

1. Cut ribs into lots of four, then cut between each rib right up to the head, leaving them attached by gristle at the top.
2. Parboil ribs for 10 minutes in enough water to cover.
3. Turn off flame; let fat accumulate on top, then pour off all liquid.
4. Add fresh water to cover; then add

   1 onion, chopped
   1 cup celery
   3 carrots, sliced
   peppercorns and salt

5. Simmer for 1½ hours until tender. Serve with sauerkraut or red cabbage.

PAN BROILED PORK BARBECUE — Serves Two Per Pound

1. Cut pork ribs as for previous recipe.
2. Brown each set of ribs thoroughly in a little oil. Cook for not less than 8 to 10 minutes per set.
3. Make a barbecue sauce, page 413, and add:

   ½ cup water per cup of sauce

4. Stack the ribs sideways in the pan and pour over all at least:

   2 cups barbeque sauce

5. Simmer over medium heat for 45 minutes, or until tender; baste occasionally with sauce.
6. When ribs are almost done, stop basting with pan sauce that has become very oily. Use fresh sauce, and have a little more hot on the stove to serve at the table.

A DELIGHTFUL LAMB STEW FROM BELGIUM   Serves Six

Our good friend, Francoise Henkart, from the yacht Hendriette, made this very outstanding lamb stew large enough to feed six. The other two guests never showed up, and it was just as well. The meal was so delicious the four of us finished every last lick.

1. In large pot, melt:
   - **1 tablespoon oil**
   - **1 tablespoon butter**
2. Add to pot:
   - **4 slices bacon, chopped**
   - **4 onions, chopped**
   - **1 small bulb of garlic, peeled and chopped coarsely**
3. When onions are brown, remove contents of pot with slotted spoon. Cook in oil:
   - **2 lbs. cut up lamb**
4. When lamb is browned all over, add onion mixture.
5. Season with:
   - **1 teaspoon thyme**
   - **1 teaspoon marjoram**
   - **1 teaspoon savory**
   - **1 teaspoon salt**
   - **1 teaspoon pepper**
6. Put on top of all:
   - **⅓ cup water**
   - **4 apples, peeled and chopped**
   - **1 cup canned Italian tomatoes, or 4 fresh peeled**
   - **¾ cup plain yogurt on the very top**
7. Bring to boil; reduce flame to low and simmer for 1 hour.
8. Add:
   - **2 tablespoons curry powder**

Simmer 5 minutes. Serve with rice cooked with raisins.

VEAL

Veal is meat from a young calf, theoretically still milk fed. It is very tender, lean meat, pale in color. It can get amazingly tough and dry if it is overcooked. Since veal is considered done when it is white inside, judging its doneness is a bit tricky. We usually fall back on an old trick, flouring the meat and sauteing

shearwater

until the flour is golden brown. The flour color indicates that the meat is done. The most common cuts of veal are cutlets and chops, though, of course, veal comes in as many cuts as beef. Cutlets are the leg muscles cut against the grain. Thin, lean cutlets, free of fat are called scallops, as in scallopini. Slices about ½ to ¾-inch thick, from the thigh are called cutlets; those from the lower leg are called shank cuts. Chops are upper rib cuts.

Veal is usually quite tender and does not need to be pounded. But several of the recipes in this book call for "thin scallops," which means about ⅛ inch-thick. If your cuts are much thicker, the veal may be pounded thin with the flat of a knife or cleaver, or the edge of a sturdy plate.

If you suspect your veal is from a mature animal, soak it overnight in milk. This helps restore the subtle, delicate flavor.

VEAL PARMIGIANA   Serves Four

The beauty of this dish is that the tomato sauce can be made in advance, and the veal breaded and set aside, both ready for last moment cookery.

The Meat

1. Cut into pieces about 2-in. × 3-in. × ⅛-in.:
   - **1½ lbs veal scallops**
2. Dip veal in milk; firmly press each side into mixture of:
   - **¾   cup bread or cracker crumbs**
   - **¼   cup grated Parmesan cheese**
   - **1   teaspoon salt**
   - **½   teaspoon pepper**
   - **½   teaspoon savory**
3. Saute in butter until golden brown. Do not let pan dry out; add more butter, as necessary. Handle delicately to avoid damaging the crust.

The Sauce

1. In another pot, combine and simmer for 15 minutes:
   - **1½ cups tomato sauce**
   - **3   tablespoons red wine**
   - **1   teaspoon lemon juice**
   - **1½ teaspoons sugar**
   - **1   teaspoon thyme**
   - **1   teaspoon oregano**
   - **1   teaspoon garlic salt**
2. Put veal on a bed of noodles or rice; pour sauce over all. Sprinkle with grated Parmesan cheese to taste. Serve with a green vegetable.

FIRST OFFICER'S VEAL MARSALA   Serves Four

- **1½ lbs. veal scallops, thinly sliced and cut into half-dollar size**
- **1   cup seasoned flour (with 1 teaspoon each: salt and pepper)**
- **3   tablespoons butter**
- **¾   cup Marsala wine, Madeira, or sweet, dark vermouth (we prefer Cinzano)**
- **4   tablespoons lemon juice**
- **½   teaspoon sugar**

corfu convent

1. Shake veal in seasoned flour.
2. Saute in butter until golden, about 4 minutes.
3. Add Marsala wine or Cinzano; simmer until wine thickens, about 3 minutes. Serve over rice or noodles. Absolutely delicious!

OSSO BUCO   Serves Four

Osso Buco is made from small sections of veal shin. The bone is always left in for the little plug of marrow. Young veal, identified by the thin ring of bone and absence of heavy fat, is best for this dish. Osso Buco is a classic recipe that takes hours to prepare in the normal way. But we have created this pressure cooker version; the result of many attempts, each a small improvement over the one before.

2 lbs. veal shin cut into sections 1½-inch long
1 small onion, chopped
3 tablespoons olive oil
1 chicken bouillon cube, crumbled
4 tomatoes, peeled, seeded, and chopped, or 1 cup Italian tomatoes, drained and chopped
3 cloves garlic, chopped
1 teaspoon lemon rind, grated
1 cup dry white wine
flour, salt, pepper

1. Dip veal in seasoned flour; brown in olive oil, using pressure cooker pot.
2. Add onion and saute until golden.
3. Add tomatoes, garlic, chopped lemon rind, and wine.
4. Pressure cook for 15 minutes. Serve over rice or noodles.

HEARTY VEAL STEW   Serves Four

1½ lbs. veal shank, cut in 2-inch long pieces, or veal shoulder cut into golf ball-sized pieces
2 cups water
3 chicken bouillon cubes, dissolved in water
1 cup dry white wine
12 small white onions
4 cloves
2 cups mushrooms, caps whole, stems chopped
3 carrots, large slices

        3   potatoes, diced
        1   teaspoon marjoram
        1   teaspoon thyme
        1   teaspoon salt
        1   bay leaf
        1   teaspoon celery salt
        1   teaspoon pepper

   1. Parboil veal in pressure cooker pot for 5 minutes; discard water.
   2. Add to pot all other ingredients; pressure cook for 15 minutes.
   3. Add more salt and pepper, and a few drops of lemon juice, as desired. Very good with black bread and cheese.

VEAL CUTLET SCALLOPINI   Serves Two
   1. Coat in seasoned flour:
        4   thin veal cutlets
   2. Saute in butter for 3 minutes on each side, or until the flour is nicely browned. Use at least:
        ½   cup of butter
   Add more to prevent drying out.
   3. Remove veal when browned; add to pan:
        ½   cup chicken bouillon
        ½   cup sweet, white wine, such as vermouth or Marsala
   4. Stir with the drippings; thicken by adding:
        1   teaspoon flour dissolved in ¼ cup water.
   Pour sauce over veal and serve.

SALAMI
   Salami is of particular interest to the yachtsman since it lasts for a long time without refrigeration. There are several different kinds of salami, all of them quite expensive, often equivalent in price to steak. We find it worth the extra expense, not only for flavor, but also for convenience. There are a number of reasons why salami lasts so long. First, it is cooked meat that is inserted into a protective jacket while still hot. Second, it is very oily, and the oil acts as a preservative. Finally, salami meat is often smoked, and frequently a preservative is added, usually sodium benzoate.

All of these factors contribute to a long shelf life, measured in terms of months, or a year. But salami cannot be treated with the same indifference as canned meat. It should be turned occasionally to prevent the oil from settling out, and examined for mold. Long storage suggestions are found on page 24.
Salami may be used as follows:

Sliced thin and fried; it is a good substitute for bacon, either in sandwiches or with eggs.

Diced salami in split pea, lentil, barley, or black bean soup is great.

Small cubes of salami go very well with macaroni and cheese.

Salami dices added to Spanish rice enhance its flavor.

A piece of salami makes fantastic crab or lobster trap bait.

STIR FRIED BEEF AND PEAS IN SOY SAUCE

1. Saute two large chopped onions in a little oil until the onions are brown.
2. Add a tablespoon of oil to the pan and bring to high heat.
3. Add 1 pound lean beef chunks and stir fry until the meat is browned. Pour off pan juices as they accumulate to avoid stewing the meat.
4. Add to the pan:
   1 cup peas
   ½ cup diced carrots or other vegetable
5. Make 1 cup of the following:
   ¼ cup soy sauce
   ½ lemon (juice only)
   ½ teaspoon sugar, salt, pepper
   5 cloves garlic, chopped
   1 tablespoon cornstarch
   beer to fill cup
6. Stir out the cornstarch lumps and pour over the meat. Stir until the sauce thickens.

14
chicken and
other birds

The Bermuda petrel may fly far out to sea, the Canadian goose may span continents, but to view a really well traveled bird—behold the chicken! It seems to exist everywhere, from Godthaab's snug harbor in Greenland to Navarino Island off Tierra del Fuego. No matter how small the port, or how primitive the people, chickens are permanent residents. It holds undisputed first place as available domestic protein; and, if selected and dressed properly, it will delight your palate when prepared in any one of a thousand ways.

Not only are chickens well traveled, they are also good, if reluctant, travelers. Several may be confined to a cage, just large enough to hold them. They will live in such confined quarters, if fed and given water, for an indefinite period; no maintenance is required if the cage is lashed over the stern. Covered with a canvas during bad weather, they usually survive, if not in high style, at least well enough to brighten the middle of a long ocean passage with their presence at the table.

We think of chicken as an artist regards a blank canvas, so reponsive is the bird to the efforts of the cruising chef. Chicken responds delightfully to wine, fine herbs, garlic, and curry. It is a succulent delight with tomatoes, canned or fresh, potatoes, onions, carrots, squash, peppers, eggplant, and turnips. It may be fried, baked, roasted, boiled, broiled, or poached, depending, of course, upon the tenderness of the bird. It responds so well to pan cookery that we have not even bothered to include any of the many excellent roasting or baking recipes.

BEST BUYS

If you are buying a chicken for a single meal, it is probably cheaper to buy chicken legs, thighs, and breasts, rather than a whole bird. But if you have a large crew, and room in the refrigerator, it almost always pays to buy a number of them whole. The pieces that are wasted when cooking one bird are useful in quantity. These include pelvises, necks, feet, hearts, giblets, and gizzards; all make a fine soup. The pelvis, which seems useless, has a surprisingly large amount of meat on it; after stewing, the meat may be picked off and used for soup or salad. Chicken livers, in quantity, make a lovely pate, an excellent gravy, or a fine entree.

SHELF LIFE OF A DEAD BIRD

There is no way that we know to keep an uncooked, unrefrigerated chicken for more than 24 hours; in many cases, even this is too long. Frozen chicken seems immortal if kept frozen and never refrozen. Cooked chicken can last for about 4 days, unrefrigerated, if it is heated to a simmer about every 12 hours; this process kills any bacteria that have formed. For example, if you prepare a lot of chicken for lunch and want to serve it tomorrow for lunch, leave it on the stove, lid on, then reheat it at dinner time; do not open it until the next day. Before serving again, heat and let simmer for a few minutes, making sure the chicken is steaming hot.

plucked chicken

STORAGE OF CHICKEN UNDER REFRIGERATION

The bird should be removed from its wrapping and wiped, inside and out, with a clean, damp cloth. The cavity should be examined for pieces of viscera that may still be attached. The entrails should be washed, and the liver separated from the rest. The liver should be examined, and the gall bladder, a small greenish sack attached by a yellow cord to the liver, should be carefully removed. It is better to cut off a little of the liver itself, rather than risk breaking the gall bladder, whose fluid makes bitter all that it touches. The bird should not be skinned or cut up until ready for use. We find that fresh chicken will last two or three days if kept wrapped in plastic, and at a temperature below 40°F.

FREEZING A FRESH CHICKEN

Clean a chicken that is definitely fresh. Never use the original wrapper or tray for freezing; always use clean freezer paper, plastic pags, or aluminum foil. Examine the body cavity to be sure that entrails and lumps of fat are removed; the fat flavors the meat, if frozen for long periods. Be sure the carcass is dry before freezing; this prevents the formation of ice crystals. If you have a freezer large enough to store several chickens, you may want to first cook them before freezing. Prepared chicken holds up quite well when frozen, and has several advantages beyond the thaw, heat, and eat syndrome. The dish can be made at the dock where conditions are ideal and fresh ingredients available, then served as a treat when fresh stores are low.

CANNED CHICKEN

Canned chicken is sold either skinned, boned, and packed solid in the can, or cooked whole in its own juices and water, then canned. Regardless of the process, the poor bird has been thoroughly cooked, and we find most of the flavor in the broth. The last thing this meat needs is further cooking. A pinch of monosodium glutamate (MSG) may help a bit, but the packer usually adds as much as necessary when the bird is canned; check the contents before adding it. The goal with canned chicken is to get some flavor back into the meat without further cooking. This can usually be accomplished by making the recipes in this chapter, which all call for stewing or sauteing, but delaying the addition of the canned meat until the last minute. At least two chicken bouillon cubes should be added to the wine or

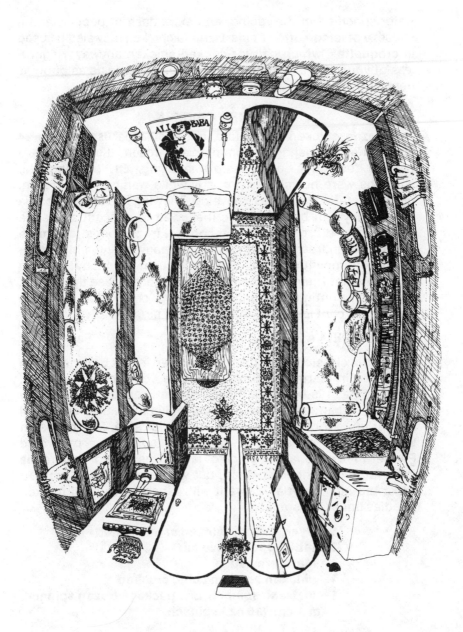

"barcarolle" salon

water specified in the recipe; and extra dash of pepper, and a squeeze of lemon often helps. Canned chicken may also be used in croquettes, which call for cooked chicken anyway. Regardless of your efforts, canned chicken will never taste as good as fresh or frozen chicken.

FROZEN CHICKEN

Frozen chicken tastes fine, but should be used within 24 hours after defrosting. If commercially frozen, there may have been a few days' delay before freezing. Or, perhaps, the chickens were not chilled properly while waiting to be frozen, giving bacteria a chance to develop. Thawing lets these bacteria loose. They can become toxic if allowed to concentrate; eat a defrosted bird promptly. When cooked, frozen birds lose more moisture than fresh. Freezing ruptures many cell membranes resulting in moisture loss, and, unfortunately, many chicken farmers water their birds before freezing to increase the weight. If you are counting the ounces for a large crew, allow at least a 10 to 15 percent loss of weight for frozen birds.

CHICKEN DELLA FLORENTINE   Serves Four

In this classic Italian dish, the chicken is first browned, then simmered in marinara sauce, and served on a bed of spinach. Fresh spinach is best, but frozen, or even canned spinach may be used. If canned spinach is your only alternative, drain and heat it in a pot with a little lemon juice, a few drops of Worchestershire sauce, a generous tablespoon of grated Parmesan cheese, and a pinch of MSG. This will not restore the food value of canned spinach, but will help the lost flavor. To make the dish heartier, serve it with a healthy layer of cooked noodles under the spinach.

        1   fryer, cut up, skinned or unskinned
        3   tablespoons olive oil
            Marinara sauce
        1   chicken bouillon cube, crushed
        1   lb. fresh spinach, or 1 package frozen spinach,
            or 1 can (16 oz.) spinach

   1. In three tablespoons olive oil, brown fryer.
   2. Make a marinara sauce, page 410; when sauce is simmering, add bouillon cube.
   3. Pour sauce over chicken; simmer, lid off, for 35 minutes.

4. While chicken is cooking, prepare spinach. If fresh, swish it thoroughly in sea, to remove grit. Break up leaves a bit; steam in pot with ½ cup water for 5 minutes, or until just tender. If spinach is frozen, follow the instructions; but be sure it is thoroughly drained before serving. If canned spinach is used, follow the suggestions above.
5. When chicken is tender, make a bed of noodles, if desired; then add spinach, butter, salt, and pepper. Finally, add chicken, pouring sauce over all. Delicioso!

CHICKEN FRIED IN ONIONS   Serves Four

1. In large fry pan melt:
   4 to 6   tablespoons butter
   Saute until translucent:
   1   large onion, diced
2. Add:
   1   fryer, cut up, unskinned
   1   teaspoon salt
   6   peppercorns, coarsely crushed
   ½   teaspoon paprika
3. Saute over low heat, lid off, turning occasionally until bird is brown. Then add:
   2 to 3   tablespoons lemon juice
4. Cover and simmer for 30 minutes, turning pieces occasionally to prevent burning. If pan becomes too dry, add a teaspoon or two of vegetable oil. Bon Appetite!

CHICKEN TARRAGON   Serves Four

1. In large fry pan melt:
   4   tablespoons butter
   Brown in butter:
   1   fryer, cut up, skinned or unskinned
   Turn frequently, adding salt and pepper to taste.
2. When chicken is brown, add to pan:
   ¼   cup dried tarragon
   6   garlic cloves, chopped
   ½   cup of dry white wine
   1   chicken bouillon cube, mixed in wine
   1   teaspoon flour, mixed in wine
3. Simmer over low heat, lid on, for 35 minutes. Do not pressure cook. Do not allow sauce to become so thick

that it burns. Add more wine or water to pan, if necessary. Turn chicken several times, and baste occasionally with sauce. Despite the large amount of garlic, the flavor will not be excessive. Serve with white or brown rice.

CHICKEN FRICASSEE   Serves Five to Six

or
What to do with a big bird of questionable tenderness

1 **stewing chicken, about 5 lbs., cut up and skinned**
3 **tablespoons bacon fat**
1 **tablespoon parsley, chopped**
2 **bay leaves, broken into pieces**
½ **teaspoon nutmeg**
½ **lb. bacon, chopped**
2 **cups mushrooms, sliced**
2 **egg yolks**
½ **cup condensed milk, unsweetened**
1 **chicken bouillon cube**

1. Fry chicken in a pressure cooker with bacon fat. Sprinkle with salt, pepper, and pre-sifted flour (no lumps). Do not brown the bird, but turn it several times.
2. Add nutmeg, bay leaves, parsley, and bacon.
3. When bacon begins to fry, cover all with water and dissolved bouillon cube.
4. Pressure cook for 30 minutes after first jiggle.
5. Remove lid; continue to simmer until tender, the length of time depending on the muscular fortitude of your bird.
6. When chicken is tender, turn off heat. Let pot stand for 5 minutes.
7. Add egg yolks mixed with condensed milk; stir thoroughly, then return pot to very low heat.

The yolks will thicken the sauce to a creamy consistency, unless overheated, in which case, the egg jells. Take it slow and easy, removing the pot from the flame several times to keep the temperature low. This dish does not reheat well.

SOUTHERN FRIED CHICKEN   Serves Four

Discussing southern fried chicken is a serious subject in the South—a debating point that is most likely to remain unresolved since there are as many variations of this dish as figs on a tree. What cooking fat to use, whether to use bread crumbs, flour, or bran meal, whether a batter is better than dusting...many a lazy Georgia afternoon has been spent arguing the various pros and cons. We, therefore, submit the following directions with humility, and beg your forgiveness if you know a different, and probably, superior recipe.

1. Cut up a 2-3 pound fryer in 8 pieces, being careful to leave the skin on all cuts.
2. Make a dipping liquid consisting of:
   2 eggs, beaten
   ½ cup condensed milk
3. Pat chicken pieces dry with a towel; dip pieces in egg mixture.
4. Allow excess egg to drip off, then gently roll chicken pieces in:
   Bread crumbs, seasoned with salt and lots of pepper
5. When all pieces are coated, set them aside on a paper towel for about 30 minutes.
6. Handling pieces very carefully, repeat steps 3 and 4, but don't pat with towel.
7. Gently place pieces in a heavy fry pan containing:
   ½ inch very hot vegetable oil
   Brown all over, turning once or twice with tongs; handle pieces as little as possible to avoid breaking off batter. Frying should take about 10 minutes.
8. Reduce flame to low heat; continue to fry for another 20 minutes.
9. Remove chicken pieces from pan, and pat off excess oil with a paper towel, or let stand on paper for a few minutes.

WHISKY CHICKEN   Serves Four

A quick, one-pot pressure cooker main course that can be served flaming on a platter. The resulting taste is not a whisky flavor.

1. Dredge in flour, salt and pepper:
   1 fryer, cut up
2. Fry in pressure cooker, lid off:
   ½ lb. bacon, chopped
3. When bacon fat covers bottom of pan, add chicken and fry until golden, turning occasionally. When the chicken starts to brown, add:
   1 large onion, chopped

4. When chicken is brown, add:
   - 1 teaspoon thyme
   - 1 teaspoon marjoram
   - 1 teaspoon tarragon
   - 1 cup mushrooms, fresh or canned
   - 1 cup cooked ham, chopped
   - 4 tablespoons whisky
   - ½ cup water
   - 1 chicken bouillon cube, dissolved in water
5. Pressure cook for 18 minutes after the first jiggle, or simmer over medium heat for 35 minutes.
6. Thicken sauce, if necessary with:
   - 1 teaspoon corn flour, or wheat flour dissolved in water

Serve over rice pilaf, page 299. To serve flambe, put chicken in warmed, fancy pan or sizzle dish; pour over it ¼ cup of just warm whisky. Flame and quickly bring to the table.

CHICKEN WITH PAPRIKA AND OREGANO   Serves Four

1. In a large fry pan heat:
   - 4 tablespoons vegetable oil
   Add:
   - 1 chicken, skinned and cut up
   - 1 onion, chopped
   Brown all over, adding salt and pepper to taste.
2. Add to pot:
   - 4 cloves garlic
   - 1 heaping tablespoon oregano
   - 2 teaspoons paprika
   - 1 teaspoon marjoram
   - 1 can (6 to 8 oz.) tomato sauce, or whole tomatoes, chopped
   - ¼ teaspoon cayenne pepper
3. Simmer over medium heat for 30 minutes, lid off, until bird is tender.

FIRST OFFICER'S CURRIED CHICKEN   Serves Four

1. In large pot make a curry by sauteing until golden:
   - 1 large onion, chopped
   - 4 tablespoons olive oil
   - 1 tablespoon sugar

277

Add:

    3   **cloves garlic, smashed**
    1   **heaping tablespoon curry powder**
    1   **teaspoon ginger**
    1   **teaspoon vinegar**

Cook slowly over low heat for 10 to 15 minutes, adding one tablespoon of water at a time, stirring constantly to make a paste of molasses consistency. Saute slowly, stirring frequently, until curry smell disappears.

2. Add to pot:

    1   **chicken, skinned, cut up**
    1½ **teaspoons marjoram**

Brown chicken all over, adding salt and pepper to taste.

3. Add to pot:

    ½ **cup nuts, preferably almonds, cashews, or hazel nuts (not peanuts).**

Saute nuts for a few minutes; add to pot:

    1   **chicken bouillon cube, crumbled**
    1   **can (6 to 8 oz.) tomato sauce or whole tomatoes**
    ¾ **cup raisins or currants**
    ½ **teaspoon sugar**

Simmer for 30 minutes, lid off, until tender; serve over yellow rice.

CHICKEN STEWED WITH VEGETABLES

    1   **broiler, cut up, skinned; include the neck, gizzard, heart**
    4   **tablespoons bacon fat**
    3   **carrots, quartered lengthwise**
    2   **medium onions, quartered**
    3   **potatoes, peeled and quartered lengthwise**
    1   **cup water**
    2   **chicken bouillon cubes, dissolved in water**
    1   **cup dry white wine**
    1   **teaspoon marjoram**
    1   **teaspoon parsley**
    ½ **teaspoon sage**
       Salt and pepper to taste

1. In large pot, fry the potatoes, the sage, and the onions in bacon fat over high heat. Turn frequently until potatoes begin to brown.

2. Add all other ingredients, beginning with carrots; simmer over medium heat, covered, for 40 minutes (or pressure cook for 18 minutes). Turn chicken several times; cook until chicken is tender.
3. The cooking liquid may be thickened into a sauce by adding a teaspoon of flour dissolved in a little wine. Simmer over low heat until it thickens.

CHICKEN HEARTS BRAISED IN WINE   Serves Four

1. Melt in pan:
   2   tablespoons butter
2. Brown in butter:
   1 to 1½   lbs. chicken hearts
3. Add to pan:
   1   cup wine
   1   teaspoon garlic salt
   1½ teaspoons bouquet garni (or ½ teaspoon each: thyme, marjoram, basil, tarragon)
   Simmer for 15 minutes. Hearts should be a little pink inside.
4. Thicken sauce with:
   1   tablespoon flour, dissolved in a little wine
   Add to the pan; simmer until thick. Serve over rice.

man-o-war cay sloop

CHICKEN CHASSEUR OF THE CAPTAIN   Serves Four

1   fryer, cut up, skinned or unskinned
1   tablespoon bacon fat
½   cup rich, red wine
1   can (about 6 oz.) Italian tomatoes, or ½ cup
     tomato puree
1   teaspoon curry powder (optional)
1   chicken bouillon cube
½   tablespoon each: basil, marjoram, chervil
     (optional), thyme, salt
2   cups mushrooms, sliced
     pepper to taste

1. In large fry pan, brown chicken in bacon fat.
2. Add bouillon cube mixed with wine; simmer for 10 minutes.
3. Add remaining ingredients, including the mushrooms if they are fresh or dried. If they are canned, wait for 15 minutes.
4. Simmer ingredients for 20 minutes, lid off. Green pepper circles, zucchini slices, or yellow squash slices may be placed on top and steamed until tender, about 5 minutes. Serve over rice.

CHICKEN WITH ARTICHOKES   Serves Four

Use the artichoke hearts packed with oil and spices in small jars. Avoid artichokes packed in water or vinegar. Their bland flavor will not contribute to the delicate flavor of this dish.

1. In large fry pan, saute over low heat until garlic is golden:
     3   tablespoons olive oil from artichokes
     6   cloves garlic, coarsely chopped
2. Add to pot, and saute over medium heat, turning occasionally:
     1   fryer, unskinned
     1   medium onion, diced
3. Brown chicken, but be careful not to burn the onions.
4. Add to pot:
     ½   cup white wine with dissolved chicken
          bouillon cube.
5. Simmer over medium heat, lid on, for 20 minutes. Add more wine if sauce thickens excessively.

6. Add to pot:
   ½ to ¾   cup artichokes, coarsely chopped
7. Continue to simmer for 10 minutes, or until chicken is tender. Serve over rice or noodles; sprinkle liberally with Parmesan cheese.

CHICKEN SALAD

The beauty of a chicken salad is that it utilizes leftover chicken in a tasty way. In addition, it is probably the very best dish for canned chicken. Last, but not least, it is a fine hot weather recipe that may be used in sandwiches, hors d' oeuvres, or as the entree. If you have refrigeration, serve it chilled. If not, cool by placing the completed salad in a damp cloth for 30 minutes in a shady, breezy spot.

CHICKEN SALAD NICOISE
2   cups cooked chicken meat, chopped
1   cup diced potatoes, boiled, but firm
1   cup cooked green beans, firm and cooled
3   fresh tomatoes (not canned), cut in wedges
½   cup black olives, pitted capers, chopped anchovies, artichoke hearts, celery hearts (any or all)
French dressing

Combine ingredients by tossing lightly: avoid smashing the vegetables.

CHICKEN SALAD—AMERICAN STYLE
1. Combine:
   1½   cups cooked chicken, diced
   ½   cup celery, finely chopped
   ½   cup mayonnaise
   ½   cup boiled potatoes, diced
   4   hard-boiled eggs, chopped
2. Sprinkle with salt, pepper and paprika. Add:
   ½   cup French dressing (optional)

LIVER

Chicken liver is not a popular dish; we suggest your asking everyone in the crew before making it. Liver is generally re-

garded with distaste because it is usually overcooked, dry, tough, and repulsive. Avoid this by cooking over low heat (high heat toughens liver), and testing the meat for doneness by opening with a knife. Liver is cooked when it is still a bit pink inside, not when it's dry and flaky.

Chicken, pig, goose, rabbit, and calves liver are particularly tender; we think rabbit liver is the best of all. Baby calves liver is on the top of the list, too. Baby beef liver comes from an animal approaching maturity, while beef liver, from the adult steer, is tough and miserable. Pork and sheep livers, if from young animals, are also excellent. Larger livers make a good pate, but avoid them for sauteing. All liver, regardless of type, should have any surface membranes, the gall bladder, and adhering fat removed. Larger livers, such as baby beef, should be soaked for a half hour in milk, then patted dry before cooking. The pan drippings from these larger livers should not be used for a sauce since they are often bitter.

If your crew is not particularly adverse to liver, it is well worth including in the menu. Liver is full of vitamins, and is a fine supplement to a high protein diet that is a little deficient in fresh vegetables. The recipes included here may be used for all types of liver, either whole or cut into manageable slices. Since liver is very rich, 1½ pounds serves four.

LIVER LYONNAISE   Serves Four

Chicken liver should be separated into individual lobes, and other livers cut to this size.

1. Make a dusting mixture of flour, salt, and pepper in a plastic bag; Add to bag and shake:
    ½   **lbs. liver, calf, chicken, rabbit, goose, kid**
2. In pan, saute until onions are golden:
    2   **tablespoons butter**
    1   **medium onion, diced**
    ½   **cup green pepper strips (optional)**
    ½   **cup mushrooms, sliced. If mushrooms are canned, add them just 1 minute before onions are complete.**
3. Slide onions and mushrooms onto a plate. Add to pan:
    3   **tablespoons butter**
        liver
    Saute over medium heat for about 1 minute per side.

4. Slide liver onto a paper towel. Wipe pan free of butter and debris. Heat a tablespoon of butter in the pan and add all of ingredients. Toss together for a minute over low heat. Fini.

BRAISED LIVER WITH VEGETABLES Serves Four

1½ lbs. liver, chicken, rabbit, goose, calf, or kid
¼ cup bacon fat
1 chicken bouillon cube
2 carrots, sliced into rounds
2 green peppers, chopped
6 to 8 small onions, peeled
salt, pepper, flour, water

1. Place flour, salt, pepper, and liver in a bag; shake thoroughly.
2. In fry pan, brown liver in bacon fat, no more than 30 to 40 seconds per side, using medium heat.
3. Pour combined vegetables on top. Add a cup of water with a chicken bouillon cube dissolved in it.
4. Cover pan and simmer until liver is tender, not more than 15 to 18 minutes.

bahamian
light structure

15
the joys of pasta

Pasta meals rank high on the list of fine cruising foods. The pasta stores well, costs very little, cooks quickly, serves legions, and is a fine base for the sauce creations of the chef.

The sauce and other additives are usually prepared before the pasta itself goes on the burner. In fact, sauces made a day or more before use, usually taste better. In any event, the sauce or pasta stuffing should be heated and ready for action when the pasta is placed in the boiling water.

Cooked pasta doubles in weight and volume. A half pound of dried spaghetti, for example, will weigh one pound when cooked, which is a most adequate serving for two. An adequately large pot and plenty of salted water are the secret of successful pasta cookery. Two quarts of water per half pound of pasta is adequate. Two teaspoons of salt should be added to raise the boiling temperature. If water is on ration, one quart of fresh water may be mixed with a quart of sea water; in this case, no additional salt should be added. Unfortunately, pure sea water cannot be used because it makes the pasta taste bitter. We usually add a generous tablespoon of olive oil, corn oil, or butter to the boiling water before adding the pasta. The oil prevents the pasta from clumping or sticking to the bottom of the pot. The uncooked pasta should be added a little at a time to the briskly boiling water. This keeps the water at a high temperature and prevents clumping.

The Italians prefer their pasta al dente, not completely soft and offering a bit of resistance to the teeth. Taste the pasta frequently as it cooks since cooking time varies considerably according to the thickness of the pasta, its age, and the wheat from which it was made. When its taste suits you, it's cooked. It is extremely difficult to give accurate cooking times. Let it suffice to say that pasta usually takes from 5-15 minutes to cook. It is unwise to mix two different packages of pasta together in one pot, especially two different brands. The result is usually a disaster—half of the pasta overcooked, and the other half still hard.

BUYING AND STORING PASTA

Regardless of what kind of pasta you buy, examine the packages or boxes carefully. We've been in some out-of-the-way stores where the pasta has been on the shelf for years. Look for roach holes, chewed ends, black droppings, and hairs. Also check the ends of noodles or spaghetti for mold or mildew. Don't even buy it if it just looks old; old pasta takes longer to cook, and frequently takes on the flavor of its container.

The storing procedure we have developed over the years guarantees fresh pasta that seems immortal. We use wide mouthed plastic jars that have been washed in a strong solution of bleach, then dried thoroughly in the sun. When the jar is thoroughly dry (an essential), we sterilize it (but not long enough to burn the plastic). The pasta is added, and the jar put in the sun for several hours with the lid on, but loose. The lid is then tightened, and the jar stored out of the sun. The air inside cools and forms a slight vacuum, which helps to preserve the pasta.

MEAT AND MUSHROOM SAUCE OF THE CAPTAIN

Serves Four

1. Saute in skillet:
   - ½   **cup olive oil**
   - 4   **cloves garlic, coarsely chopped**
   - 1   **teaspoon salt**
   - ½   **teaspoon pepper**
   - 1   **large onion, well chopped**
   - 2   **cups mushrooms, prefried**
2. When onion begins to turn golden add:
   - 1   **lb. ground beef (fresh is best), as lean as possible**

Saute, turning frequently until meat is gray (or if canned meat is used, until it is hot).

3. Thoroughly drain off liquid.
4. Add to pot:

2 to 3 cups Italian tomatoes, canned, thoroughly drained and crushed
2 cans (6 oz.) tomato paste
3 teaspoons oregano
2 teaspoons marjoram
1 teaspoon sugar
1 teaspoon salt
1 teaspoon pepper
3 tablespoons vinegar

Simmer over low heat for 30 minutes, stirring occasionally.

DRIED MUSHROOM AND TUNA SAUCE   Serves Two

Dried mushrooms are superior in flavor to the canned variety and are easy to prepare. Just buy fresh mushrooms and pass a thread through them, forming long chains. Then hang them in the hot sun for a few days until they feel tough and leathery. Store them in a clean, wide-mouthed jar, preferably with a packet of desiccant. They seem to last forever. This recipe specifically calls for dried mushrooms. If those lovely black Chinese mushrooms are available, please use them.

1. Saute in skillet for 2 minutes:
   3 garlic cloves, finely chopped
   ¼ cup olive oil
2. Add and simmer over low heat for 20 minutes:
   1 handful dried mushrooms, presoaked in warm water for 30 minutes
   1 cup tomato puree
   ½ teaspoon ground pepper
3. Add and heat until simmering:
   1 can (6 to 8 oz.) tuna, packed in oil. (Be sure the tuna is thoroughly drained and well flaked.)
4. Mix thoroughly; pour over:
   1 lb. cooked pasta

TOMATO (MARINARA) SAUCE   Serves Four

A simple, blue water sauce for spaghetti
1. Saute in skillet until onions are light golden:
   2 onions, chopped
   5 cloves garlic, coarsely chopped
   5 tablespoons olive oil

2. Add and simmer for 15 minutes:
   2½ cups canned Italian tomatoes,
   1   cup tomato sauce
   ½   teaspoon basil
3. Add and simmer for 5 minutes:
   3   anchovies, chopped
   1   teaspoon sugar, salt, and pepper
   4   teaspoon oregano
   ¼   teaspoon vinegar
4. Pour over:
   2   lbs. cooked spaghetti
   Sprinkle liberally with grated Parmesan cheese.

SAUCE MILLANNAISE FOR PASTA   Serves Four

1. Saute in skillet for 5 minutes:
   3   tablespoons butter
   ½   cup mushrooms, fresh or reconstituted dried
   ¼   lb. smoked ham or Danish salami, finely diced
2. Add and simmer for 5 minutes:
   1   cup tomato puree
   ½   teaspoon sugar
   salt and pepper to taste
3. Pour over:
   2   lbs. spaghetti
   Sprinkle generously with grated Swiss cheese.

SPAGHETTI SAUCE DELLA FLORENTINE   Serves Two

4   tablespoons butter
4   tablespoons flour
2   cups milk
¾   lb. diced ham
1   cup Parmesan cheese
½   teaspoon thyme
½   teaspoon basil
½   teaspoon salt
½   teaspoon pepper
1   tablespoon Worcestershire sauce
1   tablespoon horseradish (optional)

1. Melt butter; stir in flour. Saute over medium heat, stirring constantly, until sauce turns golden, about 2 minutes.
2. Add milk; stir until thickened.

3. Add remaining ingredients except cheese; simmer 5 minutes.
4. Add cheese a little at a time, stirring constantly.
   Pour over:
   1   lb. cooked spaghetti

view from a bistro

SPAGHETTI CARBONARA
Courtesy of Yacht HENDRIETTE
A one-burner, two-pot transatlantic meal

This lovely, easily prepared dish, is esteemed throughout Italy. But the Italians aren't the only people who enjoy this fine meal. Rebecca learned the recipe from a Belgian girl one cold, windy day. We were harbor-bound in Estapona, a little port not far from Gibraltar, waiting for a vicious Levanter to blow itself out. There was no fresh food left in the house, the nearest store was a few miles away, and we really didn't feel like another evening of bacon and eggs. Then along came Francoise, whose very presence seemed to make that gloomy day brighter. "If you have bacon and eggs," she said, "Why not have spaghetti carbonara?" And so we did.

1. Fry:
    1   lb. bacon, cut into 1-inch squares.
2. Boil and drain:
    1   lb. spaghetti.
  Boiling time is approximately 11 minutes.
3. Combine:
    bacon and grease
    ¼   cup olive or corn oil
    spaghetti, piping hot
    3   egg yolks, well beaten
    1   cup grated Parmesan cheese
    6   cloves garlic, finely chopped
  Mix thoroughly, salt to taste, and serve.

spaghetti curbonara

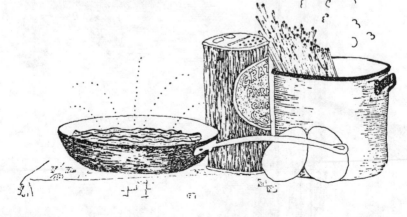

capo trionto light tower

MACARONI AND CHEESE   Serves Three to Four

This traditional dish is usually baked, and we have included baking instructions for those who have a galley oven. Since we don't have an oven, our macaroni casserole is prepared on top of the stove; it tastes just fine.

1. Combine in pot:
   - **1½ lbs. cooked macaroni**
   - **1½ cups grated cheese (a mild cheese such as American, Gruyere or Gouda)**
   - **2 eggs, well beaten**
   - **1 cup milk, or ¾ cup condensed milk and ¼ cup water**
   - **2 tablespoons butter**
   - **½ teaspoon salt**
   - **¼ teaspoon paprika**
2. Mix thoroughly. If you have an oven, sprinkle with generous handful of cheese and butter dots; bake at 400° F until cheese is browned. If you do not have an oven, simmer over low heat, stirring frequently, for 5 minutes until cheese is melted. Do not let mixture thicken excessively; add milk if it does. Sprinkle generously with cheese and butter dots; cover until cheese melts.

MACARONI IN TOMATO SAUCE   Serves Three to Four

1. Combine in pot over medium heat:
   - **1½ lbs. cooked macaroni**
   - **1 cup grated cheese, half Parmesan and half mild cheese**
   - **2 eggs, well beaten**
   - **½ cup condensed milk**
   - **1 cup tomato puree**
   - **½ teaspoons sugar**
   - **1 teaspoon dried basil**
2. Simmer over low heat for 15 minutes, stirring constantly.

TUNA AND MUSHROOM SOUP ON NOODLES   Serves Two

We normally avoid "just pour from the can" recipes, but the results here are quite tasty. This recipe is so fast that if you start lunch when the hook goes down, it should be on the table by the time the sails are furled.

1. Cook until tender or "al dente":
   ½ **lb. broad noodles (makes 1 lb cooked.).**
2. Drain and mix in thoroughly:
   3 **tablespoons butter**
   1 **teaspoon salt**
3. Pour noodles into large, shallow dish.
4. Sprinkle with:
   1 **can (7 oz.) tuna, drained and flaked**
5. Cover with:
   1 can (10¾ oz.) cream of mushroom soup, undiluted and warm
   1 **teaspoon Worcestershire sauce**
   Garnish with chopped parsley.
   Stir and heat until warm.

CLAM AND TOMATO SAUCE FOR SPAGHETTI

The Italians are extremely fond of this sauce which they make with small cockles or wedge shells. Served after a crisp green salad and helped along with a good bottle of Chianti or Bardolino, well-prepared spaghetti della vongola is dangerously addictive. We came to know and love this sauce when our sloop, the Fire Witch, was moored for the winter in the Tiber River, about 10 miles from Rome. In the Club Nautico, down the road, there was a restaurant we visited several nights a week just to have a plate of spaghetti della vongola. The road was long and dark, muddy as a swamp when it rained (which was often), and full of holes. There was always a mean dog somewhere along its length which necessitated carrying a large club. In addition, motorists heading down this quagmire held the popular Italian belief that the ride would be smoother if you just go fast enough to keep the tires out of the bumps, say about 100 miles per hour. This meant that when we spotted headlights coming in our direction, the safest way to see the sun again was simply to dive into tall marsh grass that grew beside the road. As a consequence, we often arrived at Club Nautico a bit wet, bedraggled, and always ravenous. The clams were absolutely fresh and alive, living happily in a big pot full of sea water by the stove. They were speedily transformed into this epicurian delight by the matron of the house while we sipped our Cinzano and tuned our appetites. A lovely salad invariably came first, consisting of several kinds of lettuce, escarole, sliced fennel, onion, sweet olives, garlic oil dressing with slices of fresh Italian bread and Mozarella cheese on the side. Then came the spaghetti portions big enough to lift with both hands, well covered at our special request with the lovely vongola sauce. Walter, the waiter, always the paragon of diplomacy, would then saunter over with a huge, 2-liter (½ gallon) fiasco of wine and suggest we help ourselves. We always did. By the time we had our espresso, a dish of wonderful chocolate ice cream, and a generous shot of the sweet Italian anise liquer, Sambuca, we were feeling no pain; even the mean dog on the long walk home seemed more friendly.

SPAGHETTI DELLA VONGOLA   Serves Four

Any type of sweet, tender clam may be used; but if the meat is larger than a penny, it is better to open the shells and chop the meat, reserving the liquid. Canned clams, including cockles, may also be used; add them a few minutes before serving, cooking them just enough to warm the meat. Their flavor is definitely wounded in the canning process, but a few drops of lemon restores some of the loss. Small clams, such as wedge shells, may be added unshelled to the sauce, leaving the individual diner the fun of sucking the meaty morsels free.

1. Fry in sauce pan:
    4   cloves garlic, chopped
    ¾   cup olive oil
2. When garlic begins to turn golden, add to pot:
    3   cups Italian tomatoes (fresh or canned) drained and chopped
    1   cup tomato paste
    1   teaspoon thyme
    1   teaspoon oregano
    1   teaspoon salt
    ½   teaspoon pepper
    1   tablespoon dry red wine
    ½   teaspoon sugar
    ½   teaspoon fresh lemon juice
3. Simmer over low heat for 15 minutes, stirring occasionally; add
    1½   quarts live clams, or 1½ cups raw clam meat
    Simmer another 10 minutes, stirring occasionally. (If canned clams are used, add 1½ cups of meat, drained, and a teaspoon of lemon juice to correct the flavor. Simmer for just 3 minutes, stirring frequently.)

Serve over spaghetti or linguini, about ½ pound per portion. This sauce, if any is left over, is even better the next day.

SPAGHETTI A LA VONGOLA (WHITE SAUCE)   Serves Four

1. Saute for 3 minutes:
   - **4   tablespoons olive oil**
   - **4   tablespoons butter**
   - **3   cloves garlic**
   - **6   tablespoons (¼ cup plus 2 tablespoons) shallots or onion, finely chopped**
2. Add:
   - **½   cup clam juice**
   - **3   tablespoons dry, white wine**

   Simmer for 3 minutes.
3. Add:
   - **clams (Follow proportions and directions in previous recipe for spaghetti della vongola.)**

   Simmer over low heat for 5 minutes; serve tossed into 2 pounds fo spaghetti. Sprinkle generously with Parmesan cheese.

RICE

There are many varieties of rice, and, as is true with pasta, it is difficult to give accurate cooking times for them. The cooking time varies with the age of the rice, its length, and how much it has been milled. The resulting taste also depends on whether the rice has been milled, the length of the grains, and the quality of the water in which it is cooked. In the most sophisticated kitchens, several different kinds of rice are stocked: brown rice for eating with fowl, long grains for soups and stuffings, and short grain for sauces. This is not practical on a boat; a single choice should be made. We prefer unmilled brown rice, despite its long cooking time, because of its chewy consistency, superior flavor, and nutritional value. If you are on short fuel rations or just prefer to get the job done quickly, there are always products, such as minute rice, that do not require any boiling. But remember, the shorter the cooking time, the less nutritional value from the rice.

In order to save fuel and time, we pressure cook brown rice for 20 to 25 minutes. Since it normally takes 40 to 50 minutes to cook, the savings is considerable. White, long grain rice usually takes 20 to 30 minutes regular cooking time, only 4 minutes in the pressure cooker. Never exceed these times for pressure cooking. Don't forget, undercooked rice can be simmered without pressure for a few extra minutes until cooked, but overcooked rice is unredeemable.

One cup of uncooked rice makes about 3 to 3½ cups of cooked rice. Allow two cups of water for every cup of white rice, 2½ cups of water for brown rice.

One of the outstanding problems for the galley chef is weevils in the rice. These little devils appear out of nowhere and feast on packaged rice, flour, and other cereals. Their ability to

fortress of the haj

penetrate cardboard and cellophane packages is uncanny; the only weevil-proof container we know of is a kitchen jar, preferably plastic, with a good lid. Thoroughly examine all rice prior to departure, and seal it well. There are many places where rice and weevils are as inseparable as dogs and fleas. The Costa del Sol, in Spain, is one, but their delectable brown rice is so cheap that we just can't pass it up. Immediately after purchasing this rice, we put in a big pan and bake it at 400° for about 10 minutes. This process kills the one or two weevils that would soon become 100 or 200 if given the chance.

FRIED RICE

Rice may be fried before or after boiling, depending on the result desired. Rice is fried prior to boiling to firm it and help keep the granules separate. Frying rice after boiling, usually with herbs and vegetables, changes its flavor from the usual bland taste into the chef's speciality. Both are correct but produce entirely different results.

BOILED RICE   Serves Four

1. In pot, bring to rolling boil:
   2 cups water, or stock (if canned, use condensed consomme')
   1 teaspoon salt
   1 teaspoon oil or butter (to prevent clumping)
2. Add:
   1 cup rice
3. Approximate cooking times:

TYPE	BOIL	PRESSURE COOK
Brown	40 to 50 min.	20 to 30 min.
White long	20 to 30 min.	4 to 6 min.
White short	15 to 25 min.	3 to 5 min.

About ¾ of the way through cooking time begin sampling the rice; cook and sample rice until it is cooked to taste. We prefer ours like pasta al dente, which means a little bit chewy.

When the rice is almost but not quite cooked, turn off the flame, drain the pot, and fluff the rice with a fork. Keep it covered, flame off, for several minutes to complete cooking and absorb excess moisture.

CURRIED RICE

The wind howls mournfully around the Rock of Gibralter in the winter time. The sun doesn't manage to get up till about 10 a.m., and the town, with its huge, fortified walls, seems perpetually damp. Perhaps that's why two Indian-Pakistani restaurants there do a brisk business serving many varieties of curried rice. Another reason, we suppose, is that most shops on Main Street are owned by indefatigable East Indians who certainly hold the prize for being the most determined small businessmen in the world. When the American Navy lands, the street is all red, white, and blue bunting; big signs say Welcome Yanks. The business is brisk. Everyone has to have a watch, a camera, and a beer can all at once.

Then a few days after the Yanks leave, the Russians come. Indians, being a practical people, reason that a piece of cardboard has two sides and why waste two pieces of cardboard when one will do. So the Welcome Yanks signs are reversed and what we assume is Welcome Ruskies is on the other side. We called the Russians "those boys with the brown paper sacks," because they cared nothing for the watches and cameras. They wanted clothes to take home, so you would see them loaded high with paper packages as they staggered back to their ship.

As with everyone else in that crazy country, Indians followed the Spanish custom of having a very long (2 to 3 hour) lunch break, and they could invariably be found "warming up" over a bowl of curried rice. In fact, this curried rice recipe was given to us by the proprietor of the best Indian-Pakistani restaurant in town, Mrs. Kriklewi.

CURRIED RICE   Serves Four

1. Make curry paste, page 277, in pot large enough for rice.

2. Add:
    - ½ cup Italian tomatoes, well drained and chopped
    - 1 teaspoon salt
    - ½ onion, chopped
    - ¼ cup green peppers, chopped (if available)
    - 3 tablespoons butter

3. Saute over medium heat until onions are golden, stirring frequently.

4. Add: **2   chicken bouillon cubes, crumbled**
   2   cups water
   1   cup rice
Simmer until rice is cooked, stirring frequently. Serve as
a side dish.

RICE WITH VEGETABLES COOKED IN CHICKEN OR BEEF
STOCK   Serves Four

1. Saute in pot:
   ¼   cup butter
   ½   onion, chopped
2. Add any of these optional ingredients:
   ½   small carrot, finely chopped
   **3 to 4   mushrooms, chopped (fresh or recon-
   stituted)**
3. When onions turn golden, add and stir for 30 seconds:
   1   cup rice
4. Add:
   2   cups chicken stock or beef stock
5. Bring to simmer; cook until rice is tender.
6. Add:
   salt, pepper, and butter to taste
Serve as a side dish.

RICE PILAF   Serves Four

Rice pilaf is a main course dish that includes
chopped shrimp, seafood, or chicken livers. That way is
fine, but plain old rice pilaf without anything is one of
our favorite side dishes. It's our guess that it will go well
with your crew.

1. Boil until rice is not quite cooked, rather chewy:
   1   cup rice
   **2   cups beef stock (use homemade stock,
   canned consomme, or bouillon cubes)**
2. Add:
   **2   cups Italian tomatoes, canned, well drained
   and crushed**
   ½   bay leaf
   **3   medium stalks celery with leaves, chopped or,
   if unavailable, ½ teaspoon celery seed**
   1   can (6oz.) tomato paste
   1   teaspoon salt

1 teaspoon pepper
1 teaspoon sugar
¼ teaspoom paprika
Simmer over medium heat until rice is cooked, stirring frequently.
3. If desired add:
1 cup cooked shrimp, fish, chicken livers, or chicken parts fried in curry.
4. Sprinkle with grated cheese to your taste; brown in oven.

BASIC SPANISH RICE   Serves Four

1. Saute in large pot until golden brown:
6 slices of bacon, more if desired
2. Add to bacon drippings and fry until light brown, stirring often:
1 cup white rice (brown rice doesn't do well in this recipe because of its long cooking time)
3. Add and cook until golden:
½ onion, chopped
4. Add:
1½ cups Italian tomatoes, chopped
½ cup chicken stock
2 tablespoons white wine (optional)
1 teaspoon pepper
1 teaspoon paprika
3 cloves garlic, coarsely chopped
1 green pepper, seeded and chopped (optional).
bacon crumbled
5. Simmer over low heat until rice is cooked al dente stirring frequently. Do not let dish dry out; add more stock or water as needed. Correct the seasoning for salt and pepper. Serve as a side dish.

RICE AND HAM CASSEROLE   Serves Four

1. Cook:
1½ cups rice (use chicken stock instead of water)
2. While rice is cooking, dice:
1 canned (1 lb.) ham
Brown in a little oil.

3. When rice is cooked, combine with it:
   2   eggs, beaten
   1   can condensed cream of mushroom soup
   ½   cup milk
   ½   teaspoon salt
4. Toss rice mixture over low heat until it thickens a bit, then add:
   1   cup cooked peas (optional)
   the ham
   Mix with a few strokes of the fork and serve.

RICE WITH MIXED GRAINS AND VEGETABLES

1. Saute in a pressure cooker:
   2 medium onions, chopped
   1½ cups sliced mushrooms
2. Reserve the onions and mushrooms and add to the pot a mixture of the following, enough to make 2 cups:
brown rice	**garbanzos**
lentils	**red beans**
wild rice	**groats**
3. Pressure cook the grains in six cups of water for ten minutes, let the pot cool and thoroughly wash the grains.
4. Add to the pot:
   1 can beef stock
   1 teaspoon salt, pepper, celery seed
   2 teaspoons pepper, butter
5. Simmer with the lid off until the grains are done, about 15 minutes, adding more stock as needed.
6. When the grains are amost done, add to the pot enough broken up spaghetti to absorb the remaining free standing liquid. Simmer with lid on for 5 minutes, then turn off flame.
7. Add 1-2 cups chopped fresh vegetables such as peas, green beans, broccoli. Allow to stand with the lid on for 10 minutes.
8. Add onions and mushrooms and serve.

16

salads for the galley gourmet

Webster defines a salad as "a dish of lettuce or other vegetables, herbs, meat or fowl, fish, eggs, fruit, etc., prepared with various seasonings or dressings." The "etcetera" explains more than all the rest. More informative, perhaps, is the location of this work in the dictionary, between salacious (which means lustful or possibly lusty) and Saladin (who was a sultan). And that is exactly how we think of a salad, as a lusty etcetera fit for a king!

The word "salad" usually brings to mind a combination of lettuce, onions, tomatoes, and a dressing. This combination is delicious, but what happens when the last head of lettuce is just a memory, the last tomato a moldy red dot in the wake? And what happens when provisioning in some isolated port that has never seen a head of lettuce? Oh, yes, there are many, many places like that! Know the comfort, then, of the many salads that can be created by the galley gourmet entirely without lettuce or tomatoes, salads that are possible in port or on the last day of a long ocean passage, crispy, delightful little nothings that sharpen the appetite and satisfy the soul.

There are, we must admit, a number of prepared salad dressings on the market that are very good. We can recommend some of them recognizing the convenience to the galley gourmet. But we are at the same time disappointed by the growing trend toward total reliance on the contents of a bottle or packet. What ever happened to the taste-tempting practice of

creating your own fine dressing at the table while everyone waits with bated breath. If prepared salad dressings are to be taken on a cruise, why not make several small bottles of your own special dressing, ready for instant use. Lettuce salads are dressed with a number of classic dressings, but many of the salads discussed here taste absolutely ghastly with them. In these cases a particular dressing has been specified. We suggest that you experiment with your own variations after you have tasted ours.

The best way to store lettuce is to wash it in the fruit and vegetable dip, page 28, sun dry it upside down, then keep it wrapped in a damp towel in a cool, airy place. It will last about a week without refrigeration. Refrigerated, it may keep for two

fiumaro grande
light tower

weeks or a little longer. If your cruise is under two weeks in length, or you plan to stop in a port where lettuce is definitely available, your worries in the salad department are over. If your cruise is "beyond-lettuce-range," consider the many uses of cabbage, which lasts twice as long as lettuce, can be served in many of the same ways, and is a rich source of vitamin C. If your voyage is more than a month, carefully read the section in this chapter entitled "End-of-the-Passage Salads." These salads are made from tender seed shoots that you can sprout in your galley in 3 to 4 days.

There are a number of bottled or canned items that may be added to a fresh salad base to enliven it and to add variety. These include garbanzos (chick peas), kidney beans, artichokes packed in seasoned oil, pickled vegetables, bottled mushrooms, and cooked chilled macaroni noodles. In addition, tuna, salmon, and sardines can turn a salad into a meal-in-a-bowl. When planning a voyage, don't forget to include these supplies.

Referring again to our definition of salad as "a lusty etcetera fit for a king," you will find in this chapter a number of "one off" designs, such as potato salad, beet salad, and salad Nicoise, which are not made with crispy vegetables. But the "etcetera" must have a line drawn across it somewhere; therefore, we have omitted such entries as shrimp salad, chicken salad, crab salad since they are really more meat than salad.

Since a great many salads are dressed with oil, some mention of the many types should be made. In Italy most salads are dressed with olive oil. It comes in many different grades; the best, "pure virgin oil," can be fantastically expensive. We love olive oil but realize it does have a definite flavor some dislike. Should this be the case, feel free to mix good olive oil with any of the other light, mild-flavored oils, such as safflower, corn, or peanut oil. Our favorite alternative to olive oil is coconut oil, which has a delicious flavor all its own; but coconut oil is hard to find in many places. Regardless of what you use, remember that dressings are added to a salad just before eating. Tossing the salad and dressing long before the meal is ready produces a wilted and soggy mess.

"Be sure you don't eat the salads!" How many times we have heard that advice given to travelers. While we suspend judgment on that dictate for restaurant cuisine, we are certain that it need not apply to salads made by the cruising chef. We have gone to some very humble vegetable markets in some very,

very humble corners of the world and eaten the leafy vegetables that we have found there. An ounce of prudence is, of course, necessary. After cutting or breaking the leafy part of your salad, thoroughly agitate it in the fruit and vegetable dip, page 28, to kill bacteria, then dry it in the sun. Thin-skinned vegetables, such as tomatoes, should always be washed before use; and other types, such as onions may be washed, then skinned. We have sailed 24,000 miles and never had a single case of dysentery. There is, nevertheless, always a chance that a problem may occur, if not from the salad, then from something else, such as the water. Precautions are fine, but cures should be on hand. A prescription bottle of Lomotil tablets is good on-board insurance. Of greater danger is cholera, which comes from contaminated food, water, or sea food. It is such a dangerous disease that one would be foolish to visit a country where cholera exists without obtaining a vaccination against it. The warm months are most dangerous since cholera is inhibited by low temperatures.

GARLIC

If God allowed us but one spice in the world, our vote would be solidly for garlic. This pungent member of the onion family, found in the Egyptian tombs, has been used since the birth of civilization not only as a spice, but as a medicine for the control of blood pressure. Primitive man soon learned to appreciate it not just for its flavor, but because its presence in the garden acted as a powerful repellent of many insect pests. The ancient Egyptians thought that onions and garlic promoted resistance to disease. Their diets contained lots of both, and this is speculated to be one of the important reasons why the closely packed crews who built the pyramids did not perish from disease.

As much as we love garlic, there are others who dislike it almost as much. Usually, we have found that even these people are pleased when small, relatively unnoticeable amounts of garlic are present in their food. It is, indeed, the wise gourmet, who asks his guests before seasoning the salad with garlic. Ironically, it is not the garlic itself, but its oil that flavors the food. The bulb has a bitter flavor, which is only partially destroyed in cooking—as any one who has unknowingly bitten into a cooked garlic clove well knows! Because of this, many ingenious methods have been developed to extract the garlic flavor from the bulb. These include soaking the bulbs overnight in oil, cook-

ing in oil then disgarding the garlic, wiping dishes and pots with crushed garlic cloves, and rubbing on transfer materials such as crackers and toast.

This is not to say that whole garlic should not be included in cooking. In fact, many recipes call for large quantities of it, relying on the slightly bitter taste of the bulb as a flavoring. When garlic is gently cooked in oil (avoid browning), its flavor is considerably altered, the classic garlic taste being much reduced. For this reason, the amounts of cooked and raw garlic used vary greatly.

Garlic salt is often disdained by fine chefs for a number of reasons. Most of them are concerned with rancidity and stale flavor. But both of these problems are also typical of the bulb itself and merely call for a reasonable degree of vigilance. We like fresh garlic salt and never hesitate to use it, especially in those isolated ports where fresh garlic is not available. Use a teaspoon of garlic salt in place of a large clove of garlic, but remember that you are adding salt as well.

Fresh garlic, if sun-cured till the skin is white, will last many months. Since the oil is what keeps the garlic fresh, the larger the bulb, the longer it lasts, and the easier to work with. These giants are usually reserved for restaurants, and it takes some hunting to find them. With any luck, you can purchase a good load with the stems intact and braid them into a long chain, which can be hung in the galley. They are sold that way in the Mediterranean and North Africa. The hanging technique seems to extend the bulb's life.

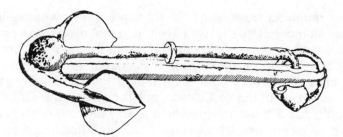

ONIONS

Members of this ancient family, widely represented in markets all over the world, began their close association with man before the dawn of recorded history. Onions have been found in Egyptian tombs and American Indian burial mounds. The Indians recognized the onion not only for its quality as a food, but also for its powerful antibacterial properties. They used freshly cut onion as a poultice for wounds, a technique not rediscovered by western man until the twentieth century.

No family is more widely represented in the modern kitchen than the onion. Garlic is a member of the same family, as are chives, shallots, leeks, scallions, and the many varieties of the common onion. Garlic and the dry onion are the most important for the sailor since they are among the longest lasting, and most easily stored fresh vegetables.

Generally, the larger the onion, the milder its flavor, and the shorter its shelf life. The big Bermudas and huge, flat Spanish reds, highly esteemed for salads, become dry and lifeless after two weeks, while the strong flavored, smaller American cepa onion lasts in a sack for months. The sprouting of onions is triggered by moisture and light. If, therefore, they are kept in a dark, closed box with an open container of salt or rice, the chances of their remaining unspoiled are improved. But do not make the box airtight; this promotes decay. Once an onion has a sprout a few inches long, its taste is permanently impaired. But do not throw it overboard in disgust. The shoot is tender and delicious, and it may be used in salads, especially bean sprout salads, with great effect. Just give the root system a bit of water, and, in a week or less, you will be rewarded with a long, scallion-like shoot that adds variety to your end of the passage meals. Onions become virtually immortal if refrigerated. We do not know the precise number of days in eternity, but do know that an onion stored 6 months in our refrigerator was a bit stale, but still hanging in there. On the other hand, cut onions deteriorate very quickly even if refrigerated and carefully wrapped. They will last a day or two without refrigeration if a few drops of lemon juice are squeezed over the cut onion, then carefully wrapped in foil.

Both texture and flavor of onions are considerably altered when they are cooked. Strong flavored onions are preferred since the mild ones, such as Bermudas, become tasteless and mushy when cooked. One of the most common cooking errors is to add raw onions to simmering food. This technique is often used in stews that call for pearl (or boiling) onions, and the result is a boiled onion whose flavor we all know. In most other recipes, onions should be sauteed in a little oil or butter, until translucent or golden. before being added to a dish. This process is enhanced by adding a pinch of salt, which helps retain firmness.

Some recipes call for browned onions; there are several ways to do this. The French add a pinch of sugar to the fry pan as the onions cook. The sugar caramelizes, producing a pleasant brown color that is very effective for soups, such as French Onion, and stews. Another technique for browning onions is to fry them in a scant amount of oil, usually just a teaspoon, over very high heat, stirring constantly. The onions will burn instantly if you stop stirring. These onions are often used to surround cooking meat or fish.

Onions are easy to peel, especially in quantity, if they are dipped in boiling water for a half minute; the skins slip off easily. If you get "soap opera eyes" when chopping onions, we can recommend for the sailor two techniques: first, chill the onion as much as possible, but don't freeze; second, wear a diving mask. We know it sounds bizarre, but many a bowl of onion soup has been produced in our galley using this technique.

Many famous recipes call for specific onion varieties, such as shallots and leeks. These two are the aristocrats of the allium family, and their subtle flavor is distinct. But they are hard to find, even in many Mediterranean places where you would expect to find them, and peeling a bunch of tiny shallots is a tedious job. We, therefore, admit the limited possibilities of shallot and leek cookery for the galley gourmet and limit their use in this book. If, however, a recipe calls for them, a combination of 1 clove minced garlic to ½ sliced onion approaches their flavor.

GROWING SALADS UNDER SAIL

No seagoing chef ever needs to feel that fine salad makings are unavailable, even on the last day of a long ocean passage. The lettuce may be just a memory, the last carrot limp and

wooden, but fast growing seed sprouts of several different varieties have crisp, excellent flavors. They may be combined with long lasting onions, chick peas, or cold macaroni noodles to make a fine salad treat that needs no refrigeration.

We have tried a number of different varities of sprouts, including alfalfa seeds, mung beans, wheat seeds (too bitter for salads), and soy beans. These may be purchased in health food shops and stored in a tight jar kept out of the sun. They will last for more than a year this way, and a healthy supply takes almost no space. Our favorite seeds are alfalfa; their culture is typical of most. Place a quarter cup of seeds in a wide-mouth gallon jar; cover with water for 24 hours. After 24 hours, drain off the water; keep the seeds moist for 2 to 4 additional days. The resulting growth produces a highly compact mass of tender, white shoots about an inch long. If kept moist, they will continue to grow at an amazing rate for 4 to 5 days and provide several fine salads for four. Lift the mass of sprouts from the container and discard the ungerminated seeds on the bottom. Pull the mass apart to fluff it, and rinse the portion to be used in seawater. This not only washes the sprouts, it salts them as well. The sprouts are now ready for salad use. The remainder should be moistened with fresh water twice a day.

Soy sprouts lead all other in food value. Almost half of their dry weight is pure protein; they are also a rich source of vitamins A, B, and C. Soy beans sprout at the same rate as the other seeds and respond well to Chinese quick frying. Like all sprouts, soy produces a very low carbohydrate meal, subtly nutlike in flavor and delicious.

END-OF-THE-PASSAGE BLUE WATER SEED SPROUT SALADS
Serves Four

I.

1 quart seed sprouts
1 large onion, sliced into rings
1 small jar artichoke hearts packed in seasoned oil (add half the oil, about 2 tablespoons)
1 teaspoon celery salt
1 can (7oz.) tuna, fluffed into flakes
1 tablespoon vinegar
1 cup cold chick peas, cooked, or cold macaroni, cooked

1 tablespoon olive oil
salt
pepper
lemon juice

1. Combine all ingredients except tuna and onions.
2. Serve on individual platters; place tuna around sides and arrange onion rings artistically over all.
3. Sprinkle a few drops of lemon juice on tuna; serve as a hot day main course.

Serves Four

II.

1 quart seed sprouts
1 onion, cut into rings
4 hard-boiled eggs, chopped
6 to 8 anchovies, coarsely chopped
1 cup canned sliced beets, rinsed
1 tablespoon celery salt
½ teaspoon marjoram
½ teaspoon thyme
¼ cup olive oil
2 tablespoons lemon or lime juice
1 cup bread cubes, fried in butter or oil with a pinch of marjoram and ½ teaspoon salt
½ cup Parmesan cheese
pepper

1. Combine sprouts, eggs, beets, seasonings, and bread crumbs.
2. Arrange onions and anchovies on top. Sprinkle on Parmesan cheese. Diced and chilled boiled potatoes may be added to make this a meal-in-a-bowl.

MUNG BEAN TREATS

Mung beans are grown like alfalfa seeds, but the resulting sprouts are much thicker. They are interchangeable in all bean sprout salad recipes; but because of their size, they may be treated as a vegetable as well. Several "End-of-the-Passage" mung bean vegetable combinations are given here.

END-OF-THE-PASSAGE HOT CHINESE VEGETABLE SALAD

1. Chop into bite size pieces and fry until cooked:

1 lb bacon

Reserve bacon drippings; carefully wipe pan clean of bacon debris.

311

2. Slice very thin, diagonally:
   4 carrots
3. Add to pan:
   1 tablespoon bacon fat, strained
   Bring to high heat.
4. Add:
   carrots
   3 cloves garlic (optional)
   Cook for 3 minutes, turning often. Discard garlic cloves.
5. Add to pan:
   1 quart mung beans sprouts, thoroughly washed and drained
   1 tablespoons soy sauce
   ¼ teaspoons celery seed
6. Toss vegetables over high heat for 1 minute. Add:
   bacon
   Serve immediately. Do not let this meal linger in the pan; the internal heat will overcook the sprouts.

If your mung bean sprouts seem too limp, try soaking them for 1 hour before cooking in a saturated salt solution, enough to cover; rinse before using.

END-OF-PASSAGE HOT SPROUTS 'N SHRIMP SALAD
Serves Four

This recipe calls for canned mushrooms and shrimp. The mung bean sprouts, of course, should be fresh. All ingredients must be ready for the pan since total cooking time is just 3 minutes.

1. Bring to high heat:
   1 tablespoon oil
   Add:
   2 cups canned shrimp (precooked if fresh)
   1 cup canned or reconstituted mushrooms, well drained sliced
   1 teaspoon soy sauce, or Worchestershire sauce
   3 teaspoon celery seed
2. Toss over high heat for 1 minute, then add:
   1 quart mung bean sprouts, washed in sea water and well drained
3. Continue to toss for 1 minute, then turn off heat and cover for 1 to 2 minutes. Serve immediately. Pepper to taste.

END-OF-THE-PASSAGE PICKLED BEET SALAD   Serves Four

This salad is made one day before eating. The ingredients should be allowed to stand unrefrigerated in a loosely covered jar. Canned shrimp may be added and pickled with the other ingredients.

    1. Combine in pot and bring to a boil:

        ½   cup vinegar
        ½   cup beet juice (from canned beets)
        2   tablespoons sugar
        3   cloves
        ½   teaspoon salt
        1   bay leaf, whole (remove after boiling)
        ½   teaspoon prepared mustard

"puff" the cat boat

2. Pour over:
>   **1   can (16 oz.) sliced beets**
>   **1   small can shrimp (optional)**
>   **1   onion, sliced**

Store according to the directions given above. This is a fine dish to serve with sardine pate sandwiches, page 379.

END-OF-THE-PASSAGE RUSSIAN SALAD Serves Four

Canned vegetables may be used, but we urge you to include as many fresh ingredients as possible. By garnishing with thinly sliced ham, salami, cheese, or hard boiled egg halves, this becomes a one-course meal.

1. Dice and combine:
>   **1   cup cooked carrots, chilled**
>   **1   cup boiled potato, diced and chilled**
>   **1   cup cooked beets, chilled**
>   **½   cup cooked peas, chilled**
2. Toss with:
>   **Mustard or garlic mayonnaise, page 324.**

CARROT AND RAISIN SALAD   Serves Four

        8 carrots, grated
        ½ cup raisins
        1 apple, grated
        1 cup walnuts, hazel nuts, or almonds
        1 tablespoon mayonnaise (as a variation sub-
           stitute yogurt or sour cream for mayonnaise)
        2 tablespoons honey, combined with mayon-
           naise
        1 teaspoon lemon juice

Combine all ingredients and chill.

CREAMY COLESLAW   Serves Six

    Unlike lettuce, cabbage is a vegetable that lasts a long time
without refrigeration, especially if it has been soaked in the fruit
and vegetable dip, page 28, and dried in the sun. If stored in a
cool spot, cabbage often lasts more than a month; refrigerated,
it lasts even longer. Cabbage is a good source of vitamin C.

    1. Shred:
        ½ medium cabbage
    2. Combine, add, and toss:
        ¾ cup mayonnaise
        5 cloves garlic, minced
        1 teaspoon celery seed
           salt and pepper to taste

    Instead of the classic dressing given above, vary your cole-
slaw with any of the conventional salad dressings: French,
Thousand Island or Roquefort. Or try any of the following added
to 1 cup of sour cream:

        1 teaspoon dill
        1 teaspoon chili powder
        2 tablespoons anchovies, chopped
           parsley
           chives
           onion, finely chopped

FRESH FRUIT SALAD   Serves Four to Six

    1. Chop and combine:
        4 to 6   cups mixed fruit, any that is available
        4 teaspoons brown sugar

4 tablespoons fresh lemon juice
1 teaspoon cinnamon
1 teaspoon vanilla
1 tablespoon kirch, or rum (optional)
3. Let stand an hour in refrigerator if you have one.

If you are a bit short of fresh fruit, this dish may be expanded with drained, canned fruit.

HEARTS OF PALM

Almost everyone who has tasted hearts of palm has had them canned. Unfortunately, the relationship between fresh and canned palm hearts is about the same as between fresh and canned green beans. Considering how well the canned variety is received and the fancy prices that some restaruants charge for it, imagine the superb taste of fresh palm heart. The heart of the palm is the tree core just at the top where the green fronds are growing. It is white, tender, and crunchy like celery heart, very solid and about 6 inches thick.

Never chop a palm tree down to get its heart, but should you find a tree overturned by a storm or cut down, seize this fine opportunity to sample one of the gastronomic pinnacles of the salad world. Use an ax to chop away the tough exterior. Make the crew take turns since it is not designed to come apart easily. You know that you've arrived when the white interior begins to be chewable. It will be worth the trouble.

Palm hearts have a very delicate, somewhat nutty flavor all their own. They are best of all in a salad of fresh mung beans sprouts with chopped onion and green pepper, seasoned with lime juice and oil. Absolutely delicious. Another extravaganza is to have them as a substitute for water chestnuts in Cantonese recipes. They are delightful with raisins, cinnamon, and a lime juice with honey dressing. Cooked with cuts of fish in coconut butter and lime, they are a delight. Palm heart is so delicious and easy to store that no vigilant galley gourmet should miss an opportunity to try it.

END-OF-THE-PASSAGE POTATO SALAD   Serves Four

Since potato salad is more potato than salad, it goes in that spot on the plate where starches belong. It does not really provide the essential roughage that a leafy or sprout salad provides, but it is tasty and nutritious and goes a long way toward filling those empty holes in a crewman's stomach. People occasionally use leftover boiled potatoes for this recipe, but they are usually too mushy in texture for good results; leftover boiled potatoes do best as hash browns. Small red potatoes or prediced baking potatoes should be used. We like predicing because it allows more rapid cooking and even texture.

1. Pressure cook for 2 minutes in enough water to cover:
    2½ cups diced potatoes
    1   teaspoon salt
    The potatoes should be just done, firm, and not mushy. Drain and rinse.
2. Add to pot:
    2   tablespoons onion, finely chopped
    2   hard boiled eggs, chopped
    1   tablespoons prepared mustard
    1   tablespoon relish
    ½   cup celery if available, or ½ teaspoon celery seed
    ½   cup mayonnaise
    1   teaspoon garlic salt
    1   teaspoon pepper
3. Toss lightly. Allow to completely cool; refrigerate if possible. Potato salad goes very well at the end of a long passage with kippers or canned fish in tomato sauce.

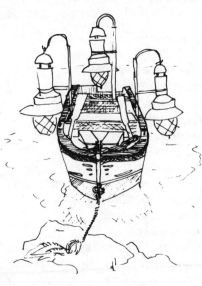

mediterranean octopus fish boat

SALAD NICOISE   Serves Four

This popular Mediterranean salad takes lots of fresh ingredients, but is a fine change from the usual tossed salad. There are many variations; feel free to add small pieces of raw cauliflower, fresh uncooked green peas, salami or ham dices, crumbled blue cheese, cooked asparagus tips, or anything that suits your taste.

3 tomatoes, quartered
1 cucumber, peeled and sliced
8 anchovy fillets, chopped
1 cup pitted black olives
2 potatoes, cubed, cooked
½ onion, diced
1 teaspoon garlic salt
½ teaspoon pepper

Toss lightly and pour French dressing over each portion.

END-OF-THE-PASSAGE POTATO SALAD NICOISE
Serves Four

This is a European version of potato salad. Every open air restaurant along the Mediterranean coast has a big plate of it ready for instant action. It's a sort of emergency ration in those restaurants since the service is as slow as the tide.

1. Cook in a pressure cooker for 2 minutes in water to cover:
   3 cups potatoes, diced
2. Drain water and immediately add:
   ½ cup wine vinegar
   ½ cup chicken consomme or bouillon
   Allow to stand for 1 hour
3. Then add to pot:
   ½ onion, diced
   2 cups green peas or beans, cooked
   ½ cup carrots, diced and cooked
   ½ cup black olives
   2 tablespoons capers
4. Toss and pour French dressing over each portion. Crisscross each portion with 4 to 6 anchovy fillets and garnish with hard-boiled egg and tomato wedges if available.

TOMATOES

Tomatoes, if purchased quite green, will last up to four weeks without refrigeration. They should be washed in the fruit and vegetable dip, page 28, then dried in the sun. As soon as they are dry, they must be wrapped in new tissue paper and stored (in a flat tray if possible) in a cool, dark spot. They should be inspected periodically, and those developing mold or black spots should be removed. If you are running out of tomatoes and the last few are a bit moldy, an attempt to save them can be made. If the mold is still limited, wipe with a solution of 1 teaspoon clorox in 1 pint of water. If the mold is heavy, cut away the bad spots. Tomatoes thus affected should be left in the sun to ripen and brushed frequently with vegetable oil, especially the bad spots. This prevents air from reaching the mold and inhibits its growth.

Tomatoes have a slightly acidic pH which helps them to resist mold and development of the botulism bacteria. They, therefore, last a long time if precooked, then poured into a canning jar and steamed for forty minutes. If a canning jar is not available, a regular jar can be used and paraffin wax or 2 in. of cooking oil may be poured on top to prevent contact with the air. Tomatoes are easly skinned by dipping them for a mnute in boiling water, then cold water. Sea water may be used. The skin slips off easily. The tomato is then squeezed to remove the seeds. Sauces such as marinara can be made in advance and will last for months.

While at the supermarket, you have probably noticed that several different kinds of tomatoes are sold. There is usually a pile of odd-shaped tomatoes, frequently with a few blemishes on them, and then there are those neat little packets of beautiful, smooth, perfectly round and evenly-sized tomatoes. The latter are a monument to the triumph of machine over man. Technocrats, attempting to develop a tomato-picking machine, met initial failure because tomatoes ripen at their leisure and have the bad habit of growing to different shapes and sizes. This

319

affront to technology was soon corrected, however, for an American university took the problem under consideration and soon developed what we call the machinato—the first vegetable designed to be eaten by a machine. We think it might have been good when they developed the right size, shape, and ripening time, if our boys in the ivory tower had also developed a bit of flavor. But then, machines don't have palates. You do, so buy the ones that look like God might have had something to do with them. They taste better and are your contribution to the war against the Great Machine.

Italian tomatoes, usually found canned in the USA, are often available fresh in other countries, especially those bordering the Mediterranean. Italian tomatoes are normally used for cooking since they are much firmer and less watery than the salad variety. Italian markets sell them in astonishing 2-kilo (4½ pound) packages since no Italian housewife worth her salt would consider making marinara sauce from canned tomatoes. Fresh marinara sauce is delicious, but unfortunately takes a lot of cooking. Italian tomatoes also make fine pickles.

Tomatoes are members of the Solanaceae family, whose members have brought both happiness, comfort, and death to humanity. Millions of people happily consume fresh tomatoes and smoke tobacco, not realizing that they are close cousins and that both are closely related to the deadly nightshades, belladonna, henbane, and mandrake. Happily, all varieties of tomato, even wild ones, are never poisonous.

TOMATO SALADS

When we consider tomato salads, our thoughts are invariably wrenched to a small but excellent Spanish restaurant in downtown Miami named El Minerva. We started dining there years ago before learning the language and had long, occasionally difficult discussions with the waiter who spoke no English. One of these difficult interludes came when we ordered a sliced tomato and onion salad. We finally succeeded in remembering that onions are celbola in Spanish. After getting that message across, we made hand motions somewhat akin to karate chops in the air. Our efforts were rewarded with a plate of onions and tomatoes sliced as desired. But where was the dressing? We wanted the creamy garlic dressing that we had there before. We talked this over for a long time with our friend, the waiter, and many words were said; but in the end, the waiter, with a confused look on his face, went to the kitchen and returned with a half pint of ghastly looking mush awash in oil. It turned out to be a huge load of finely chopped garlic covered by peanut oil (for lightness) and a little olive oil (for flavor). This mixture was used in the kitchen for cooking. We were now as confused as the waiter, but decided to put a dab on the tomatoes and give it a try. The result was so extraordinarily delicious that we ate the whole pot of garlic, wiping up the last bits with pieces of bread. We returned home with a garlic halo that lasted for days, made the dog whine and hide under the bed, turned friends into strangers, and made the postman wince. But it was worth it. The recipe for this social atomic bomb follows.

If you're not up to consuming a half bulb of garlic, there are a few other classic garlic dressings you should consider. They won't make the dog whine and hide under the bed, though rumor has it that garlic repels werewolves. Garlic mayonnaise, page 324, also called allioli sauce or Sauce Provincal, is one of them. All of these fine sauces may be used over tomatoes, cabbage, hard-boiled eggs, cold boiled potatoes, or chicken, shrimp, crab, and potato salads.

ALLIOLI SAUCE—CATALAN BOMBSHELL   Serves Four

1. Finely chop:
      2   bulbs of garlic
   Cover with,
      ¾   cup peanut oil, or other light oil
      ¼   cup olive oil
           pinch of salt
   Let stand overnight. Stir a few times.
2. Slice for each diner a small plate of:
      tomatoes, ¼-in. slices
      Spanish or Bermuda onions, ¼-in. slices
3. Sprinkle tomatoes and onions with:
      salt and pepper
   Spoon on:
      garlic and oil
   Sprinkle with:
      vinegar
   Be sure everyone in the crew eats some of the salad; that way no one will realize how outrageous the others smell.

The residual aroma created by eating huge quantities of garlic may be considerably dispelled with lemonade. Fingers may be washed in lemon juice or baking soda.

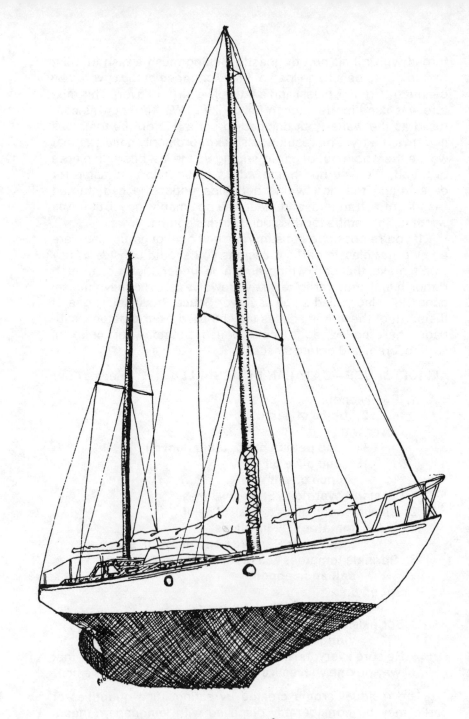

"barcarolle" hauled out

CAESAR SALAD   Serves Four

1. The night before serving combine:
   2 to 3   cloves garlic, chopped
   ½   cup olive oil.
2. The next day before making the salad, dice:
   2   cups dry bread
   Lightly brown in:
   3   tablespoons garlic oil (above)
   ½   teaspoon marjoram
   Reserve croutons.
3. To make dressing, combine:
   2   egg whites
   1   teaspoon salt
   ½   teaspoon pepper
   6   anchovy fillets, crushed
   3   tablespoons vinegar
   1   teaspoon dijon mustard
   ½   teaspoon Worchestershire sauce
4. Break into bite-size pieces:
   2   heads of romaine lettuce
5. Pour dressing over lettuce.
6. Sprinkle over all:
   Juice of 1 lemon
7. Throw on croutons, toss lightly.
8. Pour on remaining garlic oil; toss very lightly.
9. Sprinkle over all:
   ½   cup Parmesan cheese; Serve immediately.

MAYONNAISE AND RELATED SAUCES

To most Americans, mayonnaise is something that comes out of a jar. But fresh, homemade mayonnaise is so different from the commercial variety and far superior because of both its lightness and fine, unpreserved flavor. In France, particularly in the provinces, competition for making the finest mayonnaise is intense. Surprisingly often, the job is left to Papa. Fresh mayonnaise is a recipe that originated 300 years ago. It was finally named to celebrate a French sea victory over the British off Port Mahon, Minorca (Balearic Islands). But the Spanish dispute this and claim mayonnaise as their own, which attests to its popularity. It is a delicately flavored sauce that has, traditionally, been made by hand; any other way is really not as good. Fresh mayonnaise is so superior to the bottled variety that it really should be tried. In addition, it can be combined with other ingredients to make many other sauces, giving the simple mayonnaise base even greater flexibility. One last word: Fresh mayonnaise is a fair weather dish. It simply will not bind together if it is raining or if the bowl is sliding off the galley counter. We must admit, however we cannot imagine anyone wanting to make mayonnaise on a boat in such weather.

BASIC MAYONNAISE   Makes 2 Cups

1. In large mixing bowl combine:
   - **2   egg yolks**
   - **1   teaspoon lemon juice**
2. Add, a spoonful at a time:
   - **1   cup olive oil**

   While adding oil, stir constantly with a fork or whisk; do not whip. Each spoonful of oil must be completely absorbed by the egg before the next spoonful may be added.
3. Add:
   - **½   teaspoon salt**
   - **½   teaspoon pepper**

This is the basic mayonaise that can be served on fish, salads, and boiled meat.

GREEN SAUCE FOR FISH   Makes 2 Cups

To 2 cups basic mayonnaise add:

- **1   tablespoon capers, fresh chopped tarragon, or fresh chopped basil**

GARLIC MAYONNAISE   Makes 2 Cups

If you like garlic, this mayonnaise is good spread on crusty French bread. It is also great for salads and on boiled beef. The Spaniards are fond of it over small, boiled new potatoes served cold, over hard boiled eggs, or as the mayonnaise base for potato salad, which they call ensalada Ruske.

Follow recipe for basic mayonnaise except replace mustard with:

- **3   cloves garlic, minced**

SKORDALIA—A SAUCE FOR FISH   Makes 2½ Cups

This sauce is really lovely served over a sauteed, delicately flavored fish.

To 2 cups garlic mayonnaise add:

- ½ cup almonds, ground
- ¼ cup fine bread crumbs
- 3 teaspoons lemon juice
- 1 tablespoon parsley, chopped

SAUCE ANDALOUSE   Makes 3 Cups

This is another Spanish favorite used over cold vegetable salads, egg salads, or cold, poached fish.

Add to 2 cups basic mayonnaise:

- ½ cup tomato puree
- ½ cup chopped pimento, canned or freshly boiled

DEEP SEA FRUIT SALAD MAYONNAISE   Makes 2½ Cups

This sauce is great over fresh fruit salad, but it will definitely improve the canned variety, which should be half drained before serving.

To 2 cups basic mayonnaise add:

- ½ cup pineapple juice
- 1 teaspoon Grand Marnier

GREEN GODDESS SAUCE   Makes About 2 Cups

A basic mayonnaise sauce usually served on cold, steamed or poached shellfish, such as shrimp, lobster, crab, mussels, or delicately flavored fish.

To 1 cup basic mayonnaise add:

- 11 clove garlic, minced
- 2 anchovy fillets, minced
- ¼ cup onion, finely ground
- 1 tablespoon vinegar
- 1 tablespoon lemon juice
- 1 teaspoon tarragon
- 1 teaspoon salt
- 1 teaspoon pepper
- ½ cup sour cream
- ½ avocado, mashed

Serve cool, but not cold.

RUSSIAN DRESSING Makes About 1⅔ cups

The Spanish call it Salsa American and the Russians never heard of it. This is the popular Russian salad dressing but it is far superior to the bottled, prepared item.
Combine with 1 cup basic mayonnaise:

    1   tablespoon bottled horseradish
    1   teaspoon Wochestershire sauce
    ½   cup catsup
    1   teaspoon onion, grated

Russian dressing is also good on hard-boiled egg halves, french fries, boiled potatoes, or many sandwiches where butter is normally used.

TARTARE SAUCE Makes About 2 Cups

A basic sauce served with fried fish. This fresh sauce is so completely different from the bottled variety that your crew will probably not recognize it as tartare sauce, which it certainly is.
Combine with 1 cup basic mayonnaise:

    1   tablespoon French mustard
    1   tablespoon parsley, chopped
    1   tablespoon sweet pickle, chopped fine and drained.
    1   tablespoon green olives, finely chopped
    ½   tablespoon onion, minced
    1   hard-boiled egg, finely chopped
    1   teaspoon lemon juice

Let stand a few hours, if possible, before serving.

IMPROVED BOTTLED MAYONNAISE Makes About 1¼ Cups

We have saved this for last because we would like to see you give fresh mayonnaise a try. But bottled mayonnaise, not salad spread or any imitation mayonnaise, will definitely be improved by the follow procedure.
Beat into 1 cup commercial mayonnaise:

    3   tablespoons olive oil, added one at a time and allow to be absorbed before continuing.
    1   teaspoon lemon juice, added slowly with the oil.

For additional lightness, beat thoroughly with a fork.

THOUSAND ISLAND DRESSING　　　　Makes About 2 Cups

Combine with 1 cup mayonnaise:

1　teaspoon dijon mustard
½　cup catcup
2　tablespoons green pepper, very finely chopped
2　garlic cloves, minced
1　hard-boiled egg, chopped
1　tablespoon hamburger relish
1　teaspoon salt

FIRST OFFICER'S VINAIGRETTE DRESSING

Makes About 1 Cup

This dressing is made in large enough quantity to last for several meals. The garlic flavor strengthens as the dressing ages. If you are not a garlic freak, go easy on it.

Combine and shake:

⅓　cup vinegar
1　teaspoon mustard
4　cloves garlic, chopped
2　teaspoons tarragon
1　teaspoon basil
⅓　cup oil

Shake before using.

For variety, add Roquefort or Parmesan cheese.

THE CAPTAIN'S ROQUEFORT DRESSING　Makes About 2 Cups

Combine and serve chilled:

1　cup sour cream
1　cup Roquefort or bleu cheese, well crumbled
1　teaspoon Worchestershire sauce
1　clove garlic, minced
¼　teaspoon dill

THE FIRST OFFICER'S AVOCADO DRESSING
Makes About 2 Cups

1.　Thoroughly mash:
1　ripe avocado
1　teaspoon lemon juice
1　cup sour cream

          2   cloves garlic
          a pinch of cayenne pepper
2. Mix, don't beat or whip. For best results, let stand overnight.

CREAMY GARLIC DRESSING   Makes About 2 Cups

This version of Spanish allioli was originally written in the late 9th century. The recipe is certainly much older than that, possibly of Egyptian origin. This gives you some idea of how universal the appeal of garlic and oil is. The dressing is somewhat similar to fresh mayonnaise, but no attempt is made to create a mayonnaise consistency.

1. Thoroughly combine:
          2   cloves garlic, minced
          1   tablespoon lemon or lime juice
          2   raw egg yolks
2. Keep stirring and over a period of 2 to 3 minutes add:
          1½   cups olive oil
   Add:
          salt and pepper to taste

THE CAPTAIN'S SPECIAL SALAD DRESSING
1. Combine the following:
          2-3 cups light cooking oil
          ⅓ cup vinegar
          1 teaspoon sugar, oregano,thyme
          2 teaspoons salt, pepper
          2 hard-boiled, grated egg whites
          ½ cup grated cheese
          1 cup combined of any or all, chopped parsley, scallion ends, green pepper, raw cauliflower, black olives or sauteed mushrooms.
          3 tablespoons chopped garlic
2. Let stand at room temperature for a few hours before use.

17
vegetables and the cruising chef

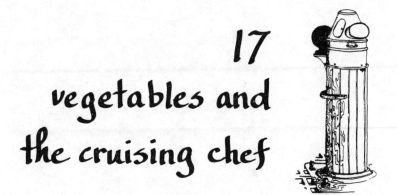

BUY FRESH VEGETABLES

This is certainly easier said than done, especially on a yacht. If you are planning an extended cruise, we heartily urge you to buy freshly picked vegetables from a farmer. Supermarket vegetables have been sitting around for awhile, even before they are first put on the shelf. You might even find a place to pick your own vegetables. The big danger here is going berserk in the vegetable patch and picking enough for the crew of the Pequod. To avoid overpicking, make a list and pin it to the shirt of the captain of the cucumber caper.

Except for tomatoes, vegetables cannot be purchased green, like fruit, and allowed to ripen. They must be purchased when ripe, and the longer they stand, the less tasty they become. The notable exceptions are potatoes, yams, turnips, carrots, beets, squash, eggplant, onions, and cabbage, all of which deteriorate relatively slowly, even without refrigeration. The perishables—fresh peas, asparagus, broccoli, peppers, brussels sprouts—usually keep less than a week. When planning the

sardinian vegetable vendor

menu for a cruise, don't expect, for example, to have fresh peas three weeks into a Pacific crossing.

The taste and shelf life of most vegetables is determined to a considerable extent by the care with which they are stored. Inedible leaves should be removed because they hasten the drying-out process. All vegetables should be washed in the fruit and vegetable dip, page 28, before they come aboard and then allowed to dry in the sun. This process not only kills mold, but it prevents insect pests from infesting the boat. When dry, vegetables may be wrapped in an unread newspaper or in brand new, unopened paperbags. Both of these paper products, if not previously handled, are relatively clean.

The skins of most fruits and vegetables emit toxins or gases that retard the development of bacteria. But the gases of one fruit or vegetable are often detrimental to others. Apples, for example, emit ethylene, which makes carrots and turnips bitter. Onions and garlic hasten the spoilage of potatoes, yams, and bananas. We don't know all of the various "no-nos" and simply recommend that produce be isolated by species and stored in a well ventilated spot.

Head vegetables, such as cabbage, broccoli, and cauliflower, last longer if wrapped in a damp rag. But the cloth must be moistened with chlorinated water (as in the fruit and vegetable dip) or mold rapidly develops. If mold does develop, rewash the head in the vegetable dip, scrub away the mold, and dry in a sunny place; the sunshine will kill the mold.

The maximum shelf life of vegetables will be achieved only with the vigilance of the chef. Stocks must be examined regularly; items beginning to spoil must be eaten, treated, or disgarded. The old saying about "one rotten apple" is true!

If a vegetable shows early signs of deterioration, the best solution is to cut the bad part away and eat the rest. If there is too much to eat at one time, cut away the bad part and enough of the healthy part to eliminate reinfection. Plug the hole with margarine or other vegetable shortening. In most cases, these treated vegetables will last an additional few days.

The life of most vegetables is extended if they are stored in a dark spot. Onions and potatoes may be hung in a mush sack or hammock. But more delicate vegetables bruise if stored this way. The best storage container is a dish drainer. The plastic-coated wire does not rust and air circulates around the vegetables. Dish drainers are space savers too, since they may be stacked conveniently under the galley sink.

sand dollar

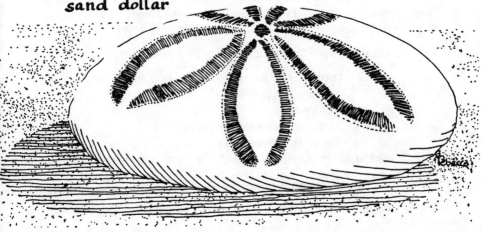

Freeze dried vegetables are often as tasty and nutritious as frozen vegetables. Peas, green beans, and carrots taste best, last longest, need no special handling, and are easily cooked. They are extremely expensive if purchased as yacht or trail food, but the cost for commercial quantities is significantly less. Unfortunately, all freeze dried foods are not excellent like the whole vegetables. The soup is usually ghastly; the entrees are usually fair, better for hiking where weight is a major consideration. Prepared freeze dried food is usually quite expensive.

BREAK OR CUT VEGETABLES JUST ENOUGH TO HANDLE

Do not finely chop vegetables unless a recipe specifically calls for it. Try to avoid mashing or grinding hot vegetables since this results in vitamin breakdown. The exceptions are potatoes and yams which are not affected by mashing or grinding.

COOK VEGETABLES JUST ENOUGH TO MAKE THEM TENDER

Nothing destroys food value like overcooking, and vegetables are most easily murdered. Canned vegetables are overcooked if safely processed. For this reason they are virtually worthless and must be synthetically fortified to make them nutritious. Maximum food value and flavor are enjoyed if the vegetable is cooked "al dente," offering a bit of resistance to the teeth. This is just a little bit crispier than most Americans like, but the increased food value is tremendous. Pressure cooking is an excellent technique for the cooking of vegetables.

VEGETABLE AND FRUIT TENDERIZER

Time makes most vegetables tough and slightly bitter. There is no way to restore their garden freshness. The following dip is not a vegetable fountain of youth, but it usually helps.

1. Soak not-so-fresh vegetables for 2 hours in:

>   2   **tablespoons meat tenderizer, made with papin or papaya juice**
>   1   **pint water**
>   2   **tablespoons lemon juice**
>   2   **tablespoons sugar**

2. Drain off most of the liquid; steam or simmer vegetables in same pot.

Another method is to simmer the vegetables in milk, which may be fresh, canned, or reconstituted. The milk, like the marinade above, tenderizes, stabilizes color, and extracts bitterness.

VEGETABLE COOKING TECHNIQUES

Our two favorite approaches are pressure cooking, page 56, and Chinese or stir frying.

Stir frying consists of cooking the sliced vegetable in a scant amount of very hot vegetable oil (1 or 2 teaspoons). Never use butter or margarine because they burn over high heat. The vegetables are turned **constantly** with a spoon to avoid burning. No time to answer the phone. Stir frying cooks vegetables in 3 to 5 minutes and retains their crispness. A fine mixed vegetable dish can be created if vegetables are added to the pan in the proper order, the most delicate added last. When seasoned with soy sauce and served over rice, it can make a fine main course.

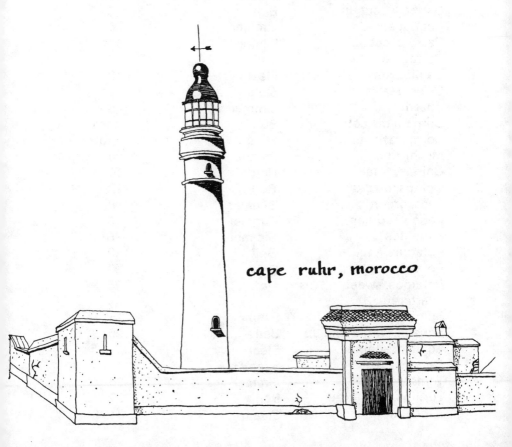

cape ruhr, morocco

COOKING CHART
FOR
BOILING, STEAMING, OR SIMMERING FRESH VEGETABLES
(Pressure Cooking Vegetables, page 56)

VEGETABLE	METHOD	TIME IN MINUTES
Artichokes, whole	Boil	25
Asparagus	Steam	8
Bamboo shoots	Boil	8
Beans, fresh	Simmer	8
Beans, lima	Simmer	15
Beans, pinto	Boil	20 to 30
Beets, cut up	Simmer	10
Breadfruit	Boil	60
Broccoli	Steam	10
Brussels Sprouts	Steam	10
Cabbage, cut up	Boil	8
Cabbage, red	Simmer	30
Carrots, cut up	Simmer	10
Carrots, whole	Boil	13
Cauliflower	Steam	10
Celery stalks	Steam	6
Chard	Simmer	45
Corn on the cob	Boil	4 to 6
Corn, fresh cut	Steam	2 to 3
Mushrooms	Steam	20
Onions, small	Boil	10
Onions, medium	Boil	12
Peas, green	Simmer	8
Peppers, green	Simmer	6
Pimentos	Simmer	6
Potatoes, small	Boil	20
Potatoes, cutup	Boil	20
Potatoes, sweet, quartered	Boil	25
Spinach	Simmer	15
Squash, winter, cut up	Boil	25
Squash, summer	Steam	3 to 5
Taro	Simmer	45
Tomatoes	Simmer	20
Turnips, quartered	Boil	20
Zucchini	Steam	3 to 5

ARTICHOKES

Globe artichokes, not Jerusalem artichokes, rank high on our list of fine cruising vegetables. If properly treated, they last a long time, cook easily, taste delightful both hot or cold, and inspire many excellent sauce creations. Their long cooking time assures the diner that they are sterilized and will remain edible for many days.

STORING ARTICHOKES

If purchased fresh and young with at least 2 inches of stem, then properly prepared, artichokes will last three weeks or more of an ocean passage without refrigeration. To prepare it for storage, soak the artichoke for an hour in the fruit and vegetable dip, page 28, then sun dry. Next cut off an inch of the stem exposing a moist and obviously alive cross section. Saturate a cotton ball with chlorinated water (1 teaspoon Clorox per gallon) and place it over the cut. An aspirin tablet goes on next, then the whole stem is covered with plastic and secured with a rubber band. The 'chokes should be stored upright in a cool, dark spot. Examine the stem pack weekly. More chlorinated water may be added with a syringe; just push it through the plastic and give the cotton a shot.

COOKING ARTICHOKES

1. Pull off any brown or leathery leaves.
2. Cut the stem within a half inch of the flower.
3. Pressure steam on a trivet in 1½ cups of water for 10 minutes, or steam in a covered pot for 45 minutes. (Very small 'chokes need only 10 minutes pressure cooking or 35 minutes of normal steaming.)
4. Turn upside down and allow to drain.

EATING ARTICHOKES

This is a bit of an art since the major part of the globe is tough and inedible. Only the heart and the small lump of flesh at the base of each leaf are tender and delicious. Small, white, transparent leaves at the center of the flower conceal the "choke," tough fibers that will catch in your throat; this part should not be eaten.

The outer leaves are usually tough, and at least one or two rows should be discarded. The remaining leaves are pulled off one at a time, dipped in sauce, and the little lump of flesh on the

inside base of each leaf is eaten. This is done, traditionally, by placing the base of the leaf in your mouth, holding it with the teeth, then pulling it out; the flesh remains in your mouth while the rest is discarded. The heart of the artichoke, located at its base, is tender and very delicious. Scrape or cut away the immature leaves and the hairy choke. Be sure to remove all of the hair. The remaining base is dipped in sauce and enjoyed.

ARTICHOKE SAUCES

We must admit that the sauce is often the most outstanding and delicious part of the artichoke! The easiest cruising sauce is made by mixing your own combination of hot, melted butter, grated Parmesan cheese, and enough condensed milk for the desired consistency. Other outstanding sauces are: Hollandaise, fresh mayonnaise, mustard or garlic mayonnaise, vinaigrette, or good old melted butter.

EXTENDING THE LIFE OF COOKED ARTICHOKES

You may on occasion come upon a treasure trove of cheap, delicious artichokes. Artichokes are particularly inexpensive and common in Africa and California, two jumping off places for trans-ocean passages. Stock up when the price and quality are right and pack the hearts in oil and spices.

1. Remove leaves and choke; quarter the heart.
2. Pack tightly into scalded small canning jars, ½ pint or less.
3. Cover artichokes with mixture of:

> ½   cup vegetable oil or peanut oil
> 3   tablespoons white vinegar
> 3   cloves garlic, well chopped
> 1   teaspoon salt
> ½   teaspoon basil
> ½   teaspoon thyme
>
> This is enough for ½ pint of artichokes. Fill to within ¾ inch of the top.

4. Loosely cap jar and place on trivet in pressure cooker. Fill cooker with water until it half covers the jar.
5. Pressure cook for 30 minutes. Remove jar and screw cap tight.

   Home-canned artichokes seem immortal, but turn gray if they become contaminated—a rare occurrence.

CANNED ARTICHOKES

Artichokes are very delicate in flavor and become bland and mushy when packed in water. Most canned artichokes are packed in water and should be avoided. However, if packed in a marinade, they are as tasty as those in cocktail size jars.

ASPARAGUS

This aristocrat of the vegetable world loves the light touch. Overcook it and the delightful, subtle flavor is gone. Young, thin asparagus is the most sensitive and needs nothing more than a little steam to make it tender. Older, thicker shoots should be peeled with a potato parer just before cooking.

STORING ASPARAGUS

If properly prepared, asparagus will last 1 to 2 weeks without refrigeration. To prepare it for storage, tie it with a string into one-meal bunches for ease of handling. Soak the bunches in the fruit and vegetable dip, page 28. Cut off the bottom inch of each bunch, exposing a live, moist cross section. Store the bunches upright on a cloth saturated with chlorinated water (1 teaspoon per gallon of water). The cloth should be changed every few days.

COOKING ASPARAGUS

When cooking the asparagus, steam the bunches upright, still held together with the string. It is best to keep the stems from direct heat by using a cooking trivet. Use a large pot with a lid, or two pots, one upside down on the other. Steam in 2 cups of water for 8 to 10 minutes, a little longer for very thick asparagus.

ASPARAGUS SAUCES AND GARNISHES

Asparagus well brushed with butter and garnished with a lemon wedge is always a delight. For special occasions, Hollandaise sauce complements the delicate flavor of asparagus. Fresh garlic mayonnaise is another welcome addition. Cracker crumbs that are sauteed golden in butter and seasoned with thyme and marjoram make a simple and delicate garnish.

GREEN BEANS

Green beans vary tremendously in size, color, and tenderness in different parts of the world. Those sold in the USA have been hybridized to a fine degree of tenderness, and it is usually not necessary to string them. But in many other places, they must not only be destrung, but cut up as well. The thinner and shorter the bean, the more delicate the flavor. Like all other vegetables, green or wax beans may be soaked in the fruit and vegetable dip, page 28, sun dried, and stored in a clean, unused paper bag. Green or wax beans last about two weeks without refrigeration, but become somewhat tough after four or five days and should be soaked in the vegetable tenderizer, page 332, or milk.

Like most vegetables, green beans are easily overcooked and do not stand up to several reheatings. They may be prepared in a variety of ways. They are, of course, delicious steamed for 8 minutes, or pressure steamed, and served with butter, Hollandaise, cheese sauce, fried bacon and breadcrumbs, or sprinkled with Parmesan cheese. Cooked green beans, served cold, make a fine salad when mixed with onions, black olives, anchovies, sauteed mushrooms, or cheese. As a mixed vegetable they improve canned corn and are a welcome addition to several canned soups, such as chicken noodle, minestrone, and split pea. Green bean and onion omelets make a fine beginning to the day.

When fresh stores are exhausted, we prefer freeze dried green beans. Unlike canned green beans, which we never use, freeze dried green beans are as tasty as frozen beans. They should be simmered for 20 mintues in unsalted water because presalting toughens them. Cooking in sea water makes them bitter.

SEVERAL GREEN BEAN TREATS

Parboil green beans for 5 minutes, then saute with chopped onions, a pinch of marjoram, salt, and pepper. Green peppers make a fine addition.

Brown beans and chopped almonds in butter, add to rice 1 minute before rice is cooked.

Green beans, parboiled 4 minutes, then pan fried with potatoes make excellent hash browns.

Pickled green beans are delicious when made from cooked beans, marinated in vinegar and oil with chopped, raw onions, salt and garlic.

GREEN BEAN, BACON, AND POTATO CASSEROLE

Serves Four

There are many variations of this fine recipe. Green peppers, pimentos, bits of celery, to name a few, add variety to this dish.

1. Fry until golden in pressure cooker:

    8 slices bacon, coarsely chopped

2. Remove bacon, but leave a bit of oil in bottom of pot to prevent scorching.

3. Add to pot:

    1 cup chicken stock, or 1 bouillon cube dissolved in 1 cup water

4. Add in layers to pot:

    3 potatoes, sliced
    1 pound green beans, cut up
    2 teaspoons celery salt
    2 teaspoons pepper
    bacon
    a few dots butter for each layer

5. Pressure cook for just 2 minutes after first jiggle. Cool pot with water and examine for doneness. Ingredients should be almost cooked. Simmer over low heat until done to taste.

IMPROVING CANNED BAKED BEANS

We admit to being baked bean lovers. Canned beans can be very tasty especially when you add your own special touch.

OLD-FASHIONED BEANS

Serves Four

1. Add to pot:

    1 can (28 oz.) pork and beans
    2 tablespoons molasses
    1 tablespoon catsup
    1 tablespoon mustard
    1 small onion studded with 3 cloves

2. Simmer over low heat for 15 minutes, stirring occasionally.

CURRIED BEANS
Serves Four

1. Add to pot:

   1   can (28-oz.) pork and beans
   2   tablespoons curry powder
   1   tablespoon ginger

2. Simmer until curry smell disappears.

BEANS 'N BACON
Serves Two

1. Fry in pot:

   6   strips bacon, coarsely chopped

2. Drain and add:

   1   can (16-oz) pork and beans

3. Simmer until hot.

LIMA BEANS

Fresh baby lima beans with salt and butter are a real treat. Fresh lima beans may be hulled by slitting the edge of the pod. The beans pop out easily. But remember that the pods account for almost 50 percent of the total weight. When buying unshelled lima beans, 1½ to 2 pounds are needed fo feed four. Baby limas may be steamed in a little water for 15 minutes or pressure cooked for just 2 minutes.

Large limas or dried lima beans that have been soaked for a few hours take 30 to 35 minutes of simmering or 3½ minutes in a pressure cooker. They are less flavorful than baby lima beans and are enhanced by rich sauces. Our favorite recipe for these mature beans follows.

LIMA BEANS IN TOMATO SAUCE
Serves Four

1. Combine in large pan:

   1   cup lima beans
   1   cup canned Italian tomatoes
   2   cloves garlic, chopped
   ½   cup olive oil
   water to cover

2. Simmer, lid off, until liquid thickens, about 20 minutes.

3. Add to pot:

   2   teaspoons butter
   1   teaspoon celery seed
   a pinch each of salt and pepper

4. Simmer until beans are soft, adding water if necessary. Season to taste.

BROCCOLI

Broccoli is a member of the mustard family and is a common sight at most supermarkets. The shelf life of broccoli may be extended in a number of ways. If a half inch of stem is cut away, exposing a live cross section, the plant may be placed in a glass of water like any other flower. Its life may also be extended by covering the broccoli with a towel, moistened in chlorinated water (1 teaspoon per gallon of water). This process retards the yellowing or preblooming stage of broccoli, which is tough and dry when cooked. The shelf life of broccoli may also be extended by the method used for artichokes, page 336.

The best way to cook broccoli is to steam it.

1. Cut head into a half dozen pieces.
2. Place upright in pot with 1 inch of water in bottom; be sure the delicate heads do not fall over.
3. Bring to boil; cover and steam for 10 minutes or just until tender.

We love broccoli with cheese sauce, page 406, but it is also delicious with Hollandaise, breadcrumbs, and many other sauces.

BREADFRUIT

Breadfruit is the large, starchy product of an exceptionally beautiful tree found in the Pacific Islands. The globular, greenish-brown fruit, 6 to 8 inches in diameter, was brought to the attention of the western world in the mid-eighteenth century by Captain James Cook of the research vessel Resolution. It was believed that breadfruit would be a fine supplement to the diet of West Indian slaves. Cook's sailing master, William Bligh, was commissioned to go to Tahiti and return with a cargo of breadfruit plants. Despite Bligh's long association with Captain Cook, Bligh had not learned to treat his men humanely, and he imposed harsh British Navy discipline. Floggings and short rations combined with light breezes and insufficient water soon had its effect. The ship's company mutinied on April 28, 1789. Captain Bligh and 18 men were set adrift in a 23-foot ship's boat, and the breadfruit was hurled into the sea after them. The mutineers, fearing vengence, briefly returned to Tahiti, but soon sailed with six Tahitian men and 12 Tahitian women to Pitcairn Island, an unknown, uncharted dot of rock 2½ miles long and less than a mile wide just south of the Tropic of Capricorn. The mutineers

the bark
"resolution"

burned their ship, the Bounty. Considering the hard life of eighteenth century sailors and the certain fate that awaited them in England, these mutineers were most content with life in their newly founded community. Today, Pitcairn Island consists of 100 souls.

Despite his evil personality, Captain Bligh was made of stern stuff. He sailed his tiny lifeboat 3,618 miles across the Pacific Ocean with little fresh water and short rations, living mostly on turtles and rainwater. They made several stops at small islands along the way where they found fruit and shellfish. Several of the ship's company died, but in July, 1789, after almost 3 months, Bligh sighted the island of Timor and was saved.

The mutineers were never brought to trial. By the time Pitcairn Island was discovered, all of them were dead except one, and he was an old, old man. Bligh, despite his incredible seamanship and subsequent commissions, was never able to outlive the nickname "Breadfruit Bligh" and died near the turn of the century, bitter and obscure.

And the breadfruit? It eventually reached its destination, but no one had ever bothered to ask the slaves if they liked it. Breadfruit never caught on in the West Indies. The slaves preferred plantains and black beans, which they knew how to grow and cook.

The moral of the story, if there is one, is that no cruising chef with lots of beer, wine, and juice, fine smells from the galley, and contented grunts from the table ever need fear the fate of Captain Bligh.

Breadfruit meat is slightly fibrous, light yellow in color, and somewhat sweet. Breadfruit with seeds may be eaten raw and the seeds roasted like chestnuts. Seedless varieties must be cooked. The tough core is usually removed, either before or after cooking. Mature fruit has a bit of green color. Avoid blemished or pulpy textured specimens.

To cook breadfruit:
1. Cut and pressure cook for 15 minutes in 1½ cup of water. Season with butter and cinnamon, salt, and pepper.
2. Or cut and bake with butter and cinnamon at 375° for 1 hour.

Breadfruit may be mashed, like potatoes, without nutritional loss. It may also be French fried and then dipped into poi, a dish made from taro root that has been baked, pounded, and fermented.

ABOUT CABBAGE

Of casual interest to the American chef, cabbage is highly respected in many isolated parts of the world. It may be grown in humble soil from Greenland to Tierra del Fuego. In many of these far flung places it is the principal source of vitamin C. Because of its vitamins and its long shelf life without refrigeration, cabbage is important to the cruising chef. When eaten raw, cabbage supplies roughage, which is particularly important on long passages when other sources of roughage are gone. Cabbage is best cooked by pressure steaming, a technique that minimizes the loss of water soluble vitamin C. Shredded or well chopped cabbage may be added raw to all of the legume soups just when they are finished cooking. The internal temperature of the soup will cook the cabbage "al dente," in this case half raw, a very pleasing effect and quite nutritious. Cabbage sauteed in oil or butter makes a tasty addition to any meal.

Sauerkraut is shredded, fermented cabbage; it may be baked, or simmered, or eaten with full flavor as it comes from the can. Sauerkraut is a very ancient dish long valued for its nutrition. The ancient Chinese belived it had medicinal value. For about 100 years captains who cared about their crews—and they were few—fed them sauerkraut believing that it would prevent scurvy, a disease caused by chronic vitamin C deficiency. They weren't far from the truth, for fresh cabbage would have worked very well. But the fermenting process of sauerkraut destroys the vitamin C in cabbage. It took that great humanitarian, daring explorer and navigator, Captain Cook to prove that lime juice and fresh vegetables are all that is needed to prevent this dread disease. On his second voyage of exploration, which lasted more than 3 years, he did not lose a single man to scurvy.

GRAND BANKS DELIGHT Serves Six

Rare, indeed, is the dinner of a Grand Banks fisherman that does not consist of cod, cod, and more cod. But winters on the Grand Banks are long and cold, and many a fishing boat, even today, finds itself icebound in some tiny, remote harbor with no hope of breaking out until the Spring thaw. This recipe is a favorite of the Portuguese, and it seems like heaven itself after six long months of cod. It is particularly useful to the long distance cruiser because it is made with long lasting, non-refrigerated stores. It is also a fine way to use leftover canned ham.

- 1 **medium cabbage**
- 4 **large potatoes**
- 1 **cup chicken stock or bouillon**
- ½ **cup butter**
- 2 **tablespoons dry sherry (optional)**
  caraway or celery seed
  salt
  leftover canned ham

1. Cut cabbage into 1-inch rounds.
2. Peel potatoes; slice into ½-inch rounds.
3. Shred ham, or slice finely and chop.
4. Put a layer of cabbage in bottom of pot. Sprinkle with salt and a pinch of caraway or celery seed.
5. Add a layer of potatoes; dot with butter. Then add a layer of ham. Repeat this process until all ingredients are used.
6. Pour chicken stock or bouillon over all and, if desired, dry sherry.
7. Pressure cook for 6 minutes at 15 pounds.

CABBAGE ON THE WHALE'S BACK   Serves Six to Eight

Rebecca and I once signed as crew of a 30-foot Azorian whaling canoe. The seven of us would row up to a 60-foot sleeping sperm whale and stick a harpoon in its back. Just seconds later the whale would wake up and become highly aggravated. If we were unlucky, the whale would turn around and make a very determined effort to have whalers on the half-shell for lunch—something an enraged 45-ton animal seems very capable of doing when only 3 feet away.

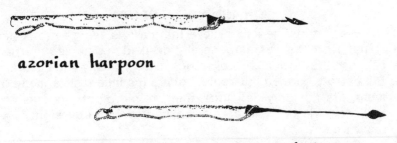

azorian harpoon

azorian whale lance

Normally the whale would run—much to our relief. Being towed at 15 knots behind a wounded whale is quite an experience. Americans call it a "Nantucket sleighride;" the Azorians call it "The Fast Boat to Lisbon." No matter what you call it, it's no row around the lake.

Eventually the whale would tire. We would then row up to it and, in the words of the harpooner, "give it a prick" with an 8-foot, razor sharp lance. Whales are not constructed to take much abuse of this type; after about 2 hours, he was ours. The dead whale was then tied to the boat, and everyone would have lunch. It usually consisted of a tomato and cabbage stew, which always tasted better when served "on the whale's back."

1. Cut into small wedges and pressure steam for 4 minutes at 15 lbs:

   1 large head cabbage
   1 cup chicken bouillon

2. Fry until just brown:
   8 slices bacon, chopped

3. In bacon drippings, fry until golden:
   2 onions chopped
   a few slices of green pepper (optional)

4. Add to pressure cooker:

   bacon
   2 tablespoons bacon drippings
   1 cup tomato puree
   2 tablespoons brown sugar
   1 teaspoon celery salt
   1 teaspoon pepper
   1 teaspoon thyme

5. Simmer until cabbage is tender and serve.

OH, NO, NOT CARROTS!

We are inclined to believe that carrots seem to rank near spinach on the list of generally disliked vegetables. Perhaps because they are usually overcooksd until mushy and flavorless. But carrots cooked "al dente," offering a little resistance to the teeth, are not only delicious, they are more nutritious as well. However, the old tale about carrots improving eyesight is not really true.

During World War II, the United States discovered that red goggles accelerated the adaptation of the eye to darkness. This was quite a discovery, one that the Germans did not make. In order to conceal from the Germans the real reason for improved night vision, the rumor was circulated that pilots were fed huge quantities of carrot juice before a mission. Apparently, the rumor was a huge success.

Carrots, fresh from the earth, store best when left unwashed until just before use. Carrots secrete natural toxins that inhibit the effects of bacteria and mold. But if your carrots come from the supermarket and have been cleaned, it is best to rewash them in the fruit and vegetable dip, page 28, before storage. We usually store carrots dry in a dark, cool spot. Moistening them induces sprouting, which spoils their taste. Carrot greens should be removed before storage; cut them back if they reappear.

Carrots become limp and woody after about 2½ to 3 weeks without refrigeration; they are also less flavorful. However, some of the crispness can be restored by slicing thinly and soaking them in a saturated salt solution for an hour before cooking. We must admit, in all fairness, that limp, wooden carrots are not high on our list of fine foods.

The life of carrots may be extended by packing them in dirt. If carrots are pulled carefully from the soil and replanted at an acute angle in a fruit box of soil, they will continue to grow for months. They do well stored on deck under the dinghy and need water only once or twice per week. The small, tender carrots make the best starters and can be packed with amazing density in good earth.

Our two favorite methods of cooking carrots are pressure steaming and Chinese frying. Small carrots may be cooked whole and unpeeled. Large carrots are more tasty if peeled and thinly sliced at an angle. Carrots simmered in water take 15 minutes to cook. Pressure steamed slices take 2 minutes at 15 pounds; larger cuts, like quarters, take 4 minutes.

Stir frying, the Chinese way, requires no water. Just saute in:

2   tablespoons butter
½   medium onion, chopped

Keep the pan covered and cook for about 15 to 20 minutes over medium heat, stirring frequently. A quarter cup of white wine, added after 10 minutes, makes a pleasant variation. Allow the wine to cook away before replacing the lid.

EGGPLANT

Cooks often avoid eggplant because of the huge amount of oil needed to fry it. Another problem is that eggplant contains a great deal of water. For best results, some of the water should be extracted before cooking the eggplant. The French and Italian solution is to slice the skinned eggplant, then salt each slice. The salted slices are placed on a cookie sheet that tilts into the sink. The salt leaches the water from the slices and reduces the cooking time. It also somewhat toughens the fiber preventing the slices from falling apart during cooking. Salted slices must be thoroughly washed before use. The English, who call eggplant "aubergine," place the slices beneath a board and stack weights on it to press the water out. This eliminates the salting and subsequent washing, but requires some degree of organization. Whichever method you choose, the result is significantly reduced cooking time and firmer eggplant.

Eggplant is one of the long lasting vegetables, particularly immune to fungus and mold. Time withers it like lines on an old woman's face. After five or six weeks without refrigeration, it is dry and bitter. Since they dry from the skin in, the big fat ones are best. This way the spongy, dry layer can be pared away, the rest used.

DEEP FRIED EGGPLANT   Serves Four

Soaking for an hour in milk before cooking leaches the bitter flavor from not-so-fresh eggplant.

1. Cut into ½-inch rounds:
    eggplant
2. Dip eggplant in:
    flour, bran, meal, or fine bread crumbs (seasoned with 1 teaspoon pepper per cup)
3. Deep fry in:
    Vegetable oil, turning once or twice and being careful not to burn.

SAUTEED EGGPLANT   Serves Four

1. Cut into ½-inch rounds:
    1 eggplant
2. Dip into:
    milk

3. Fry over medium low heat in:
   butter (may be seasoned with celery seed)
   Do not turn heat too high or the butter will burn.
4. Cook until eggplant is tender, not mushy.

LEFTOVER FRIED EGGPLANT

Leftover fried eggplant makes the most delicious cold appetizer.

1. Sprinkle each round with:
   garlic salt
   wine vinegar
1. Cover with layer of:
   tomato paste
3. Top with:
   a mushroom half, prefried in butter (optional)
4. Put in large dish and cover with:
   olive oil
5. Let stand overnight in refrigerator or at room temperature; serve the next night.

TUNA ON EGGPLANT SANDWICH   Serves Four

1. Fry floured eggplant rounds in:
   oil
2. While they are cooking; combine in pot:
   1 tablespoon hot butter
   1 can (7 oz.) tuna, flaked
   a pinch of celery seed or celery salt
3. Heat for 5 minutes, stirring occasionally.
4. When the eggplant is browned, blot it, then cover with a spoonful of tuna and place another eggplant round on top. Delicious! Goes well with applesauce.

END-OF-THE-PASSAGE LENTILBURGERS   Makes 8 Patties

When the fresh meat is gone and the crew is dreaming of milkshakes and hamburgers, these tasty lentilburgers brighten the day. You may like them so well that they become basic ammunition in your cruising arsenal. A good way to get two different meals from one pot is to first make a big pressure cooker pot of lentil soup, page 106. Remove 3 cups lentils for the burgers, then curry the soup for dinner. The burgers make a great lunch. Lentilburgers are high in protein and low in fat.

3 cups cooked lentils (or mix with cooked soy
    beans)
¾ cup onion, finely chopped and sauteed until
    golden in butter
3 cups cracker crumbs (preferably whole wheat)
3 eggs, beaten
1 tablespoon vinegar
2½ tablespoons dijon mustard
    oil
    flour
    salt and pepper
1. Mix together all ingredients; make into patties.
2. Flour the patties all over; fry over high heat, 5 minutes
   per side. Serve with hamburger relish.

DRIED MUSHROOMS

Dried mushrooms look about as promising as used chewing gum, but don't let their unappetizing appearance fool you. While their looks promise little, they possess an unseen potential that opens new vistas for the cruising chef. Soak them for a half hour in enough hot water to cover. They will soften, swelling to a respectable size full of a pronounced mushroom flavor. Stored in a jar with a few grains of rice to absorb moisture, they last for many months without becoming moldy or losing their potency. A number of varieties are commercially available, such as the famed morels, black Chinese mushrooms, cepes, and the well known mushroom relatives, truffles. In addition to those that may be purchased, you can easily dry your own mushrooms. To do this, thoroughly wash fresh mushrooms in several changes of water. Then slice them not more than ¼-inch thick and soak for a few minutes in the fruit and vegetable dip, page 28. String the treated mushrooms on ordinary sewing thread and hang in the rigging to dry, or spread a single layer in a broiler pan and bake over night at 175°, just enough heat to take away the moisture. Store in a loosely capped jar to allow the circulation of air but confine the strong aroma of dried mushrooms. Since dried mushrooms weigh less, are simple to use, and taste delicious, we prefer them to the canned variety. They may be added directly to soups, such as mushroom and barley, or reconstituted in hot water and used in omelets, stews, stuffings, and anything else that tastes delicious with fresh mushrooms. When you spot dried mushrooms for sale in some market, don't turn up your nose at their unappetizing appearance; they are the sailor's friend. No gourmet galley is truly complete without them.

ONION RINGS
Serves Four to Six

Onion rings are a special end-of-the-passage delight, but are just as good in port. The secret of success here is to reduce the labor of handling all those onion rings one at a time.

1. Cut into rings about ¼-inch thick;
   3 medium onions
2. Soak the whole lot in a mixture of:
   2 beaten eggs
   1 cup milk
3. Turn the onions until coated.
4. Lift out by the handful at a time, allowing excess liquid to drain. Drop into a plastic bag containing:
   seasoned flour
5. Fry until golden in:
   ½ to ¾-inch hot vegetable oil
6. Drain in colander and serve.

THE POTATO

The humble potato is the cruiser's best friend. We can't even tell you how long they last because we have never been on a cruise long enough to see them go bad. Our longest sea voyage was 50 days. The Atlantic whalers used to take big tubs of them to sea. We often wonder how potatoes French fried in blubber would taste—hardly the cholesterol counter's dream!

Potatoes are not only long lasting, they are also nutritious and not as fattening as you think. A potato has only as much carbohydrate as a glass of apple juice; it's all that lovely butter, sour cream, and crumbled bacon that adds on the calories. The skin of the potato contains most of the noncarbohydrate nutrition, including several vitamins and minerals, not to mention the roughage. Think twice before throwing away the skin.

SELECTING POTATOES FOR A SEA VOYAGE

Don't buy just any sack of potatoes for a long sea voyage. Select only mature baking potatoes, preferably large, smooth skinned, even textured ones, even if they cost a little more. Mature baking potatoes are best because their thick, tough

otocictrstenic tower,
yugoslavia

skins are more resistant to bruising and mold than new or boiling potatoes.

To be sure you are purchasing potatoes that will keep, follow this simple procedure:

1. Cut several potatoes open on the spot to be sure that they have not been frozen. Frozen potatoes are grey or black beneath the skin and are totally worthless. They won't last a week.
2. Cut a potato into quarters and look for pest holes or worms. If you find one, there will invariable be more.
3. Count the eyes on 3 to 4 sample potatoes. If they have more than three eyes each, they have been sitting around for a while and will soon sprout.

INSTANT POTATOES

Instant potatoes often taste a bit like paste, especially if mixed with hot water. The flavor may be improved by adding whole or condensed (not powdered) milk and lots of butter. Instant potatoes should be purchased in foil packets as the potato powder is hygroscopic and absorbs moisture from the air. It spoils quickly if packed in a cardboard box.

Instant mashed potatoes make a great topping for stews: making a beef stew, for example, into a beef pie, a particularly handy way to stretch leftover food.

PREPARATION AND STOWAGE FOR SEA

If the potatoes are fresh from the earth, do not wash them. The skins are surrounded with bacteria resistant toxins that inhibit spoilage. If there is any doubt as to their freshness, wash them thoroughly in the fruit and vegetable dip, page 28, twist off all eyes. Store in fruit trays or dish drainer trays, not in a big box or sack where the bottom ones might be damaged by the ship's motion. The damaged potatoes would decay and begin to spoil the ones above.

SAVING PARTIALLY MOLDY POTATOES

As with all fresh fruits and vegetables, frequent inspection and immediate use of bruised potatoes will help to prevent an epidemic. If immediate use is not possible, the bruise or mold spot may be cut away and the hole plugged with margarine or vegetable oil. If the damage is extensive, cut the bad half away and set the good cut end on a greased sheet of aluminum foil. These potatoes will last 4 to 5 days without refrigeration.

TYPICAL COOKING TECHNIQUES

Pressure steam large potatoes for 12 minutes, quartered large potatoes for 6 minutes, and small or diced potatoes for 3 minutes; cook all at 15 lbs. pressure.

Boil large potatoes (unskinned) for 35 minutes, quartered large potatoes for 25 minutes, and small new potatoes or diced potatoes for 20 minutes; boil all in enough water to cover.

For those galleys without ovens, potatoes can be baked on top of the stove. Bake on a trivet in a large covered pot. Cooking is accelerated if a large nail, marlin spike, or screw is pushed into each potato. Cook over medium heat for 40 minutes for large potatoes, 30 minutes for small ones. Push a fork into the potato to test it. After the initial resistance of the skin, the fork should slip easily to the center. Never wrap aluminum foil on a potato in the galley; it retards stove top cookery. Use foil only if the potato is being baked on an open fire. If this is the case, prick the potato through the foil in many places to allow the steam to escape.

POTATO PANCAKE DELIGHT Serves Six

If made properly, these potato pancakes are an absolute delight. The secret of success is to make them small, not more than 2 inches across and as thin as possible. This cooks them crispy on the outside and done, not raw, on the inside. The thinner you make them, the quicker they cook.

1. Combine in mixing bowl:
   - 4 **large, mature potatoes, shredded**
   - 1 **large onion, grated**
   - ½ **teaspoon baking powder**
   - 3 **eggs, beaten**
   - 4 **teaspoon flour**
   - 2 **teaspoons salt**
1. Toss the mixture thoroughly; shape into patties.
2. Fry over high heat in:
   vegetable oil, enough to half cover
   Turn several times until crisp, golden brown.
3. Drain on paper. Serve with applesauce or cold sour cream.

POTATO AND CHEESE CASSEROLE

Here is a fine deep water dish made quickly from long lasting ingredients.

1. In pressure cooker pot, fry:
   - 3 **large onions, diced**
   - 1 **lb. bacon, chopped**
   When onions are golden, remove them and bacon from pot.
2. Layer pot from bottom up in the following order:
   onions and bacon
   4 **medium potatoes, sliced raw**
   salt and pepper

½ lb. grated mild cheese, such as Gruyere or
Gouda
Liberal amount of butter dots
1 cup milk, poured over the top
Continue to make layers until all ingredients
have been used.
3. Pressure cook for 8 minutes at 15 lbs. The potatoes
should be cooked; but firm. Garnish with slices of
steamed green pepper.

MASHED POTATOES   Serves Four

This old favorite is more popular with the crew than the
cook. It does take a bit of work, and then there's that gooey pot
to take care of afterwards. Don't wash it in the galley sink.
Mashed potatoes can act just like concrete and plug the pipes.
But, ah, mashed potatoes are delicious!

1. Pressure cook for 15 minutes at 15 pounds:
   4 large, mature potatoes
2. Slip off skins under running water; mash potatoes with
   fork, masher, or blunt end of a wooden fid.
3. Add to pot:
   ½ cup condensed milk
   1 teaspoon salt
   3 to 4 tablespoons butter
   Combine thoroughly and serve.

HASH BROWNS   Serves Four
1. Dice and pressure steam at 15 lbs. for 1½ minutes:
   4 medium, mature potatoes
   Cool immediately.
2. Add to large skillet and bring to high heat:
   **2 tablespoons light vegetable oil or bacon
   drippings**
3. Add to pan:
   1 large onion, chopped
   1 teaspoon salt
   1 teaspoon pepper
   1 teaspoon paprika
4. Cook over high heat, tossing occasionally with spatula
   and adding more oil, if necessary, to prevent drying out.
   Cook until golden brown.

PAN BROILED GRATED POTATOES

Serves Four

This approach is becoming popular because it's easy and the skins, rich in food value, are also used.

1. Grate:
   - **3 large baking potatoes, skins included**
   - **1 medium onion**
2. Bring to medium heat in pan:
   - **2 tablespoons butter**
   - **1 tablespoon vegetable oil**
3. Add potatoes; press flat with spatula.
4. Cover; cook until potatoes are brown on both sides.

FRENCH FRIES

Serves Four

Here's one dish that never gets old. The crew can eat it one day and come back for more fries the next. Unfortunately, regular French fries require long cooking times in deep fat, although the time may be reduced somewhat by making the fries thin and long. French fries should be crisp and golden on the outside, mealy on the inside—something only achieved with high heat. We don't think good fries can be made on an alcohol burner since the heat is too low.

1. Grate and cut into ½-inch square strips:
   - **4 medium mature potatoes**
2. Bring to high heat in large pot:
   - **vegetable oil, enough to cover**

   For best results use a wire basket or tray for the potatoes.
3. Drop fries into hot oil, being careful of spatters.
4. Fry potatoes without turning them until bottoms are brown—turning uncooked fries usually results in breakage.
5. When potatoes are golden all over, they are done.
6. Remove from oil; drain on paper. Salt and serve.

THE YAM OR SWEET POTATO

This is a warm weather vegetable as important in many places as the white potato. The very word yam in Senegal means "to eat" and in most West African countries there are several varieties to choose from. The soft, moist variety is unquestionably the most tasty, but hard, gnarled yams last longer and are nearly as good. About ten days without refrigeration is tops for the soft sweet potato but the tough ones usually survive a month. If they are fresh from the earth, it is not necessary to wash them (as with the potato), but in any other condition the fruit and vegetable dip must be used. Hard yams are tough and need nothing other then a dry, warm place for storage.

Yams are long-cooking vegetables that reheat well and are, therefore quite excellent canned. We would never hesitate to use canned yams and consider them one of the cruising staples. They need only a few minutes on the stove to be warmed and, like the fresh item, mash beautifully. We like mashed, canned yams mixed with pineapple, dried fruit, or raisins, and this fine dish goes quite well with a candied canned ham. These two canned items make a first class meal. Possible variations of both tempt the culinary creativity of the chef.

MASHED YAMS WITH FRUIT   Serves Two to Three
1. Pressure cook:
   3 large sweet potatoes, pared and quartered
   Cook until soft; 9 minutes at 15 lbs. for hard yams and 6 minutes at 15 lbs. for soft yams. Heat canned yams in a pot.
2. Mash yams; add:
   3 tablespoons butter
3. Mix with 1 or 2 of the following:
   pineapple
   raisins
   dry apricots,
   carrots
   prunes
   Add, if desired:

   cinnamon
   honey

CANDIED YAMS   Serves Two to Three

1. Cut into ½-inch rounds and place in well buttered fry pan:
   3 cooked yams
2. Sprinkle with:
   ½ cup brown sugar, honey, or maple syrup
   1½ teaspoons lemon juice
3. Saute over low heat, lid on, until sugar melts.

SWEET POTATOES WITH APPLES AND RAISINS   Serves Four

This sweet and sour dish goes especially well with canned meat

1. Cook:
   - **4 sweet potatoes**
   Or heat until steaming:
   - **1 large can sweet potatoes**
2. Parboil for 2 minutes:
   - **2 cups apples, sliced**
   - **1 cup raisins**
   - **1 cup water**
3. Cut potatoes into ½-inch rounds; place in a greased pot.
4. Add apples, raisins, and half the cooking water and:
   - **½ cup brown sugar**
   - **¼ cup lemon juice**
   Sprinkle with:
   - **1 teaspoon cinnamon**
5. Simmer for a few minutes to combine ingredients.

SQUASH

Of the many varieties of squash, at least one kind is grown in almost every country of the world. The varieties fall into two categories: summer squash, which are delicate and require just a few minutes of steaming, and winter squash which are tough and require plenty of cooking time.

Soft summer squash, such as zucchini or crooked neck yellow squash, have delicate skins that easily are punctured. They last less than a week without refrigeration, bruise easily, and are, therefore, not the ideal vegetable for an extended cruise. But they and their large flowers are delicious as an in-port treat. The flowers may be dipped in fritter batter, fried in butter, then sprinkled with sugar. They make a wonderful treat for breakfast. Fresh summer squash has a shiny, unblemished skin and no trace of black decay in the stem. If not eaten immediately, all summer squash should be thoroughly washed in soapy water or the vegetable dip, page 28, since this thin-skinned vegetable is easily contaminated.

Tough winter squash is thick skinned and extremely resistant to decay. If kept too long, it dries to brick hardness but never rots. In some places gourd squash is dried, then baked extra hard and used for a water bottle. Winter squash should not have any significant bruises and should sound heavy like a melon when knocked. If the squash feels light or has a woody sound when knocked, it has probably been sitting around for a while and will be dry. Winter squash needs no special storage attention, but it prefers a dry spot that doesn't get too hot. It will certainly last for the length of any voyage and may even return home as a souvenir.

COOKING SUMMER SQUASH

Rounds of summer squash, ¼-inch thick, need only 4 to 5 minutes of boiling. When cooked; remove them from the heat immediately and drain; their delicate tissues break down easily from internal heat. Summer squash halves take about as long to cook as green beans; these two vegetables, with their sharp contrast in color, look delightful together. They may be steamed in the same pot for the same time (7 to 8 minutes), then tossed in butter and Parmesan cheese. Summer squash rounds also make a nice addition to almost all of the pasta recipes; simply toss the sliced rounds into the boiling pasta water 4 minutes before serving. All summer squash may be stir-fried in a scant amount of oil. They retain more firmness using this technique. We like cooking them in garlic oil over high heat, then adding a dash of soy sauce just before serving.

COOKING WINTER SQUASH

Our favorite cooking technique for winter squash is to halve it and pressure steam for 10 minutes at 15 pounds pressure. Then we pour sizzling hot butter into the center and sprinkle with cinnamon, a pinch of sugar, and a few drops of lemon juice. Winter squash may also be quartered and steamed for 9 minutes at 15 pounds pressure, then mashed and prepared like yams.

18

a night to remember

"That's where the *Sweet Marie* broke up, about ten years back, come Christmas," our crewman Shep said, pointing toward a spot far out on the Abaco reef, where the black water wells up suddenly from the depths and crashes heavily against white coral.

"It was sure a sad thing," he continued, shaking his head. "We all watched it from right here on the hill – hid behind the lightkeeper's shack for a bit to keep dry. The Little Harbor beacon there ..," he said, pointing aloft, "it blew right off the tower and was gone. Even here, on this hill, so far from the sea, the air was full of spray and blown sand. Ya' couldn't hardly breathe And the noise! Between the crashing of the waves and the palm fronds all beatin' together – we finally got inside the lightkeeper's shack for relief – but there was no relief for Capt'n Marcus – we could see him out there on deck, fightin' the storm the whole time, waves breakin' over him ever few minutes. It was terrible to watch, I can tell ya'," Shep said with a sigh.

"Capt'n Marcus was a fool to go out that afternoon, with the seas in such a rage. The Little Harbor beacon here just disappeared in the night. Never even found the globe. A few pieces of the lantern turned up as far away as the Bight of Old Robinson, can ya' beat that? And the roof of this shack took off like a bird and landed in the bay. That alone should have been enough for him – the bar was breaking so hard, white sea smoke was rising from it like fire; enough to chill the blood. But that old fool had the money from 26 Haitian illegals heavy in his pocket, paid in advance to make Cap Haitien before Christmas. Oh, how he smiled that morning, thinking of all the presents he could buy, maybe even an engine for the *Sweet Marie*. He could only think of the money and didn't give a damn about the rage."

"Why didn't the others stop him?" I asked.

"Marcus wasn't the kind of man you could stop once he'd made up his mind. Besides, those blacks had been building the highway up in Marsh Harbor for maybe a year. A year's a long time for a man with a family. All they could think about was hoppin' in the sack with Mama. They couldn't read the signs or just didn't care. They had their reasons, I suppose, or perhaps the sea just called them."

"Maybe Capt'n Marcus just got too good. He'd run that bar many a time in rough seas – used to delight in daring the Revenuers who were always chasin' him to follow right behind. They never did and I think they were smart. They could never go where Capt'n Marcus went, no sir, the seas woulda' got'em for sure. But Marcus always made it, slicker'n a cat. No, the signs I'm talkin' about have nothin' to do with the bar or the rough seas;" he'd seen that all before. I'm talkin' about things that tell you when the sea wants blood, that it's a great killer storm that will eat all living things – fish, birds, ships and you.

"Well, Capt'n Marcus had an onshore breeze to boot, damn fool – but he run the *Sweet Marie* way up on the inside, above North Bar channel to get a good run through the reef. Oh, that fool, that ol' smackboat could never beat into a gale at her best, let alone loaded with thirty men. Yes, thirty men with the crew and a 46 foot boat with no engine.

The *Sweet Marie* went through the breakers like a shot, disappeared into that howling smoke and we all thought she was gone. But she came through all right, sailed past the breaker line, water running like crazy off her decks, half drowned but still movin' with Capt'n Marcus standin' tall at the tiller. We had to give it to that old fool for guts then, but that wasn't the end of it. He must have parted his jib halyard or somethin' – couldn't set the jib for a bit. And that was the end. He couldn't beat past Elbow Reef. He had to tack back to the south. Not much hope after that. He was caught on a lee shore with the only chance of escape dead to windward into that storm.

"Well, Marcus wasn't thinkin' right at all that day – I guess the time for clear thinking was past. I could hardly think myself, with all the noise an' wind, and I was safe on shore! Capt'n Marcus could have turned right then and driven her down on the beach, but it probably never occurred to him – he was a fighter. He tacked back and forth all afternoon, not losin' much ground, but not gainin' any either – tackin' back and forth between the reefs, hopin' I guess for a shift in the wind.

"About six that evening, Gawd, it was a dreary sunset, like it was the end of the world. It was just about dark and there'd be no hope then, tackin' back and forth in the night, waiting for the reef to take him. Just then, I suppose Capt'n Marcus thought he saw his chance. From up here on the hill, by the wreck of the lighthouse, it looked for a bit like he made it all right. We was just ready to go down and have a few drinks to celebrate.

"I don't know if he ever saw the coral head he hit – it was getting pretty dark – or maybe he saw it and hoped to slip by on the wave crest. We saw the ship strike. Then the masts went over the side. We stood and listened to the cries of the men as they drowned. Too bad. That big head was the last bad spot befor the deep water. After that, Capt'n Marcus could have run around Cherokee Point and been gone.

"The Greeks would say he sailed off despite the omens," I said.

"Ol' Marcus didn't know about omens," Shep replied. "He just spent so many years on that old smackboat, always walkin' on the thin edge of danger, just stickin' his toe over the line now and then to bait the devil – drunk Saturday nights, whoring Sunday mornings – he'd stumble into church, late as usual and still high as a kite, but very repentant. I'd have to bite my hand to keep from laughin'. Yep, he used to repent 'til the bar opened on Sunday afternoon. It was downhill from there on," Shep said with a quiet laugh.

"But I guess you're right," Shep said, looking at the distant breakers, "Marcus sailed so far in the *Sweet Marie,* ran so many loads of beer, so many loads of illegals, got so good in her I guess he finally thought there weren't nothin' he couldn't do. Didn't read the 'omen' as you say. He lost his fear.

"That night, when the bodies floated ashore, that was a bad time. Big sharks and other things we never seen before swam the shallows, glowing all green in the darkness. We found squid 25 feet long in the surf an' other things too ugly to mention. It rained that night; black mud and dead birds fell from the sky. We was glad enough to be lying snug in Little Harbor with three anchors down and a big warp tied to a coconut palm. I don't know much about omens, but I'll tell you no man living had the courage to go out that night and look for Capt'n Marcus."

"Did anyone survive?" I asked.

"Nope – we found six bodies in the surf the next day. The masts and doghouse roof came up with them. You can still see a few pieces of iron ballast down there on the bottom. Not much, though. She was an old boat and didn't have much metal in her. Even the kids who went down to look at her a few days later didn't find much – just an old pair of Marcus' shoes and a small silver cross – musta' been a present fer someone. Yup, even the gulls got more than those kids – how the birds screamed over that spot! The sea got the rest – the hull and thirty men. Marcus' body washed up a couple of days later. He looked kinda' calm. Some folks said it served him right, blasphemin' that way against the gods. But I don't know; he was a big talker but he was a real sailor. Maybe in his heart he'd made his peace with the sea."

19
bread and
the oven

Nothing can replace the oven for cooking a perfect loaf of bread. The steady heat of a good oven bakes evenly and produces a bread that is light and fine textured. There is no way that oven bread can be made on top of the stove with consistent success. If a fry pan is to be used, it is better to make relatively flat breads, such as corn bread or Syrian bread, than to try to make raised, light golden loaves. If you have an oven, we have several basic recipes for excellent, reliable bread. If you don't, we heartily recommend the simple and reliable pressure cooker for flat breads and several versions of ship's biscuit. These should fill the hole in the most dedicated bread lover's stomach.

There are several different techniques for producing a makeshift oven. We have met cruising chefs who have thoroughly mastered them to the point of producing high-quality bread. The simplest technique is to place a trivet in a large, non-Teflon pot (not a pressure cooker as you will damage it), then preheat over a medium flame and use as a small oven. If this technique is employed, it is best to use a flame diffuser beneath the pot to further distribute the heat. A medium propane or kerosene flame produces approximately 375°F, which is just right for baking. Potato bakers or folding ovens are essentially pots with the trivet built in. They are often the tool of choice on yachts without ovens.

algerian bakery

SELECTING THE RIGHT BREAD

The galley is definitely not the ideal place to make sophisticated bread, and our selection of recipes reflects this. We expect full cooperation from our dough and no nonsense. Prima donnas, sometimes risers, and fancy dressers have no place in a cruising oven since they often reward your effort with disappointment. Bran, whole wheat, unbleached wheat, and corn meal are our special favorites because they require little or no sifting and are usually very determined about rising. For this same reason, we are somewhat inclined toward the baking powder breads, simply because the quality and nature of yeast varies so much from port to port. In addition, yeast is not the best of sailors since it does not like dampness, cold, a falling barometer, or sea breezes.

We suggest that you consider the different recipes in this chapter before you set sail. Experiment, using the same materials and conditions that you will find on board, until you find the dough that fits your needs. The most important factor to consider is consistent results. There is no time for starting over, and stores are usually too precious to consider fooling with frequent failures. Find one or two recipes that are ideal for you and stick with them. Be sure that you carefully project the various ingredients for the length of the cruise; if you don't, you may return with 20 pounds of flour and 2 ounces of baking powder. Last but not least, be sure that your ingredients are well protected against dampness, the chief enemy of the cruising baker.

BREAD AND CAKE MIXES

While packaged mixes are more expensive than "from scratch" recipes they are quite useful on a boat. The ingredients have been designed for extended shelf life, and the majority call only for the addition of an egg, some water, or little milk. Mixes never taste as good as from scratch, but the convenience, the long shelf life, and the handy unit of packaged mixes more than compensates for the difference.

Packaged mixes should be carefully purchased, preferably from stores with a rapid turnover of stock. In more isolated groceries where the volume of sales is low, packaged mixes may sit for several years. After a while, mixes lose their flavor and ability to rise. Examine the outside of the carton and reject those which seem to have been around for a long time. Check carefully for roach or ant holes, crushed ends, or signs of mold on the outside of the carton.

We recommend that packaged mixes be wrapped tightly in a sturdy plastic bag. This will reduce the chance of loss due to moisture. Packaged mixes, flour, and other grains are among the few items that may be stored in a rather warm spot, such as the engine compartment. The warmth helps retard mold and the boxes may be used as buffers between equipment to prevent rattles.

TRY ASKING THE LOCAL BAKERY...

Before your next cruise, try asking the local bakery if they will make you some sea bread. It's just their regular bread baked without salt. The lack of salt keeps moisture from getting into the bread; without moisture, mold is discouraged. Whole wheat or rye bread lasts longest. Give the baker some close fitting, double weight plastic bags. Ask him to bag the bread while it is still piping hot and leave the end open. When the bread is still quite warm, close the bag's mouth with a rubber band. The bread will last months; however, it does get dry after two weeks. If it has been kept a long time and is quite dry, it may be improved by steaming a half loaf in the pressure cooker. Set it on a trivet with a half cup of water beneath. Pressure cook for 3 minutes to soften; then slice and pan fry in butter.

SHIP'S BISCUIT   Makes 18 Biscuits

This basic biscuit is reasonably failure-proof. It can be made in a regular oven, a makeshift oven, or even in a lidded skillet with a flame diffuser. The secret of success is long beating; why not give everyone in the crew a turn.

1. Sift together:
   - **2 cups all-purpose flour**
   - **½ teaspoon salt**
   - **1 teaspoon baking powder.**
2. Combine with:
   - **½ cup shortening**
   - **½ cup water**
   Work in slowly to make a stiff dough.
3. Beat at least 5 minutes, then roll out.
4. Repeat step 3 at least 2 more times.
5. Roll out to ½-inch thickness; cut into 18 squares. Let rest ½ to 1 hour.
6. Bake at 350° to 375° for 20 to 25 minutes on greased sheet. Test for doneness with toothpick. If the tip pulls out dry, the biscuits are done.

CRUISING BREAD   Makes 1 Loaf

A simple and reliable salt water bread made in the pressure cooker.

- **1 cup lukewarm water**
- **½ cup sea water**
- **1 tablespoon powdered yeast**
- **1 tablespoon sugar**
- **4 cups unbleached flour**
- **3 tablespoons corn meal**

1. Combine water, sea water, yeast, and sugar. Let stand in temperate spot for 5 minutes.
2. Sift and stir in flour.
3. Let stand covered in temperate spot until dough doubles in volume.
4. While dough is rising, thoroughly grease sides of pressure cooker pot. Add corn meal; close lid and shake vigorously to coat pot with meal. (The corn meal acts as a separation agent and prevents burning.)
5. When dough has doubled in volume, punch down, knead, and allow to rise again.
6. When bread has increased in volume by 50 percent, punch and knead it, then shape into a ball and drop into pressure cooker pot.
7. Let stand for 15 to 20 minutes, then close lid and cook with valve off for 45 minutes over a moderate flame.

This bread does not like foul weather or a falling barometer. It is absolutely delicious served hot and does not dry out unacceptably when cool.

To vary the bread try adding:

1 handful of raisins
2 tablespoons cinnamon
2 tablespoons brown sugar

This variation makes a tasty breakfast bread.

YACHT CORINA BRAN BREAD   Makes 1 Loaf

This is a fruit loaf that is relatively failure-proof and will retain its freshness for many days.

1 cup All Bran cereal
1 cup mixed, dry fruit (like raisins and chopped apricots)
1 cup brown sugar
1 cup milk
1 cup flour, sifted
1 teaspoon salt

1. Mix all ingredients except flour; let stand in temperate spot for 1 hour.
2. Add flour; combine quickly with a minimum of beating.
3. Bake in moderate oven for 1 hour; cool before serving.

YACHT KUMBAYA OATMEAL BREAD
Makes Three Or Four Loaves

This is a heavy, tasty bread that lasts for many days without going stale. We had just gotten a taste of it fresh from the oven when the Kumbaya hit a reef and sank like a stone. Our recipe notebook got a little wet while submerged for a few days in 70 feet of water, but we helped raise the wreck and carefully dried the recipe. See what we go through for our readers!

- 2 **cups boiling water**
- 2 **cups whole wheat flour**
- 2 **cups white flour**
- 1 **cup quick oats**
- 1/3 **cup shortening**
- ½ **cup molasses**
- 4 **teaspoons salt**
- 2 **packages yeast**
- 2 **eggs, beaten**

1. Combine water, oats, shortening, and molasses.
2. Let cool to lukewarm; add remaining ingredients.
3. Knead; let rise until doubled in volume.
4. Punch down; let rise to 50 percent increase in volume.
5. Bake for 50 minutes at 350 to 375° F.

INDIAN POORIE—FRIED PUFF BREAD

Poorie is a flat bread that is treated rather like a pancake. It may be eaten hot from the pan, but we like it better sprinkled with confectioners sugar, cooled, served for breakfast. It keeps beautifully in a plastic bag. We cannot even begin to tell you how long it will last because good Poorie has a tendency to disappear quickly, particularly at night, especially during the dog watch. It makes a fine snack.

- 1 **cup whole wheat flour**
- 1 **cup white flour**
- ¼ **cup shortening**
- 2 **tablespoons water (or a bit more) to make a kneadable dough**
  coconut or vegetable oil

1. Knead until smooth; let rest for 1 hour.
2. Shape into walnut sized balls and roll flat.
3. Fry in ½ inch of hot fat.

4. Cook until edges look just dry, not brown; flip and cook until golden.
5. If sugar is to be sprinkled on, add when bread is hot from the pan.

TORTILLAS

This well-known Mexican pan bread is often available in cans and is more acceptable this way than many other breads. But there is no substitute for fresh tortillas.

1. Combine and beat until smooth:
   - **1 cup flour**
   - **¼ teaspoon salt**
   - **1½ cups cold water**
   - **½ cup yellow corn meal**
   - **1 egg, beaten**
2. Spoon 3 tablespoons of batter onto a moderately hot, greased griddle to make a thin 6-inch pancake.
3. Turn when edges look dry, not brown.

Tortillas may be bent while still hot and used to hold chili, chopped onions, peppers, and grated cheese. They may also be sprinkled with crumbled, fried bacon and a layer of hot baked beans. Or eat them as is; they're delicious.

YACHT LAMACHAN FRYING PAN SWEET BREAD
Makes 1 Cake

This easily rising cake has one secret to success: The secret here is to use a greased pan coated with corn meal, which acts as a separating agent.

1. Combine and let stand for 1 hour in temperate spot:
   - **2 teaspoons (heaping) baking powder**
   - **1 tablespoon (heaping) corn flour**
   - **enough flour (sifted) added to above ingredients to make 1 cup**
   - **½ cup brown sugar**
   - **1 egg, beaten with brown sugar until foamy**
2. Add to frying pan; cook, lid on, over low heat for 20 minutes. Resist the temptation to look under the lid.
3. After 20 minutes, test for doneness with toothpick. Plunge it into cake in several spots; it is cooked when toothpick pulls out dry.

4. Ice cool cake with mixture of:
   1 large tablespoon butter
   1 cup honey
   ½ cup confectioners sugar
   ¼ cup pineapple juice

FRYING PAN CORN BREAD   Makes 1 Pan

To prevent burning, never use more than a ¾-inch layer of batter in the bottom of a pan. About ½ inch is ideal.

1. Sift together:
   ½ cup unbleached flour
   2 teaspoons (heaping) baking powder
   2 teaspoons sugar
   1 teaspoon salt
2. Add:
   1½ cups yellow corn meal
3. Stir in:
   3 tablespoons melted butter
   1 egg, beaten with melted butter
   ¾ cup milk

Stir briefly; this bread does not like excessive handling.

4. Grease fry pan and sprinkle with corn meal.
5. Pour batter into cold pan; cook over low heat for 20 to 30 minutes, lid on, but loose. Test with toothpick; when toothpick pulls out dry, bread is done.

GARLIC BREAD   Prepares 4 to 6 Slices

This is not a bread recipe, but a nice way to salvage stale bread, dry ship's bread, or even to enliven packaged toasts.

1. Melt in pan:
   3 to 4 tablespoons butter or light vegetable oil
2. Add to pan:
   3 to 4 cloves garlic, minced
   Heat until garlic just simmers.
3. Add:
   1 teaspoon thyme or oregano
   Heat for another minute.
4. Dip into pan until garlic butter is consumed:
   4 to 6 thick bread slices, both sides
5. Cook over low heat until bread begins to brown. Serve piping hot.

SYRIAN PAN BREAD

This almost foolproof pancake-like bread is raised with baking soda. The dough is rolled into a pancake not more than ⅛-inch thick and then cooked in a sparsely greased pan. The bread is browned on one side, then flipped just like a pancake and is served hot.

1. Sift together:
   - **1½ cups whole wheat or unbleached flour**
   - **¼ teaspoon salt**
   - **2 teaspoons baking soda**

2. Combine and mix with dry ingredients:
   - **1 egg, beaten**
   - **¾ cup milk**

3. Combine quickly and do not beat excessively. Let stand one hour.
4. Take a lemon sized ball of dough and roll out into a thin pancake not more than ⅛-inch thick. Work on a floured sheet and be sure that the dough is floured when placed in the pan.
5. Wipe a fry pan with an oily rag and heat until a test drop of water jumps from the pan before evaporating. Be careful that you do not let the grease smoke.
6. Pan bake, lid on until browned, then flip and brown the other side.

PANCAKES

Pancakes and simple pan breads are more at home in the galley than good oven breads. Pancakes are almost goofproof, and a good load of them in the morning should keep the most persistent bread lover off your back. Pancake batters don't like excessive beating and should sit for an hour or two before use to obtain best results. Don't worry about a few lumps; they will disappear when cooked. The batter should run like thick honey. A little flour or milk may be added at the last moment to correct the consistency.

A certain signal of a novice or inept pancake maker is a huge, thick pancake. Pancakes should never exceed 4 to 5 inches and must be thin to be light and fluffy. Pancakes are not fried. The grease used should be just enough to keep the cake from sticking. Good Teflon pans need the barest suggestion of light oil. Apply by wiping with a greasy paper towel.

Pancakes are not lovers of heavy weather. When the barometer is falling or the sea is rough, they usually end up heavy and doughy. In addition, all the ingredients must be at room temperature since the resting process is not effective if the ingredients are cold.

Griddle heat is of considerable importance. A sure test for correct heat is to sprinkle a few drips of water on the heated pan. If the water jumps a few times before vanishing, the termperature is correct. If it simply sits there and boils, the pan is too cool; if it instantly disappears, the pan is too hot.

Pancake batter is not poured onto the griddle; it should just run off the tip of a big spoon. This assures a round and thin cake. A few moments before the first side of the cake is cooked, bubbles appear on the uncooked surface. The bottom should then be inspected to be sure that the cake is not burning. Should this be the case, the pan may be removed from the heat for a moment to reduce the temperature. When the bubbles break, the first side of the cake is done. The pancake should then be flipped and cooked until the second side is golden brown.

The following basic pancake recipes may be endlessly varied by rolling up with jelly, chopped and sauteed fruit, honey, cinnamon, raisins, chopped dates, even mashed bananas.

Crepes are a special type of pancake used for desserts or stuffed with a variety of meats, poultry, fish, or cheese to produce an elegant main course. The basic crepe may be cooked in advance and quickly warmed in a pan just before serving. Learning to make a good crepe is like learning to sail. There are a few tricks, but learn once and future success is automatic. The recipe for basic crepes follows. Dessert crepes are included in the dessert chapter.

FRENCH PANCAKES OR CREPES
      1. Sift together:
          ¾ **cup all purpose flour**
          ½ **teaspoon baking powder**
          ½ **teaspoon salt**
    2. Combine:
          2 **eggs**
          ¾ **cup milk**
          ¼ **cup water**

If the crepe is to be used for a main course, the batter is now complete. If a dessert crepe is desired, add:

- **2 tablespoons powdered sugar**
- **½ teaspoon vanilla**
- **½ teaspoons grated orange or lemon rind**

3. Let batter stand 3 to 4 hours.
4. Wipe bottom of hot fry pan or crepe pan with butter, just enough to make an oily film.
5. Let batter run off spoon into hot pan; give pan a few gentle twists to spread batter and make the crepe quite thin.
6. Brown crepes on both sides over a moderate heat. Be careful edges do not become dry and leathery.

Main course crepes may be stuffed with seafood au gratin with an added teaspoon of dry white wine. Or while the crepe is still in the pan, add a generous daub of grated, mild cheese. After the cheese melts, fold the crepe in half. Another nice version is to fold in precooked pork sausage, braised beef, or sauteed vegetables with one of several different sauces given in the sauce chapter.

BASIC PANCAKE BATTER Makes 16 Pancakes, 3½ to 4 inches

1. Sift together:
   - **1½ cups flour**
   - **1 teaspoon salt**
   - **3 tablespoons sugar**
   - **2 teaspoons baking powder**
2. Combine:
   - **1 egg**
   - **3 tablespoons melted butter**
   - **1¼ cups milk**
3. Quickly combine all ingredients.
4. Allow to stand for an hour or two before cooking for best results.

WHOLE WHEAT PANCAKES

Make as above, but use 50 percent whole-grained flour. Add 2 tablespoons molasses to batter and handle as above.

CORN FLAPJACKS

We canoed once to Baxter Lake, just northwest of Hudson's Bay. This simple flapjack, cooked over a wood fire, sure tasted good after a face wash in a bucket whose water wore a skin of ice.

1. Combine:
   - 1½   cups white corn meal
   - $^1/_3$ cup white flour
   - ¾   teaspoon baking soda
   - 1½   teaspoons salt
2. Combine and blend with dry ingredients:
   - 2   cups buttermilk or sour milk
   - 2   eggs
   - ½   cup melted butter

DEEP FRIED COFFEECAKE

1. Sift together:
   - 2   cups all purpose flour
   - 2½   tablespoons sugar
   - 1   teaspoon double acting baking powder
   - ½   teaspoon salt
2. Make a well in the center of the above ingredients and add:
   - 1¼   cups milk
   - 2   eggs, beaten with milk

   Fold and turn until smooth.
4. Heat in deep fry pan until test drop of water jumps on surface:
   - 1   inch vegetable oil
5. Put ¾ cup of batter into a bowl, then pour into oil making a tight spiral.
6. Deep fat fry for about 3 minutes on each side until golden.
7. Serve with confectioners sugar and cinnamon, or cinnamon and honey.

DOUGHNUTS   Makes 16 Doughnuts

The secret with doughnuts is to have the oil in the pan very hot, but not smoking. If the oil is too cool, it will penetrate the dough and make it oily. If it is too hot, the crust will be too hard and may burn. Don't try to cook too many doughnuts at one time. The cool dough reduces the temperature of the oil. Doughnuts should cook for about 1½ minutes per side. Add each doughnut at 15 to 20 second intervals. It is a help to have a crewman cut some of the dough and sugar the cooked doughnuts.

1. Combine:
   - **1 egg, beaten**
   - **½ cup sugar**
   - **2 tablespoons melted butter or shortening**
2. Sift together:
   - **2 cups presifted flour**
   - **¼ teaspoon cinnamon**
   - **2 teaspoons baking powder**
   - **¼ teaspoon salt**
3. Mix the wet and dry ingredients. Roll out to ½-inch thickness; cut and dry in deep fat.

FRITTERS

The several varieties of fritters vary so much from one another that the similarity is a little hard to see. In this book two categories have been included: fritters, such as corn fritters, that are similar to a fluffy pancake, and seafood or vegetable fritters that are more like seafood fried with a coating. The batter for seafood and vegetable fritters is similar to a simple pancake

flamingo

batter; but like crepes, it must stand for a while before cooking or the result will taste gluey. The onshore recipes for fritter batter call for it to stand 6 to 12 hours, but, of course, this is usually not possible on a yacht. Our fritter secret is threefold: first, minimize the amount of beating or stirring; second, use warm beer instead of water because the yeast in the beer helps to lighten the batter; third, use eggs as specified but only half of the whites because batters heavy with yolks crust better and stay light and fluffy inside. Let the batter stand at least an hour or two, even overnight. This may not be possible on a cruising yacht and is not essential with this recipe.

french angel fish

FRITTER BATTER FOR SEAFOOD OR VEGETABLES
Batter For 3 Cups of Ingredients

1. Combine in large mixing bowl:
   - 1 cup beer
   - 1 teaspoon salt
   - ½ teaspoon pepper
   - 1 tablespoon cooking oil
   - 1 egg, well beaten
2. Combine thoroughly; gradually add one tablespoon at a time:
   - 1½ cups sifted flour

Combine each addition with a few strokes of a whisk. The final batter should have the consistency of heavy motor oil; to test, it should hang about 2 inches from the spoon before breaking off. Add more or less flour as needed, but do not beat the batter with more than 12 to 16 strokes after it has reached correct consistency. If it is excessively lumpy, it is better to strain it than to overbeat. Let the batter sit for an hour or two, then use it to coat chunks of your favorite seafood or vegetable.

PEANUT BUTTER SANDWICHES

No bread chapter would be complete without a few sandwich suggestions, and no sandwich suggestions would be complete without peanut butter. Peanut butter is extremely nutritious, but hard to digest if consumed in quantity. So go easy when you spread it.

Everyone knows about peanut butter and jelly sandwiches. Jam or jelly is, of course, made from fruit. To cut down on sugar, we prefer making a fresh fruit compote to use in place of jam. Just saute a finely chopped firm fruit, such as apples, with a chopped orange and a little honey. This makes a fine combination with peanut butter that is less sweet and more nourishing, too. We also enjoy peanut butter sandwiches made with bacon, tomato, and lettuce, or fried sliced ham, or sliced hard-cooked egg, lettuce and tomato, or mild sliced cheese and onion.

TUNA SANDWICHES

To make tuna sandwiches more interesting, try flaking the tuna, sprinkling with a few drops of lemon juice, and adding any one of the following combinations:

Onion, mayonnaise, mustard, and dill weed (optional)
Onion, chopped celery, and mayonnaise
Hard-boiled egg rounds, onion, and mustard
Chopped green pepper
Tomatoes, sweet pickles, and mayonnaise or Thousand Island dressing
Chopped parsley and sliced cucumbers
Pimento, green olives, and mayonnaise

FRENCH TOAST

French toast is particularly useful on a boat because it can be made from stale bread if fresh is not available.

1. Soak bread slices in mixture of:
   2 beaten eggs
   ½ cup milk

1 teaspoon salt
1 teaspoon pepper
2. Fry over medium heat in:
butter
Fry until toast is golden brown. Serve with butter and syrup.

For lunch or supper, it may be served with several different sauces, such as cheese, marinara, or quick tomato sauce. To make quick tomato sauce, combine:

1 can condensed tomato soup
½ cup condensed milk
1 tablespoon lemon juice
2 teaspoons sugar

MODIFIED FRENCH TOAST

1. Thoroughly combine:
2 eggs
¼ cup condensed milk
½ cup condensed tomato soup
½ teaspoon salt
½ teaspoon pepper
2. Use this as the basic bread dip and proceed as for regular French toast.

GRILLED CHEESE SANDWICHES

For variety, try adding any of the following to your next grilled cheese sandwich:

Fried salami
Fried onions
Ham slices, sausage or bacon

For the ultimate treat, dip the whole sandwich in beaten egg and pan fry until golden.

SEAGOING SANDWICH DELIGHT—SARDINE PATE

For deep water cruising folk, the sandwich is often the noontime staff of life. What do you do after the fresh meat is gone, the cheese has gotten moldy, and someone has thrown a bag of tools on the tomatoes? The crew of the Fire Witch recommends this delightful sardine pate made from the long-lasting stores. It will keep several days without any refrigeration, even in warm climates. Just seal the container tightly after use.

1. Soak 2 pieces of white toast or stale bread in:
   - ½   **cup white vinegar**
   - ½   **teaspoon sugar**
   - 2   **teaspoons salt**
   - 1   **teaspoon vinegar**
   - 6   **dashes tobasco.**
2. Mash thoroughly:
   - 2   **cans drained sardines**
   - 2   **chopped medium onions**
   - 4   **hard-boiled eggs**
   - 2   **tablespoons mayonnaise or whip**
3. Mix ingredients thoroughly. Tastes much better the next day. Serve at room temperature on bread or crackers. Sardine pate also makes an excellent cocktail hour dip.

MONTE CRISTO SANDWICH

1. Dip one side of rye bread slices in:
   - 1   **egg, beaten**
2. Add:

   canned ham, sliced thin
   mustard (in the middle)
   cheese, sliced thin (Cheddar, Swiss, American)

3. Fry dipped side out, in a little butter until egg browns a bit. Serve with sliced onions. Delicious!

EGG SALAD SANDWICH

Mix lightly and spread on toast:

- 3   **hard-boiled eggs, chopped**
- 1   **small onion, well chopped**
- ½   **teaspoon celery seed**
- ½   **teaspoon dill**
- 1   **stalk celery, if available**
- 1   **tablespoon mayonnaise**
- 1   **teaspoon mustard**
- 1   **teaspoon salt**
- 1   **teaspoon pepper**
- 1   **teaspoon lemon juice**

REUBEN SANDWICH

1. Layer on buttered rye bread:
   Corned beef or thinly sliced ham
   Sauerkraut
   Swiss cheese
2. Cook open face in fry pan or under broiler until cheese melts.
3. Add:
   mayonnaise and catsup, mixed one to one.
4. Close with another slice of buttered toast.

SALAMI SANDWICHES

Try grilled salami slices, our favorite, on pan toasted bread with any of the following:

sliced mild cheese, mustard, and onion
sweet pickles, onion, and mustard
garlic mayonnaise
sauerkraut and mustard
sliced cucumbers and onions with mayonnaise
catsup and sweet pickles
cooked and curried lentils, sweet pickles, and mustard

CREAM CHEESE SANDWICHES

We can't decide which of the following is our favorite with cream cheese:

A-1 sauce and onion on black bread
black olives on whole wheat bread
anchovies on whole wheat bread
avocados on whole wheat bread
cucumber and onion on white bread
bean sprouts, oil, and cold peas, open face on white bread

BACON SANDWICHES

In addition to the traditional bacon, lettuce, tomato, and mayonnaise on toast, try adding one of following to your next bacon sandwich:

cooked lentils, sliced onion, and mustard
peanut butter, lettuce, and tomato
fried egg with mayonnaise

baked beans on toast
tomato, avocado, and French dressing
sliced chicken and crumbled Roquefort cheese

HAM SANDWICHES

Canned ham is one of the best cruising meats. Here are a few of our favorite ham sandwiches:

ham, Swiss cheese, onions, and sweet pickles on rye bread
ham, onions, mustard, and mayonnaise on white bread
ham, sliced hard-boiled eggs, and Thousand Island dressing on toast
ham, steamed cabbage, and mustard on rye toast
ham, fried egg, and catsup on white toast
ham, fried egg, tomatoes, and butter on whole wheat toast

CANNED CORNED BEEF SANDWICHES

Add any of the following to hot, flaked corn beef:

grated mild cheese, melted on the sandwich, sweet pickle, onions, and mustard on rye bread
tomato and mayonnaise on white bread
baked beans with curry powder on rye bread
fried egg, open face on whole wheat bread

EGG SANDWICHES

For sandwiches, the traditional "over easy" egg is fried a bit more than usual so that the yolk is somewhat gluey. No one enjoys biting into an egg sandwich and having the yolk run between his fingers and down his shirt. A second technique is to break the yolk when you turn the egg; we never have any trouble doing that! A hot fried egg on buttered whole wheat or an English muffin tastes delicious with any of the following:

grilled ham, mustard, and mayonnaise
grilled tomato, lettuce, butter, and scallions
baked beans
mild grated cheese, mustard, and butter
marinara sauce and Parmesan cheese
fried onions
anchovies and onions
deviled ham and black olives

FONDUE

1. Add to a saucepan over low heat:
   2 cups dry white wine
   ¼ cup Kirsch
   2 teaspoons cornstarch
2. When the mixture starts to simmer, slowly add:
   ½ lb. gruyere cheese, grated
   2 cloves garlic, minced
   ⅛ teaspoon nutmeg
   ½ teaspoon salt
   ½ teaspoon white pepper
3. Add more cheese as the mixture melts. Do not simmer.
   Serve with toast or crackers.

OPEN FACE SANDWICHES

Welsh rarebit

1. Combine and warm in a saucepan:
   1 lb. cheddar cheese
   2 tablespoons butter
   1½ cups milk
   1 teaspoon mustard (Grey), salt, pepper
   1 tablespoon sherry
   1 teaspon Worchestershire sauce
   2 egg yolks
2. Warm until melted, thin with more milk. Serve over toast.

FISHERMAN'S SANDWICH

We have seen this sandwich eaten by fishermen in so many different places that it is impossible to guess its origin. The bread of tradition is white, rough, crusty, and usually a day old. The dryness of slightly stale bread makes it soak up the fine flavors of the pan. It also is good with sea bread for the same reason.

1. Fry until light golden:
   - **1 onion, finely chopped**
   - **4 cloves garlic, peeled**
   - **½ cup olive oil**
2. Pour off half the oil into another pan.
3. Add to onions:
   - **1 teaspoon basil**
   - **1 teaspoon thyme**
   - **1 teaspoon oregano**
   - **1 small can (6-oz) tomato paste**
   - **1 can (16-oz) Italian tomatoes, well drained and chopped**
3. Simmer for 10 minutes.
4. In remaining oil, fry until slightly browned:
   - **4 large slices of bread**
5. Turn bread; fry one minute, then pour on sauce and continue cooking for 5 minutes.
6. Criss cross each portion with anchovies and serve. This sandwich is traditionally eaten with the hands. Lots of luck.

THE POOR BOY, HERO, OR ZEP

1. Cut in half lengthwise:

   - **1 loaf of crusty bakery bread**
2. Spread both slices with:

   - **mayonnaise**
3. On the bottom half, arrange layers of any or all of the following:
   - **sandwich meat**
   - **shredded ham**
   - **sliced salami**
   - **spam**
   - **bologna**

pepperoni
cheese slices (provolone, Swiss, American,
 mold cheese)
tomato
pickles
boiled egg slices
sauerkraut
lettuce
onion
anchovies
4. Spread generously with mustard.
5. If desired, sprinkle lightly with oil and vinegar.
6. Cut into manageable portions.

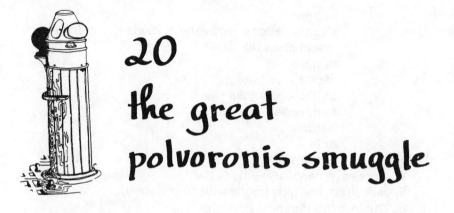

20
the great polvoronis smuggle

"We need a man with a boat who can operate at night and doesn't mind taking a few risks. It's worth 500 pounds for a night's work with no questions asked." Our onboard visitor was a small man with broad shoulders, swarthy skin, and a fine handlebar mustache that pointed proudly toward the sky. His arms were disproportionately large with deceptive flabbiness that often conceals the strength of a boxer. He had a thick neck and bulldog face with heavy jowls that quivered when he talked. He held a Morrocan pipe in his teeth, and as he talked, smoke wafted from his mouth, filtered through his great mustache, then drifted upward to obscure his face in a gray cloud. His words were intoned with a unique accent: a mixture of Moorish, Spanish, Arabic, and English that identified the native Gibraltarian.

Spanish authorities had closed the border several years before making the tiny peninsula a political island—a symbol of British tenacity, not an actual fortress. The Gibraltarians, long accustomed to siege, have since tightened their belts a little and increased trade with Morocco by buying foodstuffs, raw materials, and unskilled labor. Because of increased trade by sea and the strategic location of the rock, smuggling flourishes. Cigarettes, whiskey, and television sets are smuggled out: jewels, hashish, and hard drugs are smuggled in.

As for our nameless messenger, he stood right in the middle of our companionway, completely blocking it with his stocky frame, as though to prevent escape.

"Well, what do you say?" he asked, looking fi[...] Rebecca, my first mate, and me. His offer was almost a de[...]

Five hundred pounds is a tidy sum. A tidy sum indee[...] evening's work. It was nearly Christmas, and the extra [...] would go a long way toward making it festive. Rebecca [...] buy lovely clothes, and I could outfit our 39-foot sloop with[...] of new sails. But what kind of cargo was worth that m[...] money? Surely it had to be heroin or raw opium to be worth [...] pounds per run.

"What's the load?" I demanded, determined to be just [...] stubborn as the dark stranger who confronted us.

"No questions are part of the deal." he replied. "You just b[...] at a certain spot down the coast and a boat will come out to loa[...] you up."

"What's the cargo and quantity? If you can't give us answers, we aren't interested," I said, already dismissing the possibility of an agreement. The man looked thoughtfully at us for a moment, pulled a tobacco pouch from his pocket, reloaded his pipe, and fired it with great care. Smoke reeled overhead and swirled around a kerosene lamp giving the tiny cabin a softer hue. We could almost see his mind swaying like a pendulum, and soon it polarized.

"It's Polvoronis and Spanish hams from Tarifa. About 5000 polvoronis and as many hams as the boat will hold to top off the load," he said.

"Polvoronis? You don't mean Spanish Christmas cookies?" I said incredulously.

"That's it," he replied.

"What kind of a fool do you think I am, expecting me to buy a fairy tale like that? You're running junk or hash or refugees, something really seamy I'll bet, and you think that by whispering a few words in my ear I'll go floating off down the coast to give you a hand. Well, just hop on up those steps behind you and flit off." I was furious—sure by his answer that his game was junk.

"Shut your gab, wind your neck in, and I'll tell you a few things, my friend," he said with a patient smile; he was not at all disturbed by my words. "Most of the people in this town are Spaniards or, at least, have some Spanish blood in them. It was once the tradition around here for men to go to Spain, usually Algeceris or San Reque, and find a wife. Many families around here speak Spanish and eat Spanish food...or at least they did until the blockade. When Spain closed the border, they also em-

barred all exports, particularly food, hoping to force the Spanish people off the rock. Well, it takes more than that to break the people in this place," he said, gesturing upward toward the huge, craggy cliffs that rose from the bay behind us. "But people certainly do miss their "cafe con leche" in the morning. "English coffee is vile. It tastes like boiled tires! You know if you've ever tried the local variety. And they also miss their cheese, like Roncal or Burges, light fluffy tortillas like Hueves a la flamenca, and sweet little nothings like bizcocho. Then the wine ran out." he said, a little sadly. "The Alella was the last to go," and a hopeful gleam of remembrance flickered in his eyes. "Ah, it was so light and sharp. It crept into your soul like a little devil and made you both sad and happy at the same time."

"We have Portuguese wine now. It tastes like rabbit droppings. Well," he said drawing himself up proudly, "it takes more than that to make us knuckle under. But now it's Christmas and that nasty Northwester has been blowing for a whole week. It's too rough for the fishing boats that normally do a little 'free trading' with friends in Estapona. So the little bit of nice cheese and wine that we used to bring in are gone. But that's okay. We can do without. But now it's Christmas and we have no polvoronis." A sullen look came into his eyes. "The English, they ship us the flour and the nuts and so forth and all the shops try to make it, but it comes out like dirt with little cinders in it. The ingredients are all wrong. And then there is the ham. What is Christmas without a nice ham? Our ham comes from Italy and it's not too bad, but it's Italian ham; they don't age it in nice, cool caves like the Spanish ham. No, my friend, it's very different. Christmas will be very sad indeed without the polvoronis and the ham. Very sad." He mumbled to himself as he turned to leave.

"Wait!" I cried. "Maybe we'll give it a try. By the way, what's your name?"

"Call me Nicholas," he replied.

The sky was the color of boiled lead and the barometer was still dropping as we pointed the bow of the Fire Witch toward the straights of Gibralter. The Northwester had been hurling gusts of up to 60 knots through the mouth of the straights, lashing the water into a fury, creating huge overfalls, columns of water which shot out of the sea like the blast from a volcano, flinging everything in its path aside. Rebecca manned the tiller. I stood watch up forward with a pair of binoculars and was often covered to my waist by the frothing sea. That 500 quid was begin-

ning to look smaller and smaller as the Fire Witch bucked the turbulent sea. Night rolled over us like a miasmal cloud; we tried to stay in the lee, hugging the northern shore precariously close to those watchful eyes in Spain. Huge super tankers lumbered by, virtual mountains of steel and speed, loaded so heavily with crude oil that only a few feet of their incredible freeboard could be seen. The skipper of one once told me it takes 18 miles just to stop the brutes—in an emergency! So, regardless of the "rules of the road," we avoided them with scrupulous care.

Finally, we heard the mournful siren on Pointe del Tarifa long before we saw its red and white flash flicker through the gloom. It took us six hours to make the 12 miles from Gibralter to Tarifa, so it was well past midnight when we received the recognition signal from the little fishing vessel that chugged out to meet us.

Although it was impossible to see more than a few hundred feet in the turbulent darkness, we were so close to the lighthouse that I felt naked and trapped every time the light flashed. The Fire Witch rolled drunkenly on the swells—first one rail under, then the other. The fishing boat eased slowly and cautiously nearer, then was caught on a breaking wave and smashed violently into us crushing a rub rail and scraping our side. With curses and shouts in many languages, lines were flung and made fast, tires were dropped between the boats to reduce damage, and Rebecca jockeyed our now appended Fire Witch to face the storm.

Then the loading began; it was a murderously dangerous job in rough seas. Each box of Polvoronis became an evil personality on those tossing decks. Each box, safely loaded, became a major triumph. We filled the entire forward compartment then started loading hams. They were in sacks, so a well timed heave got them aboard quickly. We must have loaded two hundred before the first rays of dawn put an end to our struggles.

With the wind behind us the Fire Witch fairly flew toward home. Now all we had to do was slip past the Spanish patrol to be 'longshore in no time, with a long, hot shower and a big breakfast in the offing. We sped down the strait with the gale behind us, flogging the Fire Witch with every foot of sail that we dared. But we had tarried too long loading the hams, for I spotted a Spanish E-boat plowing water behind us. She was making great speed and threw a huge bow wave as she thundered ahead.

Our engine came to life with a roar making the poor Fire Witch shudder as we fairly flew along at 15 knots, surfing on the crests of the waves. But I knew it was a losing race, for the monster machine behind us could do twice our speed. It was fascinating to watch her approach as that ugly hull became ever more distinct through the spray. Then she slowed perceptively, maintaining her distance, and I realized they were waiting for us to get closer to Gibralter so the people there could see our capture. The Fire Witch continued to give us her best, and soon the rock loomed above us. Then, as the E-boat gunned her engines and began to close the gap, the first shot from her bow cannon roared toward us and erupted water a scant hundred yards away. Were they trying to sink us without the usual warning shots? It seemed so. And the rock was so near; so near we could see buildings plainly and cars moving along narrow streets in the morning's early light. The second shot thunked into the sea, much closer this time, throwing a huge, greasy water column high into the air to shower us with spray. I gave Rebecca the helm and started cutting the lashings on the life raft. Perhaps we could abandon ship before the Spaniards found us with their gun. Then, from behind the rock came an eerie sound: whoop, whoop, whoop...and a gray destroyer appeared, starboard rail awash in a tight turn around the rock, searchlights trained on the E-boat. She was easily making 30 knots as she roared toward us. But the E-boat had increased its speed and was moving in to board us. Without reducing speed, the destroyer slid between us and the Spaniards, shuddering as she came, her engines full in reverse. As she slid to a stop abeam of us, I read her name on the bow—Protector.

They were all waiting for us on the sea wall. Thousands of people, some dressed in Moroccan jalabas, some in heavy, dark fishing garb, even pretty girls in scanty miniskirts. They were all waving and cheering as we tied up at the dock just behind Protector. Still a bit weak in the knees and queasy in the gut, I walked over to the big boat to give the captain our thanks. I stood there on the bridge shaking his hand surrounded by grinning sailors.

"By the way," I asked the Captain, "What piece of luck put your vessel in a position to aid us?"

"Well," he said thoughtfully, "we received a call on the radiotelephone that you might be in trouble. The chap called himself Saint Nick, or something like that. So, we decided to have a look. Lucky we did."

Rebecca and I walked down the wharf, that December 1971, with everyone slapping us on the back and talking in many languages. Never again, I vowed. One smuggling run is enough for a lifetime. But then, what's Christmas without a little polvoronis?

the strait of gibraltar seen from africa

21
desserts

We enjoy simple desserts—a bit of cheese, some fruit, or a few nuts and a glass of port. Dessert, as our old grandmother used to say, should be "a little something sweet in the mouth," not the sugary bombshell so often served. Highly sugared desserts, such as cakes, cookies, and chewy candies, are nutritionally poor, fattening, awful for the teeth, and zilch for the digestion. Who needs them. They are among the chief villians in the battle of the bulge, and we shall risk your ire by omitting them completely.

Nevertheless, we have not forgotten grandmother's old saying, and have provided a few sweets that are nourishing—dessert omelets and crepes. But we hope the majority of your desserts will be prepared from fruit and cheese. In addition to being healthy and easy to prepare, these desserts are in keeping with the simplicity of life under sail.

DESSERT OMELETS

Somewhat neglected in the dessert world, light and lovely dessert omelets seem made just for the cruising chef. They are nourishing, easy to make, and sweet enough to be satisfying. Dessert omelets are thin and light; this means 1 egg per person and no more than a 4-egg omelet in a large fry pan. The pan is brought to high heat, the egg poured in, and the flame immediately reduced. The initial high heat gives the omelet some color, but it must be cooked slowly or it will be tough. Read more about omelets on page 115.

BASIC DESSERT OMELET   Serves Four

1. Combine by beating for not more than 20 seconds:

   4   egg yolks
   3   egg whites
   2   tablespoons cream or condensed milk
   3   tablespoons sugar
   1   teaspoon vanilla
   Optional additions:
   1   teaspoon grated lemon or orange rind
   2   teaspoons raisins or currants (sprinkled on the
   egg as soon as it is poured into the pan)
   1   teaspoon almond extract
2. Add to large, slope-sided fry pan:
   1   generous tablespoon butter
3. Pour in egg mixture and reduce to low heat. The omelet should take about 4 minutes to cook. It is done when the top is just set and still rather glistening.

Desert Omelet Stuffings, Quick and Easy

   jam
   chopped dates and nuts
   cranberries, sweetened and chopped
   canned fruit, finely chopped
   canned pie filling

Dessert Omelet Topping

   confectioner's sugar
   honey
   maple syrup
   cinnamon
   jam

DESSERT APPLE OMELET   Serves Three

1. Saute in sauce pan over medium heat:

   1   tablespoon butter
   2   apples, cored, peeled and chopped
   ¼   cup raisins
   2   tablespoons rum
   1   tablespoon cinnamon
   1   tablespoon brown sugar

Stir frequently to avoid burning. Saute until apples are soft.
2. Make basic 4-egg dessert omelet; pour apple mixture in a broad band across center of omelet, fold in edges.
3. For the finishing touch, sprinkle with:
   Powdered sugar

FRUIT PRESERVE OMELET   Serves Two

Any good quality preserve with lots of fruit pieces may be used.

1. Warm jar of **preserves** in pot of water over medium heat.
2. Make a basic dessert omelet:
   4 egg yolks
   3 egg whites
   1 tablespoon sugar
   (You may choose to add a half cup of finely chopped fruit, such as **bananas, mangos, peaches,** or **canned fruit,** such as **cherries** or **apricots.**)
3. Pour egg mixture into very hot pan containing:
   3 tablespoons butter
   Reduce heat immediately and cook until top is just set.
4. Add generous portion of preserves in a broad band across middle of omelet; fold edges.
5. Sprinkle with **powdered sugar.**
6. As an elegant last touch, warm a quarter cup of rum and pour over omelet; flame at the table.

THE CAPTAIN'S FAR OUT FRUIT FILLING FOR DESSERT OMELETS

Firm fruit, preferably fresh, must be used for this filling. Apples and bananas make a good combination. **Do not use citrus fruits.** We usually add raisins to the mixture. If you have just one fresh fruit, canned fruit may be used to supplement the filling.

1. Saute for 3 minutes:
   1 cup mixed chopped fruit
   1 tablespoon butter
2. Add to fruit:
   1 tablespoon rum
   2 tablespoons Grand Marnier or other liqueur

>   1   teaspoon lemon juice
>   2   tablespoons brown sugar
3. Simmer until liquid is like syrup.
4. When omelet is just set, pour fruit in a broad strip across center and fold. A bit of the juice may be poured on top; or sprinkle with confectioner's sugar, pour on a thin strip of honey, add 3 tablespoons brandy, and bring flaming to the table.

THE CAPTAIN'S FRUIT OMELET   Serves Three

I save this one for special days in the middle of a long passage. That is the time for occasional culinary wonders to brighten the evening watch. There is contentment after a good dinner; we sit by the companionway watching Venus rise in the east, feeling the breeze, and wondering to what green land it will blow us.

1. Saute on low heat in sauce pan:
>   4   tablespoons butter
>   2   tablespoons dark brown sugar
>   1½ cups fruit (fresh or canned apples, peaches, bananas, mangos, apricots)
>   1   tablespoon cinnamon
2. When fruit has cooked until soft, add to sauce pan:
>   ½   cup Grand Marnier
>   ¼   cup rum mixed with 1 tablespoon corn flour
>   Stir frequently to avoid burning; cook until sauce thickens.
3. Make basic 4-egg dessert omelet; mix by beating for 20 seconds:
>   4   egg yolks
>   3   egg whites
>   3   tablespoons cream or condensed milk
>   1   tablespoon sugar
4. Mix in:
>   2   teaspoons vanilla
>   1   tablespoon orange rind, finely grated (optional)
5. Pour mixture into very hot pan, reduce heat immediately; cook for approximately 3 minutes. (The top of the omelet should not be quite set.
6. Pour fruit sauce in broad band across middle of omelet; fold and sprinkle with powdered sugar.

ibeza

Optional Instant Topping. While sauce pot is still warm, add ½ cup Grand Marnier and combine with pan drippings. Pour on the topping at table and flame.

BANANA OMELET   Serves Three

1. Saute in pan over low heat:

   3   tablespoons butter
   2   bananas, sliced lengthwise in halves
   Saute until bananas are just soft, moving them with spatula to prevent sticking.

2. Then add:
   ½   cup of banana liqueur or rum
   ½   cup water mixed with 1 tablespoon corn flour or arrowroot
   When the sauce thickens, remove from heat.

3. Mix by beating for 20 to 30 seconds
   4   egg yolks
   3   egg whites
   3   tablespoons cream or condensed milk
   1   tablespoon sugar
   1   tablespoon vanilla extract

4. When omelet is just set, soft on top, slide on the bananas, keeping them intact. Add some of sauce. Fold omelet, sprinkle with powdered sugar; pour on remaining sauce and serve.

CREPES REBECCA A LA BARCAROLLE—A DEEP SEA TRANSATLANTIC EXTRAVAGANZA TO PLACATE ANGRY WIVES AND JADED PALATES

Christmas, mid-Atlantic, 20°36′N, 55°00W, a fond hello and "Seasons' Greetings" to Ocean Station Echo, U.S. Coast Guard at 35°06N, 48°00W.

Hell hath no fury like a woman scorned or a wife used to big Colorado Christmases who must spend her Christmas at sea. Tears. Sulking. Too many cigarettes smoked. Silence. But then dinner time came and we had a candied ham with sweet potatoes that couldn't be beat, and I whipped up these lovely crepes from materials at hand.

Crepes suzette are used to emergencies. They were invented by the great chef, Henri Carpentier, for Prince Albert of Wales. Henri accidentally set fire to the delicate crepe sauce literally under the nose of the prince, much to everyone's horror. Never

daunted in the face of disaster, Henri quickly poured the burning liquid over the pancake and served at once, hoping, we now guess, to minimize the damage. The effort was a resounding success and Henri, as much a politician as a chef, named the dish Crepes Albert. But there was a young lady present and the prince, a master himself at diplomacy, asked if the lovely dish could be renamed after the lady. We have followed suit.

CREPES REBECCA

The Crepe

1. Combine and sift:
    - ¾ **cup flour**
    - 1 **teaspoon baking powder**
    - ½ **teaspoon salt**
    - 2 **tablespoons sugar**
2. Mix and combine with dry ingredients:
    - 2 **eggs, beaten**
    - 1 **teaspoon vanilla**
    - 1 **teaspoon orange rind, grated**
    - ⅔ **cup milk**
    - ⅓ **cup water**
3. Allow to stand at least several hours before cooking.

Cooking the Crepe

1. Wipe a hot skillet with scant amount of butter. **Be sure sides of pan are buttered.**
2. When butter bubbles, pour in about ¼ cup batter, enough to cover bottom of pan with a thin layer. As soon as crepe begins to solidify, give pan a shake to loosen crepe.
3. After a minute, turn crepe over with spatula and cook for another minute. **Fini!**

The crepes may be made in advance and reheated in a pan at the last minute.

The Fruit Filler

1. Chop into small pieces:
    - 1 **banana or ½ cup raisins**
    - 1 **apple, peeled or other firm fruit**
    - 1 **teaspoon grated orange rind (the orange part only)**

2. Saute fruit until soft in:

    1 tablespoon butter

    Then add:

    2 tablespoons banana liqueur or rum

    2 tablespoons Grand Marnier

    2 tablespoons brown sugar

Simmer and stir for 3 minutes.

The Sauce

The sauce may be made in advance and reheated.

1. Melt in small pan until bubbling:

    ½ cup butter

    Add:

    1 teaspoon lemon rind

    1 teaspoon orange rind

    1 oz. Grand Marnier

    1 oz. rum

    2 tablespoons sugar

2. When sauce bubbles, ignite and let it burn out.

The Combination

1. Dip both sides of crepe in sauce.
2. Add generous tablespoon of fruit to one side of crepe and fold into a triangle; dust with confectioner's sugar if desired.
3. As a last, extravagant touch, pour on a warm tablespoon of Grand Marnier and serve flaming. Turn down the oil lamps, me hearties, serve at once!

NUT AND CURRANT DUFF   Serves Four

1. Combine:

    6 tablespoons sugar, granulated

    ¾ cup milk

    2 tablespoons baking powder

    1 cup currants, raisins, or 3 heaping teaspoons jam

    ½ cup walnuts

    2½ cups flour

2. Place in greased pot just big enough for the dough.
3. Place inside a larger pot on a few bolts; cook for 30 minutes at 350°. Check occasionally with a toothpick. When toothpick emerges clean, it is done.

zabaglione

ZABAGLIONE

Serves Four

This delicious light custard is the essence of simplicity. It takes no more than 6 minutes to make; but like Hollandaise sauce, it can be ruined easily by fast cooking. Use a double boiler or fill a large pot with water and rest a small pot on the water. Bring to a fast simmer, not a rolling boil.

1. Beat until light, then add to pot:

    6 egg yolks
    ½ cup sugar

    Whip constantly, preferably with a whisk. When mixture begins to foam and thicken, slowly add one of the following:

> ½ cup Marsala wine, Madeira, sherry, or (we prefer)
>
> ⅓ cup Grand Marnier

2. Continue to beat constantly until mixture thickens and has consistency of very soft ice cream. This process cannot be accelerated by turning up the heat which would only scorch the ingredients.
3. Pour into large wine or sherbet glasses; serve at once.

The whites may be beaten stiff and folded into the custard or used as a topping when combined with:

> ¼ cup confectioners sugar
>
> 1 teaspoon freshly grated orange rind
>
> ½ teaspoon vanilla

END-OF-THE-PASSAGE ORANGE CUSTARD   Serves Four

The process for making this quick dessert is quite similar to that of the previous recipe for Zabaglione. It takes only 7 to 8 minutes to cook; be sure all ingredients are ready for instant use. This custard may be served either hot or cold.

1. Combine:

> 6 egg yolks
>
> ½ cup sugar
>
> ½ orange rind, grated

2. Heat mixture in double boiler, or makeshift double boiler, over simmering water. Stir constantly until liquid foams slightly and begins to thicken.
3. Then add slowly:

> 1 cup warm milk

Stir constantly until mixture turns into custard.

4. Remove from heat and add:

> 2 oranges, well chopped and seeded
>
> 1 oz. Grand Marnier (optional)

5. Top with (optional):

> egg whites, stiffly beaten
>
> 1 teaspoon vanilla
>
> ¼ cup confectioners sugar
>
> 2 teaspoon lemon juice

Fold ingredients into egg whites.

CHOCOLATE CUSTARD

This dessert is in no way similar to instant commercial chocolate pudding. It takes two pots and about 8 minutes to cook.

1. Combine over low heat, stirring constantly until chocolate is dissolved:

    1½ cups condensed milk or fresh half 'n half (tastes better)

    4 to 6 oz. grated milk chocolate bars

2. Heat in double boiler, or makeshift double boiler, until it begins to thicken:

    5 egg yolks

    2 tablespoons sugar

    1 tablespoon rum

3. Slowly add the melted chocolate, a little at a time, stirring constantly until each addition thickens. Serve hot or cold.

MOUSSE AU CHOCOLATE

The above recipe becomes mousse au chocolate by folding in after chilling the custard:

¾ cup stiffly whipped cream

1 teaspoon vanilla

1 teaspoon brandy

END-OF-THE-PASSAGE RICE 'N RAISIN PUDDING Serves Four

This old favorite is made from long-lasting ingredients, but must steam in a double boiler for about 30 minutes.

1 cup rice, cooked

¾ cup milk (condensed)

3 tablespoons sugar, or 4 tablespoons brown sugar

2 eggs beaten

½ teaspoon lemon rind, grated

½ teaspoon lemon juice

½ cup raisins

¼ cup chopped almonds, walnuts, or hazelnuts

1 tablespoon rum

1. Combine all ingredients and stir thoroughly.
2. Grease a double boiler with butter; cook pudding for about 30 minutes or until set.
3. Sprinkle each serving with cinnamon.

TAPIOCA PUDDING Serves Two

Tapioca stores well, cooks quickly, and makes a fine base for a variety of desserts. A double boiler, or makeshift double boiler, should be used; the water should be boiling when the tapioca is added.

1. Combine and pour into double boiler:
   - 3 **tablespoons quick tapioca**
   - 1 **egg, beaten**
   - ½ **cup sugar**
   - 1 **teaspoon vanilla**
   - **a pinch of salt**
2. Cook without stirring for 7 minutes. Stir a few times and cook for an additional 5 minutes. Cool.

   Try adding alone or in combination any of the following:
   - **almond extract**
   - **grated orange or lemon rind**
   - **cinnamon**
   - **honey**
   - **shredded coconut**
   - **chopped nuts**
   - **canned fruit, chopped**
   - **fresh fruit, chopped**
   - **raisins**
   - **chopped dates**
   - **chopped figs**

DESSERT CHEESE

The classic soft dessert cheeses such as Camembert and Liederkranz, are delicate and must be refrigerated. Use them when you can, but don't expect a ripened soft cheese to keep for more than a week, even with refrigeration. Canned cheese, though not quite as delicate in flavor as true fresh cheese, lasts indefinitely if refrigerated, but breaks down in consistency if unrefrigerated for more than a month. Processed cheese, sold in little foil triangles, has preservative added to it and will last a month, unrefrigerated, if kept cool. Its flavor may be improved by combining with grated hard cheese, which lasts much longer.

Fine desserts may be made from nothing more than pieces of hard cheese, such as provolone, aged Romano, and sharp

chedder served with nuts, olives, and crackers. After-dinner wines, such as port and sweet sherry, add the finishing touch. Hard cheese may be grated and mixed with a little butter and a dash of flavoring, such as vanilla, almond extract, brandy, or Grand Marnier. Grated hard cheese mixed with cream cheese is delicious. The truly hard, aged cheeses, such as old provolone, Romano, and very sharp cheddar, last a long time without any sort of preservation. Other hard cheeses may be cut into small rectangles, perhaps 2 to 3 inches long, and all sides firmly pressed into a plate of coarse pepper. The cheese may then be placed in a scalded jar and covered with light oil that has been heated, then cooled. Cheese treated with sterile oil will last indefinitely.

DRIED FRUIT

No cruising galley is really complete without a jar filled with dried fruit. It lasts four months or more, is very nutritious, and can be made into a variety of desserts. Since dried fruit weighs about 80 percent less than when fresh, a little goes a long way. It can be eaten as is for a snack or "plumped" by simmering for 15 minutes in all sorts of delightful liquids such as liqueur, lemon juice and sugar, or wine, cinnamon and cloves. Reconstituted in this way, dried fruit makes a fine filling for a dessert omelet or, mixed with a bit of honey, a fine syrup for pancakes.

Drying fruit is easy and a good way to take advantage of the many fruit bargains that a cruising chef often finds. All you need is a hot sunny day, a pest free spot, and a few newspapers. All fruit should be prepared in the fruit and vegetable dip, page 28. Hands should be thoroughly scrubbed and several clean, unopened newspapers spread and held by weights on the deck. Seedless grapes are removed from their stems and dried as is. Apples are peeled and cut into wedges. Apricots and peaches are pitted and quartered. Plums are pitted and quartered if large. The fruit is then laid on the newspapsr, skin side down, and allowed to dry. They should be covered at night and turned the next morning. The fruit is dry if no liquid appears when squeezed. Commercial processors use sulphur dioxide to stabilize color. This is not really necessary except from an aesthetic standpoint. When the fruit is dry, place it in a tightly capped jar and examine occasionally for any signs of mold. Should some appear, throw the infected pieces out, wash the rest of it and the jar in the fruit and vegetable dip, then redry.

Mold does not usually develop, because the enzymes in the fruit retard its growth.

DRIED FRUIT DELIGHT

1. Soak 1½ cups dried fruit overnight in:
   - **2 cups water**
   - **½ cup lemon juice**
   - **1 tablespoon cinnamon**
2. Bring to simmer and sweeten to taste with:
   - **Honey or brown sugar**
3. Add 3 tablespoons of your favorite liqueur (optional)

FRIED FRUIT WITH FRESH CITRUS

Citrus fruit usually lasts for a month or more if first washed in the fruit and vegetable dip. The experienced cruising chef always has a decent supply.

1. Soak dried fruit for a few hours in:
   - **citrus fruit juice**
   - **brown sugar**
2. Simmer for 15 minutes. Eat as is or serve over cake. Delicious!

22
sauces

Sauces are the secret weapons in any good chef's arsenal. They can perk up dishes that would otherwise be drab, or they can provide the crowning touch for a culinary work of art.

SHELLFISH COCKTAIL SAUCE   Makes 1 Cup

If you run out of canned sauce or just prefer making your own, here is a recipe you are sure to like.

1. Combine:

    ¾   cup tomato sauce
    1½ teaspoons lemon juice
    ¼   cup horseradish
    ½   teaspoon tobasco
    1   tablespoon dill, finely chopped (optional)

CHEESE SAUCE FOR VEGETABLES   Makes About 1 Cup

1. Melt in sauce pan:

    3   tablespoons butter
Add:
    ½   cup Parmesan cheese
2. Slowly add, stirring constantly:
    ½   cup condensed milk (less if thicker sauce is desired)

406

3. Season with any of the following:
      celery seed
      chopped celery
  1 teaspoon finely chopped onion
      nutmeg
      paprika
4. Tastes especially good when poured over broccoli or cauliflower.

FRIED BREAD CRUMBS AND BUTTER VEGETABLE SAUCE

1. Parboil or steam vegetable for ⅔ of its normal cooking time.
2. While vegetable is cooking, saute:

    2 to 3 tablespoons butter
  ½   cup bread crumbs

3. When bread crumbs turn golden, add vegetable and any of the following:
      crumbled bacon
      chopped almonds, hazel nuts, or walnuts
      chopped anchovies
4. Saute until vegetable is soft.
5. Sprinkle with Parmesan cheese if desired. Salt and pepper to taste and serve at once.

limpets

QUICK MUSHROOM CREAM SAUCE

1. Heat:

   1 can condensed cream of mushroom soup
2. Stir in and blend:
   - **½ cup condensed milk**
   - **½ cup Parmesan cheese**
3. Salt and pepper to taste.

BREAD CRUMB AND ONION SAUCE

1. Melt in a sauce pan:
   3 tablespoons butter
   Fry until golden:
   ½ small onion, well chopped
2. Add:
   2 heaping tablespoons bread or cracker crumbs
   Saute until golden.
3. Add:
   - **1 teaspoon marjoram**
   - **salt and pepper**
4. Toss vegetables in the mixture.

ANCHOVY BUTTER AND ALMONDS

1. Melt in pan:
   3 tablespoons butter
   Fry until golden:

   2 to 3 tablespoons almonds, chopped
2. Add:

   4 to 6 anchovies, chopped
   Saute for a few minutes.
3. Toss vegetables in this mixture; add salt and pepper to taste.

QUICK CHINESE SAUCE

1. Melt:
   3 tablespoons butter
   Saute until golden:

   2 tablespoons bread crumbs

2. Add:
   - **1 tablespoon mustard**
   - **1 tablespoon vinegar**
   - **1 tablespoon Worcestershi**
   - **¼ teaspoon hot sauce**

   Pour over vegetables.

MARINARA SAUCE

1. Saute in skillet until golden:
   - **2 onions, chopped**
   - **2 cloves garlic**
   - **½ teaspoon salt**
   - **½ teaspoon pepper**
   - **5 tablespoons olive oil**
2. Discard garlic and add:
   - **2½ cups Italian tomatoes, chopped and drained**
   - **½ teaspoon oregano**
   - **½ teaspoon sugar**
   - **½ teaspoon lemon juice**
   - **4 teaspoon red wine**
   - **2 anchovy fillets, well chopped**

Simmer for 30 minutes over low heat, stirring occasionally. When serving over pasta or veal, it is traditional to sprinkle each serving with Parmesan or Romano cheese.

CURRY SAUCE A LA GALLEY GOURMET
Serves 4 to 6

This simple sauce, so varied in its uses, was taught to us by a Pakistani lady in Gibraltar. The sauce is usually prepared first and the other ingredients are added to it in the same pot. Curry dishes are good the first day, but even better the second. The sauce then has time to work its magic. There is no one right way to make curry paste. If you have a tried and true method, by all means, use it. The secret of making a good curry paste is to fry it gently until the curry smell disappears, about 5 to 10 minutes.

1. To pot, which will be used for entire dish, add:
   - **4 tablespoons butter or oil (Use oil if you plan to fry something like chicken, or butter if you are going to stir the curry paste into something like rice.)**
   - **1 medium onion, chopped**
   - **1 heaping tablespoon curry powder**
   - **1 teaspoon ginger**
   - **1 teaspoon vinegar**
   - **3 cloves garlic, crushed**
2. Slowly saute over medium heat for 5 to 10 minutes, adding a tablespoon of water at time, stirring constantly until molasses-like consistency is achieved. Continue to cook until curry smell disappears.

HOT CURRY SAUCE

Follow previous recipe, but add:

>   ½ to 1 teaspoon pepper
> 2   additional cloves garlic, crushed
>   BON APPETITE!

FOUR SAUCES

The basis of many French sauces is a roux, which is nothing more than flour sauteed in butter. There are 2 secrets here: first, be sure that the flour and butter are thoroughly combined before cooking to eliminate lumps; second, cook over moderate heat and keep a good eye on the pan. A roux burns easily.

SAUCE BECHAMEL OR BASIC WHITE SAUCE

1. Combine in sauce pan:
   >   2   heaping tablespoons soft butter
   >   1   tablespoon flour

   Fry for 2 minutes over low heat.
2. Add:
   >   1   cup milk
   >   ½   teaspoon salt
   >   1½   teaspoons pepper

   Simmer gently for 5 minutes, but **do not boil**.

This sauce is used for creaming foods and as a basis for the three sauces that follow.

SAUCE MORNAY

To the hot bechamel sauce add:

>   ¼   lb. Gruyere cheese, grated
>   Melt into liquid like heavy cream.

This sauce is the basis of all au gratin recipes and can be poured over an omelet, steamed vegetables, or fish.

SAUCE AURORA

To the hot bechamel sauce add:

> 1   can (8 oz.) tomato puree

This goes well with poached eggs and steamed fish.

410

SAUCE POULETTE

Add to the bechamel sauce:

- **2 teaspoons lemon juice**
- **½ cup dry white wine**
- **1 egg yolk, beaten into wine**
  Do not let sauce boil.

This tastes especially good over chicken baked, broiled, or sauteed in garlic and oil.

BARBECUE SAUCE

Use for meat or fowl*; makes a lot of sauce so reduce quantities as necessary.

Combine and let stand overnight:

- **2 pounds tomato sauce**
- **½ onion, finely chopped**
- **4 tablespoons Worchestershire sauce**
- **2 tablespoons brown sugar**
- **2 tablespoons vinegar**
- **1 teaspoon dijon type mustard**
- **½ teaspoon cayenne pepper**
- **½ teaspoon basil, rosemary**
- **4 cloves garlic, chopped**
- **½ teaspoon celery seed**
- **3 tablespoons vegetable oil**

*If you are grilling, brown the meat or poultry thoroughly. Add a cup of water to the sauce, then brush on the meat and repeat occasionally as it cooks down.

If pan frying, cook until the meat is done, then brush on the sauce, warm and cook for a few more minutes.

If broiling, cook the meat until done and brush on sauce just once on each side, then broil until the sauce bubbles.

SOUR CREAM FISH SAUCE   Serves Four

1. Melt ½ cup butter in a sauce pan.
2. When the butter is melted, stir in
   1 cup sour cream
   2 tablespoons finely chopped dill
   1 teaspoon salt
   1 teaspoon white pepper
   2 tablespoons lemon juice

Do not let the sauce even simmer. It need only be warmed. If you overheat it the sour cream will become thin.

CHICKEN OR TURKEY GRAVY

1. Take all the unused bird scraps and boil for as long as possible in enough chicken stock to cover. Include all parts such as feet and liver if available. Add more consumee as the liquid steams down. Remove the scraps, pull off the meat and chop finely (including the liver). Add pan scrapings to the pot.
2. Mix ½ cup beer and 3 tablespoons corn starch. Add slowly.
3. When the gravy is sufficiently thick, remove it from the heat. Add cream or condensed milk as desired. Rewarm when needed but do not cook.
4. Add the scrap meat, white pepper, sauteed mushrooms if desired and salt to taste.

HOLLANDAISE SAUCE

Hollandaise is an absolutely delicious sauce with a wide variety of uses. It is well known served over vegetables but is just as delicious over poached fish, eggs and veal. There is always another use for a good hollandaise sauce and many possible modifications to make it even more versatile.

Blender Hollandaise

If you have a blender nothing can be easier than making hollandaise. Just heat ½ cup of butter until it is crackling but do not burn. Pour into a blender and put on "slow." Add 1½ teaspoons lemon juice and 4 egg yolks. That's it!

412

Quick Handmade Hollandaise

Have in hand a large wet sponge or towel. This will be used later to arrest the pot's heat.

1. Melt ½ cup butter, 3 tablespoons light oil til crackling. Use a teflon sauce pan.
2. Remove pot from the hot burner and add 4 egg yolks. Stir rapidly with a whisk.
3. If the sauce does not completely jell put it back on the flame for not more than 20 seconds at a time.
4. If the sauce starts to overcook and looks like bits of scrambled egg, quickly add 1½ teaspoons lemon juice (or a lump of cold butter) and set the pot on the wet sponge. Stir frantically. Further rapid cooling can be ahieved with cream. Salt to taste. Use white pepper.

Modified Hollandaise

Hollandaise can be "cut" with sour cream. Grated cheese is an excellent addition, particularly Romano. Cheese can also be quickly shaken into the sauce to arrest its cooking. Sauteed slivered almonds make a good addition and create a fine fish sauce. Hollandaise can be sweetened wth sugar, flavored with rum and cinnamon and served on a sauteed banana for dessert or mixed with heavy cream and combined with fruit. As a fish sauce it can be modified with a bit more lemon juice and finely chopped dill. A large amount of very finely chopped parsley will made hollandaise into a green sauce for shrimp or fish.

CRANBERRY SAUCE

Delicious with meatballs or burgers.

1. Combine and heat:
   1 can crushed cranberries
   1 lemon (juice only)
   2 teaspoons cornstarch diluted in ½ cup beer
   1 teaspoon sugar
2. Simmer over low heat until the sauce thickens.

appendix

equivalents'n things

CAN SIZE	DESCRIPTION	NO. CUPS
No. 10	largest can	holds 6½-8 lbs of anything
No. 46	large juice drink can	6
No. 2½	can or glass jar	3½
No. 2	small fruit juice or fruit	2¼
No. 303	can or jar for vegetables	2
No. 1½	usually holds fruit	2
No. 300	holds vegetables, or juice	1¾
No. 211	tall can, holds drinks	1½
12 oz.	vegetables or meat products	1½
Picnic	vegetables or meat products	1¼
Tall Buffet	vegetables or meat products	1.
6 oz.	juice drinks	¾
No. 1	fruit, usually pineapple	1
No. 1¼	fruit, usually pineapple	1½
No. ½	Fish and meat products	1

WEIGHTS AND MEASURES

LIQUID MEASURE

60 drops	=	1 tsp		
3 tsp	=	1 tbl	=	½ ounce
2 cups	=	1 pint	=	.53 liters
2 pints	=	1 quart	=	1.06 liters
4 quarts	=	1 gallon	=	4.22 liters

METRIC CONVERSION WEIGHT EQUIVALENTS
1 ounce   =   28 grams
1 pound   =   454 grams

LINEAR MEASURE

1 inch   = 2.54 centimeters
1 centimeter   = 0.39 inches
39.37 inches   = 1 meter

SUBSTITUTIONS AND EQUIVALENTS
Cornmeal—3 cups = 1 pound = 12 cups cooked
Egg Whites—8 to 11 whites = 1 cup
Egg Yolks—12 to 15 yolks = 1 cup
Flour—all purpose 1 pound = 4 cups sifted;
whole wheat, 1 pound = 3½ cups unsifted;
soy, ¾ cup = 1 cup all purpose by weight
Milk—(1 cup condensed + 1 cup water) = 2 cups whole
(⅔ cup powdered + ⅓ cup water)* = 1 cup whole
*(or as instructed)

Macaroni—2 cups dry = 4 cups cooked
Milk, Dry, Whole—
(4 tbl powder + 1 cup water) = 1 cup reconstituted milk
Mushrooms—1 oz. dry = 4 ounces fresh
Peas, dry, split—2 cups = 1 pound (5 cups cooked)
Macaroni—1 cup = 4 oz. (2¼ cups cooked)
Noodles—1 cup = 2 2/3 oz. (2 cups cooked)
Spaghetti—2 cups (½ pound) = 4 cups (1 lb. cooked)
Rice—2½ cups = 1 pound (8 cups cooked)
Tapioca—2 tbl quick = 6 tbl cooked

RECONSTITUTED EQUIVALENTS
Apples—1 pound dry = 3½ pounds fresh
Apricots—3 cups = 1 pound dry
Beans, Peas, Legumes—2½ cups = 1 lb (6 to 7 cups cooked)
Corn meal—1 cup = 5 oz. (4 cups cooked)
Eggs, dried—(2½ tbl egg + 4½ tbl water) = 1 whole egg
Gelatin—1 oz. powder makes 1 quart
Lemon—one squeezed = 2½ tbl juice

index

418